Recovering Classical Liberal Political Economy

Edinburgh Studies in Comparative Political Theory & Intellectual History
Series Editor: Vasileios Syros

Edinburgh Studies in Comparative Political Theory & Intellectual History welcomes scholars interested in the comparative study of intellectual history/political ideas in diverse cultural contexts and periods of human history and Comparative Political Theory (CPT).

The series addresses the core concerns of CPT by placing texts from various political, cultural and geographical contexts in conversation. It calls for substantial reflection on the methodological principles of comparative intellectual history in order to rethink of some of the conceptual categories and tools used in the comparative exploration of political ideas. The series seeks original, high-quality monographs and edited volumes that challenge and expand the canon of readings used in teaching intellectual history and CPT in Western universities. It will showcase innovative and interdisciplinary work focusing on the comparative examination of sources, political ideas and concepts from diverse traditions.

Available Titles:

Reforming the Law of Nature: The Secularisation of Political Thought, 1532–1689
Simon P. Kennedy

Recovering Classical Liberal Political Economy: Natural Rights and the Harmony of Interests
Lee Ward

Recovering Classical Liberal Political Economy

Natural Rights and the Harmony of Interests

LEE WARD

EDINBURGH
University Press

To the memory of my mother Catherine Ward (née Parker)

Edinburgh University Press is one of the leading university presses in the UK. We publish academic books and journals in our selected subject areas across the humanities and social sciences, combining cutting-edge scholarship with high editorial and production values to produce academic works of lasting importance. For more information visit our website: edinburghuniversitypress.com

© Lee Ward, 2022

Edinburgh University Press Ltd
The Tun – Holyrood Road
12(2f) Jackson's Entry
Edinburgh EH8 8PJ

Typeset in 11/15 Adobe Sabon by
IDSUK (DataConnection) Ltd

A CIP record for this book is available from the British Library

ISBN 978 1 3995 0059 3 (hardback)
ISBN 978 1 3995 0061 6 (webready PDF)
ISBN 978 1 3995 0062 3 (epub)

The right of Lee Ward to be identified as the author of this work has been asserted in accordance with the Copyright, Designs and Patents Act 1988, and the Copyright and Related Rights Regulations 2003 (SI No. 2498).

Contents

Acknowledgements

This book has been a real joy to work on. First, I wish to thank the Series Editor at Edinburgh University Press Vasileios Syros for his support and guidance. Without his encouragement, this book in its current form would not have been possible. I also want to thank my editor at Edinburgh University Press Ersev Ersoy for her support for this project and her suggestion to take my analysis in new, and I believe fruitful, directions.

During most of the time I was researching and writing this book, I have had the pleasure of teaching at Baylor University. I thank my faculty colleagues and the graduate students in the Department of Political Science for their support and friendship over the past four years. I am especially grateful to David Clinton, Department Chair *extraodinaire*, for his support of my successful application for a Research Leave Award. I am also pleased to thank the Baylor University Faculty of Arts & Sciences for granting me a Research Leave Award for spring 2021. This support allowed me to dedicate an entire semester to writing, and without it I would not have been able to finish the book when I did.

Numerous scholars have read parts of this manuscript, including Ruth Abbey, Theodore Christov, Alexander Kaufman, James Stoner, Monicka Tutschka, Constantine Vassiliou and Aaron Zubia. I thank them for their comments. I also am grateful to Jeffrey Church for inviting me to present my work on Hobbes at the University of Houston, and I thank him and Alin Fumurescu, Dustin Gish and Jeremy Bailey for their stimulating comments and questions. Part of Chapter 1 appeared as 'Equity and Political Economy in Thomas Hobbes', *American Journal of Political Science* 64(4)

(2020): 823–35, and some of Chapter 2 appears as 'Trust and Distributive Justice in John Locke's Politics of Money', *Review of Politics* 83(4) (2021). I thank both journals for allowing me to use this material in this book.

As always, I give my thanks to my family for their love and support. In particular, I dedicate this book to my mum Kate Ward (née Parker), a wonderful mother and, like David Hume and Adam Smith, a proud Scot.

Introduction: Rethinking the Origins of Liberalism

The idea of the liberal democratic nation-state appears to be experiencing one of the periodic economic crises of legitimacy that are a hallmark of the modern era. In living memory, we recall the challenge to the post-war welfare state posed by neoliberal economic theory in the 1970s and 1980s, even as more recently we have witnessed the neoliberal post-Cold War consensus splintering under the pressure of political populism and economic nationalism. In contrast to the Continental tradition of the *Rechstaat* or 'Legal State' generally thought to have been inaugurated by Immanuel Kant, the Anglo-American liberal tradition typically has been reluctant to identify a dominant theory of the state.[1] We are now arguably very much in need of one, or at least we need to begin to think through what the economic elements of a liberal theory of the state should entail.[2] This study proposes that there is genuine value in looking back to the intellectual foundations of British political economy in the 'classical' liberal period in the seventeenth to the early nineteenth centuries in hope of better understanding the possibilities and challenges confronting liberal democracies in our times.

The origins and history of liberalism have been the subject of considerable interest of late.[3] And there have been valuable recent studies that illuminate particular aspects of early modern political economy, such as the concept of risk, charity and political corruption.[4] There has also been renewed focus on the extent to which economic concepts such as propriety and self-ownership have long been embedded in the normative foundations of liberal political theory.[5] However, the present project is guided by a different set of conceptual concerns and theoretical questions. I operate on the assumption that the primary reason for the continuing relevance of classical liberal thought is the widely held view that it is the philosophical inspiration for the neoliberal economic theory influential today. Contemporary neoliberalism is a somewhat nebulous concept, and one which has few self-admitted subscribers, but at its core it is frequently identified with the position that the economic realm has moral primacy over political life in the sense that political institutions are legitimate in the extent to which they contribute to the creation and functioning of markets driven by the free choice of individuals, not as fellow citizens, friends, parents or colleagues, but as economic agents: consumers, producers and investors.[6] For its part, classical liberalism is also a term that eludes easy categorisation. In historiographical terms, classical liberalism is a concept perched uneasily at the intersection of two meta-narratives. The first is the well-known, and well told, story about how early modern political economy made possible the emergence of *homo economicus* and the autonomy of economic discourse from the traditional moral categories of political philosophy.[7] The second grand narrative in which classical liberalism plays a central role is the influential account of the evolution of capitalism from the laissez faire teaching of Adam Smith through to the triumphal liberalism of later times that exuded supreme confidence in the proposition that the progress of capitalism built on free markets, private property and the wage relationship produces the greatest happiness and prosperity for the greatest majority of people.[8] In terms of both accounts, classical liberalism is, then, often seen as arguably one of the most formative intellectual influences that shaped the modern world.

In this study, I avoid sweeping generalisations claiming liberalism is constitutive of modernity itself or arose primarily as a justification for the ideology of unrestrained capitalism.[9] However, while I also eschew Karl Polanyi's magisterial efforts to frame the origins of liberalism in terms of any supra-historical event that ushered in the advent of capitalism, I do endorse his profound observation that memory of the deep complexity of classical liberal political economy was lost in the transition to the later modern liberal economic orthodoxy as the 'elementary truths of political science and statecraft were first discredited, then forgotten'.[10] Following Polanyi's insight, this study aims to recover a sense of classical liberal political economy as a multifarious intellectual tradition characterised by two distinct concepts and idioms epitomised by the discourse of natural rights and the harmony of interests. To the extent that we can speak of a classical liberal theory of the state, it must include both the concepts of rights and interests. But the discrete categories of rights and interests are primarily heuristic, rather than starkly ideological. Typically, the natural rights and harmony of interests strands of classical liberalism are treated in curious isolation. Whereas the importance of the concept of 'interests' to the development of capitalism has been brought out brilliantly by Albert Hirschman and others, many prominent studies of the emergence of natural rights theory in the early modern period generally have not considered issues of political economy in great depth.[11] Thus, part of the recovery of classical liberal political economy will involve careful examination of the important economic dimension of natural rights thinkers such as Thomas Hobbes, John Locke, Thomas Paine and John Trenchard, and Thomas Gordon.

This book is neither a genealogy of capitalism from its premodern origins, nor is it a teleological account of the evolution and development of the triumphant capitalist economic system of today.[12] Rather, I propose to construct a narrative in which classical liberal political economy emphatically does not signify the liberation of economics from moral and political judgements about equity and distributive justice. Instead, in both the rights- and interests-based version of classical liberalism, I illuminate aspects of statecraft that were a vital component of liberal political economy well into the modern period. Moreover, this narrative concludes not with the familiar story of the ideological triumph of laissez faire capitalism in the nineteenth century, but instead culminates alternatively in the complex interweaving of individual and social interests that constitute the normative foundation of J. S. Mill's zero-economic growth 'stationary state', the visionary goal of his political economy.

At this point, I should clarify a few points about my methodology. The range and scope of this project is bookended, as it were, by Hobbes and J. S. Mill, arguably the first and the last important British liberal thinkers to present a comprehensive philosophy including rigorous and systematic reflections on politics, ethics, morality, logic and economics. I will begin this narrative by highlighting how the modern liberal conception of the state that owed its origins to Hobbes, would two centuries later with Mill experience its first serious encounter with the challenges of socialism and communism. Perhaps the defining characteristic throughout this narrative was the proposition that, arguably for the first time in history, individual freedom was recognised by leading political philosophers as the primary moral fact. The political economy of rights and interests are two distinct expressions of this fundamental normative commitment. Moreover, as we shall see, there were important historical events and institutional developments such as the Financial Revolution in early eighteenth-century England and the expansion of British imperialism in the nineteenth century that propelled and impacted the emergence and adaptation of the discourse of rights and interests.

Another feature of my methodology is the criteria for selecting the thinkers and issues warranting special attention. This book is not a standard account of classical political economy because the aim is to recover the profoundly political character of classical liberal economic theory. As such, important economists such as Thomas Malthus and David Ricardo, who had little to say about political theory per se, are considered only insofar as they influenced political philosophers. My focus, then, is on highlighting classical liberal *political* economy; that is, the economic thinking of recognised political philosophers. But this requires negotiating among certain different categories of thinkers. For instance, I will examine in detail the political economy of figures such as Hobbes and Thomas Paine, who are not typically seen as economic thinkers, and I will treat Adam Smith, who is best known as the pioneer of classical political economy, primarily as a moral and political philosopher; even as I try to integrate the lesser known (at least today) economic writings of other thinkers such as Locke, David Hume and J. S. Mill into their more familiar political theory. Finally, I will be sensitive to the complexity of situating figures such as Bernard Mandeville or John Trenchard and Thomas Gordon, writers well-known as polemicists or literary figures, but often undervalued as a serious political theorists.

While there is great value in attempting a theoretical reconstruction of classical liberal political economy, I recognise that it is also important, however, to be sensitive to the problem of reading concerns of contemporary liberal political theory back onto the canonical founders of the tradition.[13] Indeed, my approach will likely raise objections from some commentators who charge that it is presumptuous to even identify a 'liberal tradition' of which these thinkers are a part. For instance, Duncan Bell dismisses the idea of a seventeenth-century liberal tradition *tout court* seeing liberalism as both an 'evolving and contested historical phenomena', and at the same time as the product of a philosophical reconstruction by later scholars who sought to establish liberalism as the 'constitutive ideology of the West' either to justify nineteenth-century British imperialism or twentieth-century American anti-communism.[14] In this view, any attempt to establish a single coherent intellectual tradition out of a 'universe of liberal languages' and a multitude of 'extant thought-worlds' is fated to be anachronistic for the simple reason that even a seminal thinker such as Locke only 'became a liberal during the twentieth century'.[15] Timothy Stanton similarly excoriates the 'fable of liberalism' as an attempt by modern scholars to transpose secular concepts of individualism onto a figure, once again, like Locke, who was primarily a religious thinker for whom the 'ruling normative force' was divine law.[16] Most recently, Eric Nelson claimed that 'there is no such thing as early modern liberalism', rather that thinkers such as Hobbes, Locke and Jean-Jacques Rousseau were fundamentally 'Pelagians' inspired by the rationalist metaphysics of a fourth-century Celtic ascetic monk.[17]

A full consideration of the important historiographical issues at stake here is beyond the scope of the present study, but I can affirm that I do not mean to engage in semantic disputes regarding whether it matters if Locke or Hume among others ever identified themselves as 'liberals'. Nor do I wish to reduce the range of thinkers who fit the category of liberal into a handful of canonical doyens. I am happy to embrace a broad universe of early modern 'thought-worlds'. In the present context, it makes little difference if we accept that all of the thinkers I identify as classical liberals in this study are permitted, for the sake of argument, to stand as liberals, quasi-liberals or proto-liberals.[18] However, I believe it is important to acknowledge that these political and economic thinkers understood themselves to be engaged in an intellectual milieu deeply influenced by an identifiable set of concepts, including natural rights, civil and religious liberty, property rights and commerce; ideas that we can tolerably categorise as liberal inasmuch as this approach, as David Armitage explains, 'provides a convenient conceptual shorthand and has the virtue of familiarity as a term of art'.[19]

My methodology strives to illuminate interconnections among a group of thinkers engaged in a grand conversation in a dialogue, at times even a multilogue, of different voices and interpretations of the relation between economics and politics. The legendary economic historian Jacob Viner once said that the emergence of laissez faire doctrine in England owed a debt to moral philosophers 'whose major objective was often to rebut Hobbes'.[20] There is plenty of evidence to confirm this statement, as well as my broader claim about the dialogic character of the classical liberal tradition. For instance, Hume quite explicitly framed his moral philosophy as a repudiation of the 'selfish system of Hobbes and Locke', even as Jeremy Bentham famously claimed to have discovered the basic principles of utilitarianism in the philosophy of Hume.[21] Similarly, Paine drew from Smith, much as Smith launched an extended critique of Mandeville,[22] and, of course, J. S. Mill's entire career was distinguished by an active critical engagement with practically every prior philosophy. Indeed, lacking any real sense of the rich, interconnected texture of classical liberal thought, I worry that the recent trend labelling of 'anachronistic' to any serious effort to categorise past historical intellectual traditions sometimes leads only to ever more jarring anachronisms such as abridging the complex moral, political and scientific enterprise of seventeenth-century political thought to an alien interpretive paradigm such as early Christian patristic controversies or Cold War propaganda. For our present purpose, I identify these figures ranging from Hobbes to J. S. Mill as British liberals because their thought was organised around a few fundamental principles that most political theorists today will recognise as classical liberalism.

The structure of this book is designed to reveal the origins, development and interconnection between the political economy of rights and the political economy of the harmony of interests. This complex narrative requires us to weave together the telling features of two distinct rhetorical strategies that also reflected substantive differences regarding human psychology and the role of history in political development. There is no inevitable teleology or certain, predictable process governing this narrative. Each chapter includes an introductory discussion that situates the political economy of specific classical liberal thinkers in their relevant historical and institutional context. However, at this point I would like to provide an overview of the general framework of the book. The opening chapters begin with a careful examination of the emergence of natural rights theory in the ground-breaking liberal philosophy of Hobbes and Locke. In Hobbes and Locke's conflict with the premodern *ancien régime*, we are witness to the creation of the modern state by way of rationalist philosophy and an individualistic moral orientation that does not, as is often supposed, necessarily culminate in the defence of the acquisitive bourgeois ethos or a *homo economicus* philosophical anthropology. Instead, Hobbes' account of a political economy grounded on the norm of equity, and Locke's intervention into debates over monetary policy in

1690's England reveal how these natural rights liberals advanced an approach to political economy that combines individualist ethical principles with important features of distributive justice and prudential reasoning informing a kind of liberal statecraft.

One of the pivotal historical moments in our account of classical liberal political economy is the Financial Revolution in England. In particular, in Chapter 3 we will consider the way in which Bernard Mandeville's scandalous *Fable of the Bees* and the radical Whig classic *Cato's Letters* written by John Trenchard and Thomas Gordon reflect two distinctive responses to the first major scandal caused by the new financial institutions during the South Sea Bubble in 1720. Whereas Cato continued the natural rights discourse of Locke and Hobbes, Mandeville adopted an original formula of 'private vices, public benefits' that became the conceptual basis for a new interest-based version of liberalism that defended commerce, luxury and a morality of self-interest, but did not do so on the logic of individual rights. Instead, Mandeville's liberation of acquisitive passions from the strictures of traditional classical and Christian morality rested upon a rudimentary concept of historical progress that culminated in the inchoate form of a self-stabilising social mechanism that paradoxically promised to put individual vice unintentionally at the service of social happiness.

In our reflections upon the political economy of the Scottish Enlightenment in Chapter 4, we will consider how David Hume and Adam Smith inaugurated a crucial double-movement that deepened the fracturing of liberal political economy into a rights- and interest-based variant. The first part of this movement involved Hume's critique of natural rights philosophy and the social contract theory central for Hobbes, Locke and later for Paine. In Hume's account, justice is rendered artificial, and political legitimacy is reduced to certain habits of obedience. The second element of the Scottish reworking of the moral foundations of liberal political economy had to do with what I call, following Dario Castiglione's lead, *moralising Mandeville*. Hume and Smith agreed with Mandeville on the importance of history and developed a sophisticated stadial history for the development of commerce that was inspired by Mandeville. They also agreed with the fabulous beekeeper about the general outlines of a natural harmony of interests, but they rejected his model of pure self-interest. Instead, Hume and Smith discovered a natural basis for moral relations in certain other-regarding sentiments such as compassion, benevolence and humanity. That is to say, Hume and Smith's defence of commerce, luxury and free trade presupposed this moral foundation. It is, thus, the Scots' moralised Mandevilleanism that climaxed in the 'invisible hand' transmogrification of self-interest into the laissez faire economic system.

Chapter 5 turns to the economic thinking of Thomas Paine, who exposes the enormous impact that his predecessors Hume and Smith had on the political economy of liberal rights theory. Early in his career Paine believed that the natural rights and the harmony of interests doctrine were perfectly compatible, almost interchangeable, but gradually over time, prompted by the events of the French Revolution and his desire to rebut both Edmund Burke's influential critique of the natural rights doctrine and proto-communist French radicals, Paine came to the conclusion that the moral foundation of a natural rights society compelled the liberal state to introduce quite radical redistributionist policies such as the creation of a welfare system underwritten by a 'National Fund' designed to preserve as much socio-economic equality as is feasible in a system of private property.

The following chapter examines John Stuart Mill, who represents a kind of logical and contextual end point for the narrative of classical liberal political economy. Mill's refined utilitarianism, modified from its Benthamite original, is famous for the manner in which he almost practically fused the logic of interests and rights in his defence of free inquiry, lifestyle choices and the emancipation of women. I will focus, however, on Mill's *Principles of Political Economy* (1848), a work now often ignored, but very influential in its day. We will see that Mill's political economy was far from a dogmatic endorsement of the principle of laissez faire, as is sometimes supposed. Rather, Mill examined the limits and possibilities of both capitalism and socialism as they reflected different aspects of the historical progress of the spirit of social cooperation and the material requirements for the mental improvement of the great majority of people. I will argue that the zero-economic growth 'stationary state' – the bane of classical political economy since Smith, Malthus and Ricardo – remarkably signifies Mill's idea of a liberal best regime guided by the normative economics charged to supply the physical needs for a society directed towards individual moral and intellectual flourishing.

This historico-conceptual account of classical liberal political economy will conclude with a thematic examination of two of the most morally contentious aspects of liberalism's history; namely, liberalism's relation to British imperialism and its historical ineffectiveness at combatting the legal, social, political and economic subjection of women until very recently. Chapter 7 will engage the question: was classical liberalism complicit with, and even supportive of, empire and the subjection of women, or, rather, was it antagonistic to these violations of the liberal principle of natural equality? Not surprisingly, this is also a complex tale. With respect to empire, the natural rights tradition registered deep ambivalence inasmuch as the idea of equality and consent to government militated against any claims to empire based upon the natural inferiority of one group towards another, but both Hobbes and Locke seemed to accept the practical reality of colonisation, and even slavery in the 'New World' (although to his credit Paine represented a more direct version of natural rights anti-imperialism). The interest-based version of classical liberalism was arguably even more conflicted over the issue of colonisation with a strong anti-imperialist argument running through the political economy of Hume, Smith and Bentham as they excoriated mercantilism and the unjust domination of foreign peoples. These classical liberals believed for the most part that it was not in Britain's interests politically or economically to hold overseas possessions. However, with J. S. Mill the argument that empire was not in Britain's interests was turned on its head as he expanded the logic of interest to include the interests of humanity as a whole in accepting the governance, even including despotic rule, by culturally advanced nations over 'backwards' peoples below them on Mill's nebulous scale of civilisation progress. We will also see, however, that the principles of Mill's political economy encouraged him to adopt a different attitude towards colonisation with respect to nations supposedly at different points in cultural progress, including Canada, India and Ireland.

Finally, on the question of the emancipation of women, I will try to put classical liberal thinkers in a dialogue of sorts with contemporary feminist scholars. We will see that while there was fairly obvious emancipatory potential in the natural rights philosophy of Hobbes and Locke, their individualism was, nonetheless, undermined by their continued acknowledgement of some vague natural or quasi-natural basis for de facto male rule in the family and political society. The great shift in classical liberal thinking on gender equality occurred with Mary Wollstonecraft and J. S. Mill. Writing in the context of the transformative events of the French Revolution, Wollstonecraft advanced an argument for women's equality that combined both the rights- and interests-based liberal discourse in a complex blend highlighting both the benefits for society if women are afforded the same educational opportunities and a comparable level of economic independence as enjoyed by men, as well as the violation of fundamental rights inflicted on females when they are effectively denied the opportunity to develop the rational and moral faculties central to human dignity. With Mill, his commitment to equality for women seems to cast him beyond even the mental horizons of utilitarian interest philosophy, insofar as he insisted uncharacteristically that gender inequality is wrong in itself. For Mill, as for Wollstonecraft, greater educational and employment opportunities for women is crucial to ending their subjection, although some feminist commentators perceive lingering sexist assumptions about women's purportedly different 'nature' than men, even in an early champion of women's rights with the bona fides of Mill.

Classical liberal political economy is, then, a complex, multifaceted tradition that weaves together economic, moral and political concepts, and sheds light on issues of imperialism and gender inequality, which arguably continue to trouble liberal societies with their lingering aftereffects, as well as direct manifestations, to this very day. But in order to understand who we really are as liberal democrats today and how we got to this point in the economic and political reality of modern liberalism, we need to reacquaint ourselves with liberalism's deep connection to the theoretical origins of the modern state in seventeenth-century England.

Notes

1. Hayek 1960: 196–7.
2. C. B. Macpherson provocatively posed the question 'Do we need a theory of the State?' to modern liberal democrats decades ago (Macpherson 1985).
3. See, for example, Rosenblatt 2018; Deneen 2018; Kalyvas and Katznelson 2008; Rasmussen 2014.
4. For the concept of risk in early modern British political economy, see Nacol 2016; for the concept of charity in a set of thinkers ranging from David Hume to Immanuel Kant, see Hanley 2017; and for the significance of corruption as a theme in early modern thought in England and France, see Sparling 2019.
5. Kelly 2011: 3–6; Sklansky 2012: 239.
6. McKean 2020: 6–7. Colin Hay resists any attempt to discover a 'generic and transhistorical definition of neoliberalism' (quoted in Biebricher 2018: 11–12). Richard Epstein's recent work on the 'Classical Liberal Constitution' perhaps exemplifies the reluctance even among sympathetic scholars to embrace the term 'neoliberal' (Epstein 2014).

7. Hirschman 1977; Dumont 1977; Myers 1983; Macpherson 1962.
8. Persky 2016: 4.
9. Bell 2016: 62, 85.
10. Polanyi 1944: 33; see also Sklansky 2012: 235.
11. For influential accounts that emphasize the idea of interests as central to liberal political economy, see Hirschman 1977; Dumont 1977. For examples of important studies of early modern natural rights theory that largely do not consider political economy, see Finnis 1980; Tuck 1979; Zuckert 1994.
12. See Tribe 1981; Sklansky 2012.
13. Kelly 2011: 1–2.
14. Bell 2016: 70; Bell 2014: 704–5.
15. Bell 2014: 687–8, 698.
16. Stanton 2018: 606, 616, 620.
17. Nelson 2019: 1, 4, 16–18, 42–6.
18. Nelson, 2019: 1.
19. Armitage 2013: 90.
20. Viner quoted in Myers 1983: 6.
21. Hume 1961: 296; Persky 2016: 3.
22. Paine 1987b: 66–8; Smith 1981: 308–12.

Chapter 1

The Political Economy of Thomas Hobbes

In the political philosophy of Thomas Hobbes, arguably we are witness to one of the most important harbingers of the dawning of the modern conception of the state. Hobbes' account of the origins, character and limitations of political association displays a level of theoretical sophistication that surpassed his immediate predecessors such as the arch-realist Niccolò Machiavelli or the master *politique* Jean Bodin. The distinct historical context out of which Hobbes' political philosophy emerged is marked by both the specific political history of his native England and the more general intellectual milieu in mid-seventeenth-century Europe.

As is well-known, Hobbes' political writings are in some sense an extended reflection upon the long simmering constitutional and religious disputes in England that exploded into civil war in the 1640s. What Hobbes perceived in this conflict was nothing less than the complete shattering of the feudal order that had dominated not only England, but much of Europe, since the medieval period. Under pressure of events in the first decades of the seventeenth century, the theological and social pillars of the Stuart monarchy splintered apart as the commercial towns, dissenting Protestants and their proponents in Parliament grappled in a struggle for supremacy with the defenders of the Crown's prerogatives among the adherents of the established Church of England.

To Hobbes' mind, so complete was the disintegration of the once well-established grounds of legitimate authority that by the time the civil war broke out 'not one perhaps of ten thousand know what right any man had to command him'.[1] The centrifugal forces that tore apart the delicate Elizabethan political and religious settlement proved to be impervious to the effects of traditional modes of moral and civil discourse. Of course, Hobbes was not surprised that even the Restoration of the Stuart monarchy in 1660 could not fully resolve the crisis of legitimacy in the English government, which would not be settled, more or less decisively, until the Glorious Revolution of 1688–1690 a decade or so after Hobbes' own long life came to an end.

The events that Hobbes experienced directly in England were, however, not *sui generis*, but rather resembled just one front in a massive continent-wide struggle that Jonathan Israel describes as the 'Crisis of the European Mind'.[2] The dramatic political tumults in Hobbes' life occurred in the context of an even more transformative intellectual awakening already well under way in mid-seventeenth-century Europe. In the scientific revolution led by Galilei Galileo, René Descartes and Francis Bacon novel principles of empiricism, methodological reason and programmatic scepticism were put forth as a challenge to the intellectual hegemony of Christian–Aristotelian metaphysics and the regnant ontology of scholasticism. In a parallel track, on the philosophical and legal level this period saw Hugo Grotius inject new modern philosophical principles into the study of the Roman Civil Law tradition, even as his Dutch compatriot Baruch Spinoza pioneered the modern concept of textual criticism of scripture. In the spirit of this time of bold intellectual endeavour to break new ground in the understanding of moral and natural phenomena, Hobbes was arguably the most important distinctively English voice in this period to challenge the orthodoxy of political and religious ideas that had governed England and Europe for centuries.

Hobbes' assessment of human beings' starkly egoistic psychology would later earn him the dubious distinction of being identified by David Hume as one of the founders of the modern 'selfish system of morals', even as Hobbes' famous state of nature motif rejected the Aristotelian premise of natural sociability that had been foundational in western philosophy for centuries.[3] With this assertion of a radical individualist ontology, Hobbes sought to eviscerate the classical and Christian teaching on natural justice, for in the state of nature, 'this war of every man against every man . . . nothing can be unjust. The notions of right and wrong, justice and injustice, have there no place. Where there is no common power, there is no law; where no law, no injustice.'[4] In the asocial condition without a 'common power to keep them in awe', the primary goal of securing self-preservation is constantly jeopardised by the natural right of all other individuals to employ any means necessary to secure their self-preservation in a situation marked by 'continual fear and danger of violent death, and the life of man, solitary, poor, nasty, brutish and short' (Lev 13.8–9.76). The logic of this preservationist imperative pervades the central paradox of the Hobbesian account of government; namely, that individuals can secure their natural right of self-preservation only by largely surrendering their natural liberty to the sovereign power.

While Hobbes' status as one of the founders of the modern natural rights-based conception of the state is widely acknowledged, in our effort to retrace the philosophical origins of classical liberal political economy, Hobbes is a complex, and more ambiguous, figure. On the one hand, Hobbes' treatment of political economy has suffered neglect among scholars under the mistaken assumption that 'Hobbes said little, almost nothing about economics'.[5] But, on the other hand, on a more abstract theoretical level, Hobbes' status as one of the philosophical inspirations of the bourgeois ethos and capitalist economics was firmly established many decades ago by his central role in several influential accounts of the ideological origins of liberalism. For example, in his classic study *The Political Theory of Possessive Individualism* C. B. Macpherson argued that understanding Hobbes' political theory requires recognising that his psychological postulations are consistent with 'a certain kind of society' only, specifically one characterised by the 'compulsions and morality' of the competitive free market.[6]

While coming from a different philosophical perspective, Leo Strauss reached the same basic conclusion about Hobbes as did Macpherson inasmuch as he identified Hobbes as 'the founder of liberalism' and a vision of society dominated by 'the morality of the bourgeois world', according to which the fundamental connection between Hobbes' economic and political theory means that 'private property and private profit are . . . the inevitable condition for all peaceful life'.[7] For her part, Hannah Arendt not only identified Hobbes as the seminal proto-bourgeois thinker, who envisioned 'a society relentlessly engaged in a process of acquisition', but she also associated Hobbes with what she took to be the moral psychology of the uniquely modern totalitarian state that produced individual subjects incapable of exercising the normative judgements necessary for self-government.[8] More recently, Jürgen Habermas continued the now well-established reading of Hobbes as 'more of a theorist of a bourgeois rule of law without democracy than the apologist of unlimited absolutism'.[9] Hobbes, then, has become arguably the central figure in an important scholarly interpretation of the founding of liberalism.[10]

This chapter aims to demonstrate that Hobbes had a more complex and theoretically significant conception of the state and political economy than is witnessed in the reductionist bourgeois individualist account. In particular, it will show that reconsidering Hobbes' account of the natural law of equity can potentially allow us not only to recover a sense of the important normative dimensions of Hobbes' political economy, but also to highlight the prudential aspects of his statecraft more generally. While Hobbes did not subscribe to the model of political economy that intellectual historians normally associate with later figures such as Adam Smith, Thomas Malthus, David Ricardo and Karl Marx, it is possible to discern in his account of the 'Nutrition of a Commonwealth', which he claims 'consisteth in the plenty and distribution of materials conducing to life', an early version of the form of analytic study of production, trade and national income in their relation to government that would assume greater importance in the following centuries (Lev 24.1.159). Similarly, while the concepts of free markets and bourgeois morality are strictly speaking anachronistic for seventeenth-century thought, arguably the application of these concepts to Hobbes by twentieth-century scholars suffices to warrant taking seriously potential earlier anticipations of these ideas. I contend that Hobbes did not even adumbrate laissez faire ideology for he did not commit to an economic system revolving around the selfish acquisitive desires of individuals largely unfettered by law or morality. Rather, he proposed an economy integrated holistically into a political vision bearing a normative view of the citizen. I thus hope to replace the reductionist possessive individualist account of Hobbes with a more complex story embedded in a historical context of networks of social relations sustained by legal contracts, as well as robust norms of equity and prudence.

Hobbes recognised that with the creation of the state *qua* state there is validity, and in some respects even priority, of the moral principles of equity underlying the socially constructed idea of the public. Equity is emphatically public, is not reducible to contract, extends political considerations of distributive justice beyond procedural market principles, and is the main requirement for peace. While Hobbes did not directly seek to create the social and political conditions that would prevent the institution of free-market mechanisms, his state theory did reject scientific laws of economic determinism. For Hobbes, the scope and extent of government's practical involvement in economics was dependent on prudential judgement, even as his theoretical ambitions extended to establishing equity as a norm that could inform not only public policy, but also the behaviour of individuals in the commonwealth. But before we can fully appreciate Hobbes' seminal account of classical liberal political economy, we need to reflect in more depth upon his role in the invention of the modern liberal state.

Natural Rights and the Modern State

Hobbes is perhaps most widely remembered as the thinker who argued in his masterpiece *Leviathan* (1651) that all human beings are naturally in a state of war that does not end until every individual surrenders his or her natural liberty and agrees to obey the law established by one absolute civil authority. But Hobbes' account of the origin of political society in his earlier works *Elements of Law* (1640) and *De Cive* (1642) did not include a fully developed concept of the state of nature, and in the case of the *Elements* even largely presupposed a degree of natural sociability.[11] In *De Cive* the idea of the civil person as constructed legal entity replaced the *polis* still present in the *Elements* as the conceptual touchstone of the Hobbesian state.[12] But while in *De Cive* Hobbes insisted that the will of every citizen is 'comprehended into the will of the supreme authority of the city' (DC 6.14.84), he did not at this stage in his philosophical career offer any explanation about how to operationalise this principle of comprehension. Arguably what most clearly distinguished *Leviathan* from these earlier works was Hobbes' argument for sovereign authorisation.

In a sense, sovereign authorisation is the implicit conclusion of Hobbes' earlier thinking in *De Cive* about the idea of a civil person as a legal entity.[13] The purpose of chapter 16 of *Leviathan* , titled 'Of Persons, Authors, and Things Personated', is to define the terms involved in the idea of personhood and to examine what Hobbes takes to be the central political relationship, that being the relation of author and actor. Chapter 16 is also the final chapter in Part I *Of Man*, and thus is the last chapter before the beginning of Part II *Of Commonwealth*. Hobbes presents the idea of the 'person' as a kind of bridge between human beings and political society. It is widely recognised that defining terms and concepts was one of the main goals in *Leviathan* because Hobbes believed that agreement on the use of terms would promote peace, even as disagreement about the use of language is a fundamental cause of conflict.[14] A *person*, Hobbes claims, is '*he whose words or actions are considered either as his own, or as representing the words or actions of another man, or of any other thing to whom they are attributed, whether truly or by fiction*' (Lev 16.1.101). Perhaps the most striking feature of this definition of a person is its conceptual flexibility that covers words *or* actions, of one's own *or* another's; that represent people *or* things and may be attributed in truth *or* by fictional representation. This definition of a person intensifies the distinction between nature and convention even as it proposes to, at least theoretically, bridge it.

The common experience of personhood is in relation to the natural person; that is, a human being displaying the features of human physical form and mental life. However, the artificial person is the core of Hobbes' political teaching, and such a person can be understood only by means of the principle of representation, rather than sensual experience per se. The relation between real and unreal, or natural and artificial, persons is complicated by the fact that the idea of a 'fictional' person is dependent upon real people acting as though the natural person can or should take responsibility for certain actions attributed to an artificial person.[15] Properly identifying what Hobbes means by a 'person' requires recognising that it involves both an internal and external process. Internally it requires assuming an identity that is not naturally one's own, while externally personating involves the recognition of others. Hobbes demonstrates this complexity with the example of Cicero, who claimed that as a lawyer in a case: 'I bear three persons: my own, my adversary's and the judges' (Lev 16.3.101). Just as Cicero acts in multiple capacities so too is every person 'the same that an actor is', and Hobbes insists this is recognised both 'on stage and in common conversation' (Lev 16.3.101). How exactly is one an actor in 'common conversation'? Perhaps Hobbes means that if I relate to someone what a third party said or did, I am in effect representing them. While Hobbes presents the classical idea of the person as something pertaining to a wide range of phenomena, he noticeably does not, at least early in chapter 16 of *Leviathan*, highlight any uniquely political uses to which the classical idea of the person can be employed.

In *De Cive* and the *Elements* contract solely involved natural individuals who form the union; there is no contractual relation with the sovereign. In *Leviathan*, however, covenant and contract are redefined in terms of ownership rather than simply as consent. Or to put it differently, the idea of *person* advanced in *Leviathan* means that the author–actor relationship depends upon determining the question of ownership. As Hobbes describes the relation made possible by the extension of the idea of the person into politics, the author confers authority upon an actor and the actors act on behalf of the author. In this relation, Hobbes chooses to stress the moral force of authorised actors rather than the obligations delegated agents have to their principal.[16] For Hobbes, 'when the actor maketh a covenant by authority, he bindeth thereby the author, no less than if he had made it himself' (Lev 16.5.102). Authority means that an actor can generate moral claims for others. This concept of representation rests, according to Hobbes, upon a foundation of voluntary choice as authors give the actor legitimacy. This, for Hobbes, is voluntary in two senses: both with respect to the will of the authors and the will of the actors. Hobbes clarifies that it is theoretically possible for authors to place limits on the authority conferred upon an actor so that it would reach as far as 'their commission, but no farther' (Lev 16.5.102). Hobbes even offers a helpful warning that if you make a covenant with an actor without 'knowing the authority he hath, you doth it at [your] own peril' (Lev 16.6.102).

For Hobbes, the commonwealth or state is a person, albeit an artificial one. It is precisely the artificiality of the state that is crucial for Hobbes because it signifies his complete rejection of the naturalistic classical *polis*, elements of which still persisted in his earlier writings. The commonwealth as an artificial person with legal existence is a person capable of voluntary action and of generating collective responsibility. The legal personality of the commonwealth is inseparable from its intrinsic unity. The natural multitude of individuals become one person – a single political entity – only when they are represented by one ruler or assembly 'so that it be done with the consent of everyone of that multitude in particular' (Lev 16.13.104). The unity that characterises the unity of the state derives, however, from a very specific condition according to which it is 'the unity of the represoner, not the unity of the represented, that maketh the person one' (Lev 16.13.103). That is to say, Hobbes insists that there is no natural unity in the undifferentiated multitude for 'unity cannot be otherwise understood in multitude' (Lev 16.13.104). Embedded in this conception of unity is an adaptation to representative assemblies in which 'the voice of the greater number must be considered the voice of them all' (Lev 16.15.104). The major theoretical innovation in Hobbes' idea of the state as one person is the proposition that every individual among the multitude is an author 'of everything their representative saith or doth in their name, every man giving their common representative authority from himself in particular, and among all the actions the representer doth' (Lev 16.14.104). But by what means does the representative sovereign obtain this authorisation?

It is important to recognise that for Hobbes sovereign authorisation is not an event that occurs either before or after a political entity is formed. Rather, authorisation is identical to the very generation of a commonwealth, which requires everyone acknowledging his or her self as an author. Hobbes famously describes this process in terms of a declaration: '*I authorise and give up my right of governing myself to this man, or to this assembly of men, on this condition, that thou give up thy right to him, and authorise all his actions in like manner*' (Lev 17.13.109). Authorisation is more than simply consent or concord. It requires reciprocity: my agreement to authorise the sovereign is contingent upon your agreement to do likewise. Hobbes describes the product of this authorisation process in quasi-religious language as the 'great Leviathan', who is 'that Mortal God, to which we owe, under the Immortal God, our peace and defence' (Lev 17.13.109).

As the founding political act, or the act that makes political life manifest, sovereign authorisation by natural rights-bearing individuals introduced a degree of subjectivity and psychological depth arguably unparalleled among Hobbes' predecessors in the contractarian tradition.[17] Hobbes' deepened appreciation of the formative, constitutive powers of individuals witnessed in his account of authorisation also transforms the normative elements of contract theory that were seen as crucial supports for the idea of obligation in traditional, teleological accounts of the origin of political society. Hobbes is proto-Kantian in the sense that authorisation involves rational individuals making a contractual agreement the breaking of which must on some level constitute a contradiction of one's original rational purpose. But Hobbes' stipulation about the primacy of self-preservation means that the real normative thrust of authorisation is a displaced form of political obligation according to which the aim is to fortify the obligation of everyone else as opposed to the individual who is actually endangered by punishment. Hobbes' version of the categorical imperative (which is, of course, not categorical at all) is that it is normally in my self-interest that everyone else apart from me should do their duty! It is not, then, a matter that I authorise the sovereign to punish me, but rather that each individual firmly believes that everyone else authorised the sovereign to punish themselves. In this scenario of displaced moral responsibility, authorisation emerges primarily as Hobbes' account of political founding, and only derivatively and problematically, as a theory of political obligation per se.[18] How then should authorisation inform our assessment of the familiar claim that Hobbes' treatment of sovereignty depends upon his assumptions about the pre-political origins of political life?

Authorisation is undoubtedly a kind of liberal founding myth, but it is also disarmingly non-mythical precisely because it is so self-consciously fictive. The artificiality of the artificial person that is Hobbes' state is hardly concealed. Indeed, this artificiality is central to Hobbes' nascent idea of political obligation, and thus serves as a stark contrast to nationalist mythologies that try to establish the antiquity or connaturality of ethnic identities that came into being in time in the anthropological sense.[19] Hobbes' authorisation theory is designed in part to demonstrate that any consideration of the 'pre-political' origins of the commonwealth is politically irrelevant for a number of reasons. First, Hobbes' innovative use of the idea of representation presupposes a relationship between the social group and the putatively pre-political individual. Authorisation pertains to all as much as to each. As such, it is inaccurate to suggest that Hobbes' version of the argument for the legitimacy of civil government is simply self-referential inasmuch as the sovereign's role as representative means that individual and group claims are mutually reinforcing. That is to say, the 'people' is not a political entity separate from the sovereign because prior to the creation of the sovereign through the authorisation process, the political person of the commonwealth did not exist.[20] Second, Hobbes emphasises that authorisation is a formative, constitutive act. The founding of the commonwealth involves 'creation out of nothing by human wit' (EL 2.1.1.108). As Runciman says of Hobbes, 'the multitude makes possible the fiction that they can act as a unit',[21] but this does not mean that we can assign logical or temporal priority to any specific act in the authorisation process over and against any other. This also does not indicate that there is latent personality in the Hobbesian natural multitude of individuals. It may be said that the sovereign 'presents the person', or represents the artificial 'people' that is brought into being through authorisation but, we recall, individuals contract with each other, and thus the sovereign cannot help but 'present the person' formed (Lev 18.1.110). The atomistic presupposition of the authorisation formula is revealed by the way in which it is described solely in terms of the first person singular: '*I authorize . . . my right . . .*' (Lev 17.13.109). Thus, we likely need to avoid attributing any kind of even latent personality to Hobbes' conception of the natural multitude for fear of ascribing unwarranted essentialism to his theory.

The transformation of the multitude into a political entity is therefore not a multi-stage process, but it does involve a complex double movement. Even as the principle of representation, on the one hand, differentiates the sovereign and the people as author and actor, the concept of authorisation presented in *Leviathan*, for its part, requires practically equating the will of the multitude with the will of the sovereign.[22] What then does it mean to speak of the 'pre-political' in Hobbes' political theory? In one of his later works, *De Homine* (1658), Hobbes stipulated that 'an author must have right to act himself, if not the actor has no authority'.[23] Strictly speaking, in terms of the creation of the commonwealth, the authors do not have the prior right to act because the authors are only a people capable of authorship by virtue of having appointed a designated actor. To put it in terms familiar in contemporary democratic theory, authorisation is meant to show two things: (1) that there can be no political entity or people independent of the sovereign, and (2) to demonstrate that any *demos* is naturally bounded and only conventionally unbounded because every demos is itself a construct.[24] Of course, the key distinction for Hobbes is not between democratic and non-democratic procedure, but rather the difference between what is natural (i.e., individuals) and what is conventional (i.e., political entities). The artificiality of the *demos* is not territorially limited as it is defined by an agreement among potentially dispersed individuals who recognise the same person or body as sovereign. As the primordial political unit, Hobbes' commonwealth does not exist even in *potentia* prior to the authorisation process described in *Leviathan*.

For Hobbes, the artifice of politics is actually more inclusive than the natural condition precisely because it is social. This is the case because representation rendered necessary by authorisation makes it possible to transcend the limits of a natural person by means of the artificial person that is the commonwealth potentially to a vast proportion. As representative of the state, one person or assembly of people can govern millions. Moreover, insofar as authorisation is an inherently political act of founding, it signifies Hobbes' recognition that there must be a mechanism in place for becoming a member of the commonwealth; that is in addition to founding properly speaking. Hobbes' concept of representation is an extraordinarily flexible concept that makes modern 'indirect' government possible.[25] The state is itself a product of practical reason, and thus is characterised by a structural flexibility consistent with the goal of securing peace.

As Waldron and Kraynak remind us, Hobbes was an enlightenment figure who believed that his political project to promote peace through recognised sovereign authority can succeed only if the normative grounds of the sovereign's legitimacy is not 'opaque to the subjects' understanding'.[26] Part of this enlightenment process requires recognition of the unintuitive character of Hobbes' sovereign authorisation theory of political founding, which he admits is more prescriptive than descriptive. Hobbes' authorisation theory does, however, reveal some of the discursive architecture of the modern state, for as Hobbes insists, authorisation involves inter-subjective communication inasmuch as in principle moral obligation emerges in relation to other subjects rather than to the sovereign. The social dimensions of Hobbes' theory of sovereignty are fleshed out in later chapters of *Leviathan* dealing with the role of ministers and other civil persons that are non-sovereign institutions of civil society such as universities, churches and commercial guilds, which Hobbes treats as locations of civil discourse. While Hobbes' theory of sovereign authorisation is in some respects self-referential – reducible to the individual's pre-political rights – this hardly resolves the integral debates that Hobbes' account of sovereignty and political founding necessarily produce. Is the legitimacy of sovereign actions due to authorisation by the subjects, or is it self-generated by virtue of the fact that the sovereign is the one uncontracted agent in the state still in full possession of his or her natural liberty? And, more specifically for our purposes, does the legitimacy of the Hobbesian commonwealth depend upon a certain conception of the sovereign's role in preserving the economic foundation of the state created by natural rights-bearing individuals?

Hobbes and *Homo Economicus*

Before we turn to Hobbes' political economy per se, it is perhaps fitting to consider some of the main pieces of textual evidence drawn on to support the interpretation of Hobbes as the apostle of *homo economicus*. In his earliest political writing *The Elements of Law*, Hobbes listed as one of the laws of nature: 'That men allow commerce and traffic indifferently to one another' (EL 1.17.87). Here Hobbes observed that if the ruler allows a right or privilege to one group that is denied to another, then the effect will be to encourage war by expressing hatred towards the parties excluded from the privilege. In the later *De Cive*, Hobbes argued that individuals institute governments 'in order to live as pleasantly as the human condition allows . . . with all good things necessary not just for life but for the enjoyment of life' (DC 13.4.144). The government's primary task, then, seems to lie in providing the legal infrastructure 'in what manner all kinds of contract between subjects (as buying, selling, exchanging, borrowing, lending, letting and taking to hire) are to be made' (Lev 24.10.163). Importantly for Macpherson, Hobbes argues that government must facilitate a market for individual labour for 'a man's labour also is a commodity exchangeable for benefit, as well as any other thing' (Lev 24.4.160). Hobbes even suggests that the measure of a person's value can be determined by means of a price mechanism: 'The value or Worth of a man is, as of all other things, his price . . . And as in other things, so in men, not the seller, but the buyer determines the price' (Lev 10.16.51).

In order to place these statements in their proper context, however, it is important to consider Hobbes' account of the origins of proprietary rights. For Hobbes, the right to property is not natural for in the state of nature 'there be no propriety, no dominion, no mine and thine distinct, but only that to be everyman's that he can get, and for so long as he can keep it' (Lev 13.13.78). Moreover, 'where there is no own, that is property, there is no injustice' (Lev 15.3.89). Property rights derive from the sovereign: 'all men had right to all things which necessarily causeth war, and therefore, this propriety, being necessary to peace, and depending on sovereign power, is the act of that power in order to the public peace' (Lev 18.10.114). Not only the determination of right, but also the distribution of material resources 'belongeth in all kinds of commonwealth to the sovereign power' (Lev 24.5.160). Thus, Hobbes' statements regarding the right to buy and sell goods and labour must be understood in the light of the more fundamental truth that the very notion of property right originates in the sovereign power.[27] This explains why the subject's property rights are inherently limited: 'The propriety which a subject hath in his lands consistently is a right to exclude all other subjects from the use of them, and not to exclude the sovereign, be it an assembly or a monarch' (Lev 24.7.161). Indeed, Hobbes insists that the doctrine 'that every private man has an absolute propriety in his goods, such as excludeth the right of the sovereign' is one of a handful of 'pernicious doctrines' that every commonwealth has to suppress in order to prevent dissolution (Lev 29.10.213).

It is still, of course, an open question as to whether the bourgeois ethos ascribed to Hobbes depends upon the idea of property rights being either natural or absolute. Insofar as natural law served as a normative description of contractual relations already permeating English society, Hobbes' treatment of property in terms of the naturalness inhering in the equality of right is a means to ensure that everyone has an interest in preserving the property of the rest. For Hobbes, property was less about possession than right in terms of giving everyone their due.[28] Hobbes did not assimilate property rights into the logic of self-ownership as did John Locke.[29] By eschewing the rhetorical device of self-ownership, Hobbes rejected the natural rights basis of property in favour of an 'older notion of property bound up in social relations and obligation'.[30] Thus, while it is true that Hobbes defined injustice very narrowly as 'no other than the not performance of covenant' (Lev 15.2.89), it is also clear that his notion of distributive justice rests upon the complex relation between justice and equity.

Hobbes on Justice and Equity

Throughout his discussion of justice Hobbes frequently reminds the reader about the main features of the classical argument for justice exemplified in Aristotle's *Nicomachean Ethics*. In Book V of the *Ethics*, Aristotle explained that the term justice is used in several senses, but the equivocal uses are closely connected.[31] The just is, thus, both that which is lawful and that which is equal or fair. The lawful, or what Aristotle calls 'particular justice', can be divided into distributive and corrective justice. Distributive justice involves 'the distribution of honour, wealth, and the other divisible assets of the community, which may be allotted among its members in equal or unequal shares' (NE 1130b34). Aristotle claims that the principle of allocation for distributive justice is geometrical proportional distribution such that equal shares are given to equals and unequal shares to unequal people. Corrective justice, on the other hand, relates to private transactions not involving common property. The principle guiding allocation for corrective justice is arithmetical proportion, which is a certain idea of equality because with corrective justice the character of the individuals is irrelevant for 'the law looks only at the nature of the damage, treating the parties as equal' (NE 1132a5).

What is fair, on the other hand, deals with reciprocity which Aristotle claims is more fundamental to political life even than equality for the 'very existence of the state [*polis*] depends on proportionate reciprocity' (NE 1132b35). Equity, in Aristotle's account, is connected to fairness and operates as a 'rectification of legal justice' where the law is defective because of its generality (NE 1137b12, 27). The equitable man is not simply the law-abiding individual, for Aristotle characterises this person as one 'who does not stand on his own rights unduly, but is content to receive a smaller share although he has the law on his side' (NE 1138a1–2). Interestingly, Aristotle broke with his own practice by never providing a term to describe the opposite of an equitable person (*ho epieikes*), but perhaps a 'contentious' person or 'stickler' might be apt as one who ungraciously insists upon his or her legal rights to the exclusion of any other consideration. For our purposes, the most significant element in Aristotle's discussion of equity is his judgement that while both justice and equity are good, 'equity is the better' (NE 1137b10–11) precisely because it requires prudential deliberation about particular conditions not adequately treated by laws in their generality.

Hobbes' account of justice and equity primarily reflects a significant departure from Aristotle's influential teaching on natural right. The problem as Hobbes sees it is twofold: not only is Aristotle the great authority about justice among Hobbes' contemporaries, but his mistaken premise of natural inequality is the 'foundation of all political knowledge, that some men have been made by nature more worthy to rule, others to serve' (DC 3.13.49). In Hobbes' taxonomy of natural law virtues and vices, Aristotle's premise of natural inequality encourages the vices of 'pride' and 'encroaching' (or 'covetousness') practically inimical to peace.

Hobbes' fundamental moral premise is that the right of nature consists in 'the liberty each man hath to use his own power, as he will himself, for the preservation of his own nature' (Lev 14.1.179). The natural right of self-preservation means that there is nothing just or unjust by nature 'for where no covenant hath preceded, there hath no right been transferred ... and consequently no action can be unjust' (Lev 15.1.89). If justice and injustice presuppose a form of contractual agreement about a promise of future action, then logically the sovereign – who Hobbes insists has made no covenant or promise with the subjects – can do no injustice. Justice is strictly a matter of the 'manners' of the subject regarding their fulfilment or dereliction of their duty to obey the sovereign. Hobbes takes issue with the Aristotelian distinction between corrective justice (or what Hobbes terms *commutative*

justice) and distributive justice as a reflection of different kinds
of equality according to which commutative justice involves the
equality of value of things contracted for, while distributive justice
supposedly involves 'the distinction of equal benefit to men of
equal merit' (Lev 15.14.94). To Hobbes, Aristotle's account of
distributive justice is fallacious because it assumed a standard for
measuring value to give each their due that is independent of the
contracting parties 'as if it were injustice to sell dearer than we
buy, or to give more to a man than he merits' (Lev 15.14.94).
Thus, justice in the sense of fulfilling contracts is both conceptually very narrow (i.e., there is no natural justice operating beyond
compact), but also provides great scope for human volition as the
only real source of value or merit.

The upshot of Hobbes' account of justice is not simply that it
reduces to the obedience of subjects, but that a particular form of
distributive justice in its public aspect of the arbitrator is actually a
function of equity with far-reaching implications for political life.
Hobbes' reformulation of the Aristotelian idea of distributive justice involved collapsing equity and a version of distributive justice
to produce a distinctive interpretation of the public dimension of
justice whereby 'distributive justice is the justice of an arbitrator,
that is to say, the act of defining what is just . . . and this is indeed
just distribution, and may be called (though improperly) distributive justice (but more properly equity, which also is a law of nature)'
(Lev 15.15.95). Justice, for Hobbes, amounts to the conventional
obligation of subjects and the natural freedom of rulers. Equity,
however, has a different normative force 'to which, as being a precept of the law of nature, a sovereign is as much subject as to any of
the meanest people' (Lev 30.15.226). Thus, the traditional idea of
a limit on, or at least a measure of, illegitimate government action
retains a thin presence in Hobbes' thought in his concept of equity
rather than through the idea of justice. It is important, however,
to recognise that equity assumed increased significance over the
course of Hobbes' political writings. In the early *Elements of Law*,
Hobbes presented equity as a law of nature specifically related to
reciprocity such that 'every man acknowledges another for his
equal' (EL 1.17.88). This idea of reciprocity operated directly on
the manners of a just person, who acknowledges that 'whatsoever
right any man requireth to retain, he allow every other man to
retain the same' (EL 1.17.1.89). The vice associated with not recognising another as one's equal Hobbes called *pride*, but the breach
of equity Hobbes claims is 'that which the Greeks call *pleonexia*,

which is commonly rendered covetousness, but seemeth to be more precisely expressed by the word encroaching' (EL 1.17.2.89). In the *Elements*, then, Hobbes clearly associates distributive justice and equity with the 'manners' of individuals who possess the qualities of mind conducive to peace.

In *De Cive* Hobbes provided distributive justice with a more emphatically public sense than in the earlier *Elements*. Here we are informed that distributive justice involves 'men's dignity and deserts, so that if awards are made *kata ten axian*, more to the worthy, less to the less worthy, and it is done proportionably' (DC 3.6.46). In *De Cive* Hobbes qualifies the argument about distributive justice from the *Elements* by insisting on the subjective character of judgement about merit and desert for 'if I give a larger share of something of mine to someone who is less deserving, I am not doing a wrong to either of them, provided I have given what I agreed to give' (DC 3.6.47). *De Cive*, then, differs from the *Elements* most clearly in the sense that in the former Hobbes separated equity from reciprocity and set equity off as a separate law of nature on its own that 'forbids us from giving more or less to one person than to another as a favour' (DC 3.15.50). Hobbes' reasoning is that showing favouritism to one party over another is tantamount to repudiating the idea of natural equality. In *De Cive* the vice associated with not recognising that one must acknowledge that others retain the same rights that I do requires the introduction of a new precept 'to distribute Right to others'. Of this new natural law category Hobbes informs us, the observation of this precept is called equity, 'violation of it is discrimination; the Greek word for it *prosopolepsia*"' (DC 3.15.50).

In order to understand the subtle, but significant shift, in Hobbes' argument regarding distributive justice from his earlier writings through to *Leviathan*, it is necessary to reconsider Hobbes' interpretation of what he took to be the problematic character of the classical idea of justice, which he claims failed to recognise natural human equality. In the *Elements*, Hobbes rejected the possibility that there is a natural, as opposed to civil, basis for determination of merit, worth and value: 'the question, which is the better man, is determinable only in the estate of government and policy, though it be mistaken for a question of nature' (EL 1.17.1.88). Hobbes' reflections on equity in *Leviathan* register a deepening of his commitment to the importance of equity. In chapter 15, Hobbes first introduced the public character of justice by way of partial agreement with what he took to be the 'ordinary definition of justice in the Schools', which is that 'justice is the constant will of giving to every man his own' (Lev 15.3.89). But to Hobbes 'giving every man his own' meant that justice comes into being as a viable moral category only after the establishment of public power. The public dimension of justice restricts, without wholly eviscerating, the individual's capacity to determine just action inasmuch as 'in commonwealths, private men may remit to one another their debts, but not robberies or other violences whereby they are endamaged; because the detaining of debts is an injury to themselves, robbery and violence are injuries to the person of the commonwealth' (Lev 15.12.94).

This public dimension of justice is also exhibited in Hobbes' reconsideration of the distinction between commutative justice and distributive justice. The distinctive feature of this account is Hobbes' direct association of commutative justice with 'the justice of a contractor' and distributive justice with 'the justice of an arbitrator . . . the act of defining what is just' (Lev 15.15.95). Commutative justice requires adhering to the terms of an agreement. Distributive justice, however, adheres to basic principles of 'just distribution . . . but more properly equity' (Lev 15.15.95).[32] Equity, then, is reformulated as the distinct eleventh law of nature, to wit 'if a man be trusted to judge between man and man, it is a precept of the law of nature that he deal equally between them' (Lev 15.23.97).[33] The want of impartial arbitrators in the natural condition is one of, if not 'the cause of war' (Lev 15.23.97). It is the observance of this law of nature relating to 'the equal distribution to each man of that which in reason belongeth to him' that Hobbes claims 'is called equity . . . the violation [is called] acception of persons (*prosopolepsia*)' (Lev 15.24.97). Equity is arguably the principal law of nature because it expresses the essence of what is required to secure peace. Not only does equity require the fair treatment of individuals, it also encapsulates the moral premise of basic human equality, the appreciation of which permeates practically all of the characteristics Hobbes insists are conducive to peace such as gratitude, accommodation, pardon, as well as avoidance of vengeance, pride and displays of contempt for others (Lev 15.16–22.95–97). Hobbes' concept of equity, thus, presupposes that it is a norm that should inform not only the social, but also the economic behaviour of individuals within the commonwealth.

When we follow the development of Hobbes' concept of equity throughout his political writings at least two major points emerge. First, even as Hobbes narrowly defined justice in terms of fulfilling contracts, he presented an expansive range of public judgements about what is equitable and inequitable. Hobbes identified the fundamental characteristic of the good judge to be 'a right understanding of that principal law of nature, called equity' (Lev 26.28.184). Second, it becomes clear that it is equity rather than justice narrowly defined that represents the central normative concept in Hobbes' theory of the state.[34] *Pleonexia* or 'encroaching' is what inequitable actions look like when displayed by private persons, but from the perspective of private citizens or subjects assessing a public figure inequitable action is *prosopolepsia* or favouritism.[35] Equity is a disposition of character pertaining to the proper conduct of publicly appointed judges, arbitrators and even governors. The favouritism or 'acception of persons' exhibited by a judge or public official renders completely corrupt actions that would be fairly unremarkable for a private citizen. Presumably, corrupt actions or biased judgements could even be rendered invalid upon appeal to a higher body or investigative agency. Thus, Hobbes' idea of the common good depends upon a principle of fair treatment that transcends justice among private individuals, and extends even to the sovereign who Hobbes insists 'is as much subject' to the principle of equity as 'any of the meanest of his people' (Lev 30.15.226).[36]

What are the consequences for a sovereign who violates the natural law of equity? Hobbes suggests that a sovereign is weakened in such a case and an individual subject could arguably have grounds for resisting the inequitable sovereign by virtue of a moral power included in the liberties of a subject.[37] Conceivably, if fundamentally unfair treatment were widespread or systematic in character, this could justify something akin to a collective self-defence right as a group of similarly situated individuals treated unfairly could unite to resist lawful discrimination.[38] However, the most powerful incentive for the sovereign to respect equity is its connection to peace, for the sovereign risks sparking conflict by condoning or enacting policies that undermine the subjects' confidence in the impartiality of government.

Equity involves judgements pertaining not only to the actions of individual officials, but also extends more broadly to cover the distribution of public goods, which must be 'agreeable to equity and the common good' (Lev 24.6.160). The obvious question is whether Hobbes believed equity is a substantive concept of right or a purely procedural principle. While several commentators reject the idea that Hobbes endorsed redistributionist principles,[39] the evidence suggests that there are some basic substantive elements in Hobbes' account of equity. For instance, in *The Elements of Law*

Hobbes required that 'such things as cannot be divided, be used in common, proportionably to the numbers of them that are to use the same, or without limitation when the quantity thereof sufficeth' (EL 1.17.3.89). The main example of things held in common that cannot be divided are the 'universal practice' regarding 'the common use of wells, ways, rivers, sacred objects, &c; without it life would be impossible' (DC 4.14.63). In this sense, Hobbes anticipates his later more explicit provisions for social welfare in *Leviathan* (Lev 30.18.228). This early Hobbes insisted that common use of indivisible things should be protected as when 'a few shall make more use thereof than the rest, that equality is not observed' (EL 1.17.3.89). Hobbes did allow that an individual 'may have given way his right of common' by way of a 'covenant antecedent' (EL 1.17.3.90), but he did not explain what incentive anyone would have to give up by contract this apparently natural right to an equal share of indivisible common things. Significantly, Hobbes does not even mention the possibility of a 'covenant antecedent' in his later restatements of the use of indivisible common things in *De Cive* and *Leviathan*, perhaps signifying his mature conclusion that the equitable use of common things derives from a basic principle of equality that cannot be renounced by an individual through contract: that is, this aspect of equity is beyond the realm of justice.

If equity is the defining characteristic of the judge and arbitrator, then how is equity relevant to things not held in common and how does arbitration enter such cases when setting up the rules of property once the commonwealth is established? In the event of something that 'can neither be divided nor enjoyed in common', equity requires that the entire right be subject to 'equal distribution' determined by lot (Lev 15.26.98). The system of lot can be either natural (primogeniture or first seizure) or lot can be arbitrary in the sense of the rules being 'agreed upon by the competitors' (Lev 15.27.98). For example, the agreement between Abraham and Lot to divide their flocks in *Genesis* 13.8 that marks 'the abolition of common ownership' (DC 4.4.60) signifies the contractual basis of the mine–thine distinction, and not any presumed individual acquisition right having priority over the demands of equity relating to the retained right to the necessities of life. We only divest ourselves of those rights, 'which cannot be retained without loss of peace' (EL 1.17.2.88). The normative claims rooted in equity potentially extend to 'the right of bodily protection, of free enjoyment of air, water, and all necessaries for life' (DC 3.14.144). These are the necessities of life (as opposed to 'delectations' of living well), and thus the right of access to necessities includes basic, but important, substantive elements required to secure equal benefit.[40] Equal benefit presupposes access to some class of necessary things, but also goes beyond a strictly procedural claim towards a substantive notion of benefit for: 'There is no acknowledgement of the equality of worth, without attribution of the equality of benefit and respect' (EL 1.17.2.89). Any question of what constitutes equal benefit depends upon universal acknowledgement 'that men content themselves with equality, as it is the foundation of the natural law' (EL 1.18.6.96). Olsthoorn correctly observes that these 'retained' rights 'do not qualify as propriety in Hobbes' account', precisely because Hobbes rejected any pre-political claim for individual property rights.[41] This does not, however, contradict, and arguably even supports, the position that Hobbes' claim that common property should be distributed in terms of equity signifies a moral claim intelligible in terms of retained rights individuals have to a share of common property in civil society. Needless to say, Hobbes did not describe this moral claim as a justification for jeopardising peace, for in Hobbes' mind any 'retained' rights to essential resources must be compatible with the preservationist logic undergirding the individual's political obligation.

The sovereign who 'assigneth to every man a portion according as he ... shall judge agreeable to equity and the common good' (Lev 24.4.160–1) is both the establisher and original distributor of property rights, as well as the arbitrator who settles authoritatively disputes about property rights claims for 'the intention of the Legislator is always supposed to be equity' (Lev 26.26.182). It is for this reason that property rights are not simply reducible to individual possession. As Muldrew observes, Hobbes' intuition that trust is not possible without law was 'related to changes in English society created by the development of credit and its legal discontents'.[42] In this context, contract theory represented a state-enforced system of trust that extends to both informal networks of credit and more institutionalised 'trade fairs'.[43] For Hobbes, the role of the state was not only to ensure that people feel confident to lend money, but also to cultivate relations of equity among people in the emerging credit economy. The sovereign guided by principles of equity creates the conditions that allow the system of credit to develop wherein one individual or group may 'borrow money of a stranger ... that is not of the same body' (Lev 22.11.148). In contrast to other contract theorists of the era, including Richard Hooker, Hugo Grotius and John Selden who remained broadly within the Aristotelian tradition of natural sociability,[44] Hobbes' political economy placed a distinctively liberal emphasis on the role of the state mediating competitive desires through networks of credit, social relations and material distribution in ways consistent with the normative demands of equity.

Hobbes' Political Economy

We are now prepared to consider Hobbes' reflections on political economy as it is normally understood in terms of production and trade, and the distribution of national income and wealth. Perhaps the best description of Hobbes' preferred system is a 'mixed economy' that blends moderate free market principles with significant public regulation of private enterprises and an important welfare function built into Hobbes' conception of the state.[45] Certainly, some of Hobbes' twentieth-century critics admitted that the creation of a free-market society presupposes a potentially high degree of government regulation in order to enforce rules allowing 'peaceful competition of the market'.[46] However, this misunderstands the causal relation between Hobbes' conception of the state and of society. Hobbes is a contract thinker both in terms of the original social covenant and the many legal contracts enforceable by sovereign power. Contract and justice in the narrow sense definitely contribute to the 'commodious living' made possible through commerce. But, as we have seen, contract is only part of the story because Hobbes' political economy also rests upon the normative foundation of equity. This is not to say that Hobbes required that a regime must provide for the poor in order to qualify definitionally as a civil state. Rather, Hobbes' account of the characteristics of the commonwealth speaks in favour of instituting at least a minimal degree of public welfare, as well as a robust regulatory framework in order for the commonwealth to be stable and just. Thus, Hobbes' economic policy recommendations are informed by his theory of equity.

Perhaps the first thing that strikes us about Hobbes' political economy is the distinctively Hobbesian combination of legalism and discretionary power. On the one hand, Hobbes views the economic life of the commonwealth as embedded in a framework of laws established by the sovereign that makes possible 'all kinds of contract between subjects' pertaining to buying, selling, lending or exchange of goods and services (Lev 24.10.163). But legal justice applies only to subjects, not sovereigns, as the propriety of subjects 'exclude not the right of the sovereign representative to their goods', for otherwise the sovereign 'cannot perform the office they have put him into . . . and consequently, there is no longer a commonwealth' (Lev 29.10–11.213). Hobbes insists that all private estates originally derived from the distribution by the sovereign subject only to what the sovereign 'shall judge agreeable to equity and the common good' (Lev 24.6.160). He recognises a zone of private economic activity through the medium of what he calls 'lawful irregular' concourses of people 'not made on evil design (such as are conflux of people to markets)' (Lev 22.4.146). Hobbes herein acknowledges that the original egalitarian distribution of resources is not a static arrangement. Rather, the forces of supply and demand animating trade and exchange will predictably create over time less equitable distribution, perhaps only remediable through state action.

A central feature of Hobbes' political economy is his treatment of trade. Hobbes assumed that it is natural and beneficial for commonwealths to trade with one another. The 'most commodious' method to facilitate trade is through a 'body politic' or joint stock company in which 'everyone that adventureth his money may be present at all the deliberations and resolutions of the body' (Lev 22.18.150). The danger Hobbes saw with these import trade companies is when they are given 'a double monopoly' with sole control over buying of exports from a particular foreign country and exclusive right over selling imports to their domestic markets. Hobbes concludes that the practical effect of this arrangement is normally to exploit consumers unless every trader is allowed 'to buy and sell at what price he could' (Lev 22.19.151). In this case, competitive market principles would reduce the potential harm caused by trade monopolies. In other respects, however, the central thrust of Hobbes' teaching regarding trade requires state involvement in the economy.

For instance, the government determines the parameters of lawful trade for 'to assign in what places, and for what commodities, the subject shall traffic abroad, belongeth to the sovereign' (Lev 24.9.163). Hobbes also assumes that the government can levy a tax 'upon the body' that is understood to be laid upon 'every member proportionably to his particular adventure in the company' (Lev 22.22.151). In addition to corporate taxation, Hobbes insists that the government can impose a fine or 'mulct' upon any corporation for 'some unlawful act' (Lev 22.23.152). The deeper concern Hobbes harbours regarding corporations is the excessive concentration of wealth 'when the treasure of the commonwealth, flowing out of its due course, is gathered together in too much abundance in one, or a few private men, by monopolies' (Lev 29.19.218). This painful 'pleurisy' on the body politic is a function of oligarchical tendencies inherent in both large monopolistic corporations and by the feudalistic arrangements in which individual agents (typically minor aristocrats) are contracted by the Crown to collect taxes like 'farms of public revenues' (Lev 24.19.218). Hobbes perhaps points towards the creation of a publicly appointed civil service as a remedy to the problem of oligarchs enriching themselves from the public purse. At any rate, the primary structural challenge that the government must confront is to ensure that 'the passage of money to the public treasure' is never obstructed by non-state actors (Lev 29.18.217).

Some commentators have interpreted Hobbes' recommendation to avoid relying on publicly owned land as a source of government revenue to signify a blanket endorsement of free market principles.[47] This assessment, however, ignores the complexity in Hobbes' treatment of public land and resources. The position Hobbes rejected was the idea that the commonwealth could appropriate public land 'that such portion may be made sufficient to sustain the whole expense to the common peace, and defence necessarily required' (Lev 24.8.162). Hobbes' concern here is with the illusion that public land *on its own* would be 'sufficient to sustain the whole expense' of government. It is the uncertainty and insecurity in a dangerous world, rather than any commitment to free-market principles, that caused Hobbes to question relying solely on publicly owned resources: 'Commonwealths can endure no diet; for seeing their expense is not limited by their own appetite, but by external accidents and appetites of their neighbours, the public riches cannot be limited by other limits than those which the emergent occasions shall require' (Lev 24.8.162). Restricting public revenue can be even more decisive domestically insofar as it undermines the sovereign's capacity to govern. As Hobbes related with regard to King Charles I's disadvantage during the English Civil War: 'What means had he to pay, what provision had he to arm, nay means to levy, an Army able to resist the Army of the Parliament maintained by the great purse of the City of London?'[48] Hobbes' future-directed conception of power presupposed that no government can ever know with certainty how much money, arms and soldiers will be needed to provide for future security and, as such, in principle there should be no limits on the sources of revenue available to government. Hobbes did not, however, foreclose the possibility that public enterprises could perhaps manage the resources Hobbes associated with retained rights pertaining to the necessities of life (e.g., water and fire) that are not profit-making ventures per se (e.g., as public utilities).

The final element of Hobbes' political economy we need to consider is tax policy. Hobbes claims that 'the equal imposition of taxes, the equality whereof dependeth not on the equality of riches, but on the equality of debt that every man oweth to the commonwealth for his defence' (Lev 30.17.227). In this case, the equal benefit 'that everyone receiveth', that is, self-preservation, means that 'the equality of imposition consisteth rather in the equality which is consumed than of the riches of the person that consume the same' (Lev 30.17.228). Hobbes claims that a consumption tax is fair because it encourages hard working people who 'consumeth little' and in effect punishes both the idle who possess little and wealthy private individuals who expend their resources on 'luxurious waste' (Lev 30.17.228).[49] While Hobbes does not register any concern about the potentially regressive effects of a consumption tax, he did reaffirm the normative principle of equity: 'Whereas many men, by accident inevitable, become unable to maintain themselves by their labour, they ought not to be left to the charity of private persons but to be provided for ... by the laws of the commonwealth' (Lev 30.18.228). On the one hand, Hobbes seems to want to restrict these public charities to the disabled and dependants. However, it is also significant that these are explicitly *public* charities. The public character of these institutions signifies a potentially important welfare function built into Hobbes' conception of the state, even as it exposes his distrust of the private system of relief provided by churches and wealthy individuals and organisations that characterised the pre-modern feudal state.

The specific features of Hobbes' political economy, such as his recommendations about trade, public resources and tax policy, all point towards an economic vision that combines free-market principles of private ownership and exchange with substantial public involvement in the economy to encourage equity through fair benefit of shared goods and resources. Contrary to the argument of his twentieth-century critics that Hobbes simply imbibed and provided philosophical justification for the emergent free market he supposedly observed around him in seventeenth-century England, our analysis of Hobbes' political economy suggests that in crucial ways he sought to subordinate economic forces to the political needs of the commonwealth. Arguably, Hobbes' primary goal was to illuminate the features of a modern state unburdened by feudal

and theological assumptions. In this sense Hobbes' political economy is more prescriptive than descriptive, and more normative
than empirical. Towards the 'Conclusion' of Part II of *Leviathan*
Hobbes hinted at the radical intention of his political theory when
he admitted that even though sometimes he suspects his works
are as utopian and 'as useless as the commonwealth of Plato', he
retains 'some hope that, one time or other, this writing of mine
may fall into the hands of a sovereign who will consider it himself . . . and by the exercise of entire sovereignty . . . convert this
truth of speculation into the utility of practice' (Lev 31.4.243–4).
For Hobbes, then, the moral imperative of his theorising, in terms
foreshadowing later British liberal thinkers, directs towards the
manifestation of thought in the concrete reality of the state.

Progress or Return to Rights?

While there is little disagreement that Hobbes was 'situated at a
critical juncture in the theorization of the emerging nation-state',[50]
in this chapter I have sought to challenge the identification of
Hobbes as the anchor in an influential philosophical anthropology
of the origins of liberalism that reduced the state and political life
into an instrument designed to secure the conditions required for
free-market economics. I have argued that this account of liberalism, at least with respect to Hobbes, depends upon an historical
appropriation of his legacy that proves inadequate upon serious
re-engagement with Hobbes' most important political writings.
But this misreading of Hobbes, even by sophisticated commentators like Macpherson, Strauss and Arendt, is both instructive and
consequential as it speaks to the problem of tradition 'constructing'.[51] On the one hand, despite enormous social and technological
changes in the past four centuries, there remain clear aspects of
continuity in the way people today talk about the idea of rights and
government. Yet, on the other hand, the very recognition of intellectual traditions often occludes theoretical possibilities embedded
in the complex relation of philosophical speculation, prudential
judgement and social context.

How does recovering Hobbes' political economy help us to
understand the broader tradition of classical liberalism? Perhaps a
fruitful way to understand the theoretical significance of Hobbes'
treatment of the economic dimensions of the theoretical foundations of the liberal state is to consider this question in the light of
what Abizadeh identifies as 'foundationally normative prudential

precepts'.[52] The most important of these self-evident moral principles, I have argued, is identifiable with the natural law of equity.
While Hobbes conceived of practical reason directed towards 'science', which he defined as 'the knowledge of consequences' (Lev
46.2.454, 5.17.25), he did not hereby advance a normatively reductionist, proto-behavioural interest-based account of the civil state.[53]
Rather, by distinguishing practical reason from speculative reason,
which he associated with the metaphysical teachings of scholastic
'vain philosophy' (Lev 46.14,40), Hobbes highlighted the normative thrust of his conception of science: 'reason is the pace; increase
of science, the way; and the benefit of mankind, the end' (Lev
5.20.26). Thus, the egoistic psychology underlying Hobbes' moral
philosophy must be qualified by the important social dimension in
Hobbes' account of rationality and science as a public enterprise.[54]
The political state is, then, the culmination of the Hobbesian ideal
of reason, for it is only through the interpersonal relations of civil
life that the judgements of individual reason can be transformed
into the collective mode of scientific truth legitimised, at least in
principle, by the consent of each member of society.

The important social dimension of Hobbes' account of practical
reason permeated his treatment of the relation between the state,
the economic system and the individual. As we have seen, Hobbes'
political economy presupposed the existence of a network of social
relations, including both lawful private systems in 'markets' and bodies politic established for the 'well ordering of foreign traffic' (Lev
22.4.146, 22.18.150). The sovereign guided by principles of equity
creates the social conditions allowing a system of credit to develop
whereby people may 'borrow money of a stranger' (Lev 22.11.148).
Hobbes emphasised the role of trust as the social foundation that
allows for the exercise of practical reason as individual lenders and
borrowers, sellers and buyers make prudential judgements about the
trustworthiness of their exchange partners. This focus on social networks and the importance of opinion-formation suggests an aspect of
Hobbes' thought that is more often associated with the pluralist and
affective conceptual model of non-contractarian eighteenth-century
liberals such as David Hume and Adam Smith than the acquisitive,
individualist rights theory commonly attributed to Hobbes. Hobbes'
holistic political economy, therefore, avoids reducing liberalism to an
economic doctrine for it embeds rights in social networks sustained
by both legal contracts and norms of equity.

The model of the sovereign state presented in Hobbes' *Leviathan*
looks and feels familiar to contemporary readers, who largely take

for granted the existence of a vast network of public and quasi-public authorities with responsibility for managing and directing national resources, as well as providing material and educational services that extend into practically every aspect of life. However, the Hobbesian origins of the modern state are complicated. On the one hand, Hobbes' state of nature and contract theory de-mystified the political association presenting it as being neither a divinely ordained body nor an organic outgrowth of human rational faculties pointing towards certain identifiable moral and intellectual ends. Rather, the modern state is a product of practical reason legitimated by consent. On the other hand, Hobbes employed a novel narrative device, the theory of sovereign authorisation, to provide a model for the origins of the state constructed on the basis of the principle of natural rights. The Hobbesian state is omnicompetent as it rejects economic determinism and promotes a system of mass public political education (Lev 30.2–14) designed to inculcate moral opinions necessary not only for stability and peace, but to facilitate scientific progress.

Thus, the modern Hobbesian-inspired liberal state was born with a deep internal tension. The counterpart to Hobbes' unflattering account of egoistic and violent human psychology is his palpable confidence about the possibility for intellectual progress for 'time and industry produce every day new knowledge' (Lev 30.5.220). Hobbes' optimism was to some extent self-serving as he sought to counter the objections of critics who contended that 'there are no grounds, nor principles of reason, to sustain those essential rights which make sovereignty absolute' (Lev 30.5.220). Hobbes compared those who rejected his novel conception of the post-feudal modern natural rights-based civil state with nomadic peoples who deny that there are any 'principles of reason' capable of helping to construct durable permanent homes because 'they never yet saw any so well built' (Lev 30.5.220). For Hobbes, the progressive character of knowledge is challenged by the verbal nature of human communication which presents obstacles to learning, but can be overcome with effort: 'the faculty of reasoning being consequent to the use of speech, it was not possible but that there should have been found some general truths found out by reasoning, as ancient almost as language itself' (Lev 46.6.454). Even the 'savages of America', Hobbes' preferred symbol for the primitive condition, were 'not without some good moral sentences; also they have a little arithmetic' (Lev 46.6.454). Hobbes' confidence in intellectual progress lay in part in his recognition that despite the many epistemological and psychological obstacles to genuine knowledge acquisition, there had nonetheless been 'divers true, general, and profitable speculations from the beginning, as being the natural plants of human reason' (Lev 46.6.454). In this sense, scientific progress depends upon the development of human sociability in a mutually reinforcing process as the state allows for the conditions of peace amenable to intellectual advance, even as scientific progress ideally strengthens the social habits and practices that guarantee peace: 'Leisure is the mother of philosophy, and Commonwealth the mother of peace and leisure' (Lev 46.6.455).

Did Hobbes foresee a future stage of social development in which absolute sovereignty was no longer necessary to secure peace, that is to say, when social habits become so engrained as to basically correct our seemingly incorrigible egoistic tendencies, making it possible to appreciably reduce the need for coercive constraints on the thoughts and actions of the subjects or citizens of the polity? Perhaps Hobbes never fully resolved this tension between his pessimistic account of human psychology and his enlightenment optimism about the possibility of scientific and moral progress, but, as we shall see, the possibility of reconsidering the normative foundations of the state in terms of a political economy that balances the claims of liberty and equity, or rights and interests, would be a consuming question for his most important successors in the British classical liberal tradition of political thought.

Notes

1. Hobbes 1840: 168.
2. Israel 2001.
3. Hume 1961: 296.
4. Hobbes 1994: ch. 13, s. 11, p. 87. Hereafter in notes and text Lev chapter.section.page.
5. Letwin 1972: 143.
6. Macpherson 1962: 15, 16, 48, 85, 106.
7. Strauss 1936: 118, 121; Strauss 1953: 182.
8. Arendt 1998: 31; Arendt 1966: 137–43.
9. Habermas 1996: 90.
10. The bourgeois interpretation of Hobbes has been the subject of intense criticism practically since its first appearance (e.g., Berlin 1964; Thomas 1965; Miller 1982). Indeed, Martinich (1997: 148) announced that by the 1990s the bourgeois Hobbes had suffered 'definitive refutation'. However, this proved to be premature as in more recent times several scholars have revisited favourably the

bourgeois interpretation of Hobbes (e.g., Townshend 1999; Hillyer 2002; Bray 2007).

11. Hobbes 1969: bk 1, ch. 19, s. 8, p. 104. Hereafter in notes and text EL book.chapter.section.page.

12. Hobbes 1998: ch. 5, s. 10, p. 73. Hereafter in notes and text DC chapter.section.page.

13. See Skinner 2007: 161; Pitkin 1964: 328; Martinich 1997: 225; Zagorin 2009: 56.

14. See Abizadeh 2011; Waldron 2001.

15. Runciman 2000: 272.

16. Pitkin 1964: 340.

17. For instance, the Jesuit scholastics Suarez and Bellarmine advanced a version of contract theory in which the community of individuals acted as a kind of primordial democracy whereby power 'is given directly by God to the community' (Suarez 1950: 3.2.9.14, see also Ward 2004:42). Similarly, while Grotius affirmed natural freedom and equality and viewed government's primary goal as the protection of individual rights from harm, he also accepted the Aristotelian premise of natural sociability (Grotius 2005 proleg., s. 6; see also Ward 2004: 75–6)

18. Orwin argues that Hobbes' main aim with sovereign authorisation is to alleviate subjects of any feeling of guilt arising from obedience to sovereign commands (Orwin 1975: 32). Warrender takes the opposite view, claiming that authorisation is meant to indemnify the sovereign against charges from disobedient subjects (Warrender 1957: 110). Arguably both Orwin and Warrender are correct to observe that Hobbes' primary concern with authorisation is to identify moral responsibility for sovereign action, and only secondarily to contribute towards a revised understanding of political obligation. But Gauthier is right to highlight the 'public aim of the act of authorization' (Gauthier 1969: 140, 163). For Hobbes, authorisation *is* the founding, primal political act that constructs the idea of the public.

19. For the role of myth in nationalism, see Hobsbawm 1990: 12; Anderson 1991: 6; Miller 1995: 35; Gellner 1997: 3; Abizadeh 2004: 310.

20. Zagorin 2009: 62.

21. Runciman 2000: 273.

22. Forsyth 1981: 195.

23. Hobbes 1991: 84.

24. Hobbes thus reversed the assumptions about the meaning of what is universal and what is particular that we see in some recent commentators who endorse the concept of the 'boundless demos' according to which it is impossible for political boundaries to be 'democratically legitimized' with respect to both citizens and foreigners (e.g., Abizadeh 2012: 874).

25. Mansfield 1971: 97–8.

26. Waldron 2001: 468; Kraynak 1990.
27. Mathiowetz 2011: 121.
28. Muldrew 1998: 318, 321.
29. Locke 2016 II:27.
30. Shanks 2019: 322; Kelly 2011: 32,75,92.
31. Aristotle 1934 1129a25. Hereafter in notes and text NE and section.
32. Ron is thus mistaken to accuse Hobbes of simply collapsing distributive justice into 'either commutative justice or grace' (2006: 248). Clearly by associating distributive justice with equity, Hobbes resists the conclusion that all justice can be reduced to honouring contracts.
33. Equity in *Leviathan* is the eleventh law of nature, but in the earlier *De Cive* and *Elements* it is the tenth.
34. May 2013: 67–83.
35. Hobbes' use of the term *prosopolepsia* is curious. He attributes this term to 'the Greeks', but he uncharacteristically did not trace the use of this term back to Aristotle. Recall that for Aristotle the vice exhibited by an inequitable man is the contentiousness of a litigant prone to excessive legal stickling. Thus, for Aristotle inequity does not relate to the favouritism or discrimination displayed by a corrupt public official. Rather, Hobbes seems to draw the term *prosopolepsia* from Scripture, the New Testament in particular where we are told that 'God is no respecter of persons', who favours the rich and powerful over the poor and weak (Acts 10:34–5). We are left to wonder: why would Hobbes turn to Scripture to describe an important element of his account of equity, rather than draw from Aristotle or the Scholastics as he normally does? Klimchuk (2012: 165) suggests that *prosopolepsia* was a term used in the writings of the Digger leader Gerrard Winstanley. This, however, would represent an unlikely association between the arch-royalist Hobbes and the Civil War era radicalism of the proto-anarchist Diggers.
36. Contradicting Macpherson's charge that Hobbes expressed 'scorn' for the concept of 'equal benefit, to men of equal merit' (1962: 62–3), in the Latin version of *Leviathan* Hobbes declared 'to reproach someone for having a humble station is both inequitable and dangerous to the commonwealth' (Lev 30.16, n. 9).
37. Lev 21.11–17. See Sreedhar 2010 for the subject's limited right to rebel against the sovereign.
38. Ward 2017: 878–81.
39. E.g., Gray 1996: 10; Olsthoorn 2013: 13, 22.
40. Klimchuk 2012: 170. Lopata (1973: 210–12) claims that the retained rights in the *Elements* and *De Cive* are pre-civil property rights that Hobbes abandoned later in *Leviathan*. However, this fails to recognise that Hobbes' concept of equity in *Leviathan* also possesses an important pre-civil normative dimension that impacts his treatment of property.

41. Olsthoorn 2015: 494.
42. Muldrew 1998: 124.
43. Muldrew 1998: 324; Chown 1994: 116.
44. Muldrew 1998: 319–23.
45. See Kavka (1988) for an insightful treatment of the welfarist dimension of Hobbes' political economy (cf. MacArthur 2013: 186).
46. E.g., Macpherson 1962: 89; Arendt 1966: 141.
47. Mathie 1987: 261; Sorrell 2011: 45.
48. Hobbes 1840: 299.
49. It is, thus, perhaps ironic that Rousseau would later charge supporters of *doux commerce* as implicitly endorsing a Hobbesian depiction of amoral natural man to justify their defence of luxury and commerce (Douglass 2015: 84–5).
50. Springborg 2015: 120.
51. Bell 2016: 85.
52. Abizadeh 2018: 119.
53. Mathiowetz 2011: 129–33.
54. See Nacol 2016: 30; Frost 2008: 10–11.

Chapter 2

John Locke's Liberal Politics of Money

John Locke and Thomas Hobbes are mirror images of the seventeenth-century English natural rights tradition. Both started from a doctrine of individual natural rights and a comparable state of nature account, but they nonetheless concluded with very different political visions. For Hobbes, natural equality produced the need for a radically conventional politics; that is, only with the construction of an all-powerful, omnicompetent sovereign power is it possible to protect the individual's natural right to self-preservation. Locke believed that Hobbes' theory of absolute sovereignty was a terrible misstep. The central difference between them related to property. Hobbes famously argued that in the chaotic state of nature, there is no right of property for 'where there is no commonwealth, here is no propriety, all men having right to all things', including, quite graphically, the right 'even to one another's body'.[1] For Locke, on the other hand, the constitutional requirement of limited government derived its normative imperative precisely from the primordial moral fact that every individual owns his or her own person. Thus, *contra* Hobbes, Locke insisted that by nature human beings do not have a right to each other's bodies. This conception of self-ownership provides the logic behind perhaps the two most characteristic Lockean teachings: namely, that the powers of the civil government derive from the natural power of individuals to execute the law of nature; and that the natural right of property derives from an individual's labour, the products of which 'nobody has any right to but himself'.[2]

Unsurprisingly, the political implications of Locke's property-centric natural rights theory revolve around the notion of the purpose of civil government being primarily to secure individuals in the enjoyment of their property, a goal presupposing a high degree of liberty rendered impossible in the Hobbesian ideal of absolute monarchy.[3] Thus, in Lockean liberalism the individual right of property supplies both the object of civil government and the rationale for its intrinsic limitations.

In terms of his political economy, Locke has long been identified, arguably even more definitively than Hobbes, as one of the founding figures of the acquisitive capitalist ethos.[4] This influential interpretation of Lockean liberalism presupposed a distinct philosophical anthropology demonstrating the logical and moral priority of individual economic interests. However, I will challenge this reading of Locke by examining the normative dimensions of his most developed economic writings *Some Considerations of the Consequences of Lowering Interest and Raising the Value of Money* (1692) and *Further Considerations Concerning Raising the Value of Money* (1695). While some commentators question any relation between Locke's economic tracts and his more famous political and philosophical writings,[5] and others view the former as simply the logical deduction from what they take to be Locke's natural science of economics,[6] I will argue that Locke envisioned a holistic conception of political economy that combined normative, legal and natural jurisprudential elements in his account of the economic foundations of a society governed by the philosophy of individual natural rights. In particular, I will try to demonstrate that Locke's political interventions in the monetary controversies in England of the 1690s were grounded upon prudential judgements about the moral foundations of community in an economic network of credit, trust and social relations.

John Locke's role in the development of early modern thinking about money is well established. For centuries, Locke's opposition to currency devaluation in England in the 1690s earned him the title as one of the founders of the 'sound money' doctrine and defender of the institutions integral to the birth of capitalism during the Financial Revolution in England.[7] This narrative has proven remarkably resilient as most recent scholarship reaffirms this image of Locke, albeit with different emphases. However, there is no consensus among commentators about the political principles underlying Locke's theory of money. In the 1970s Joyce Appleby influentially argued that Locke inaugurated what would become the classical liberal idea of the naturalisation of money, an account that would effectively remove considerations about currency 'from the realm of politics'.[8] More recently, in her magisterial study of the invention of the modern idea of money in England, Christine Desan illuminates the revolutionary manner in which Locke 'fetishized money as a matter of intrinsic metal content', in order to place currency not only 'beyond control of the state', but 'out of governance altogether'.[9]

Another group of commentators reject the strict naturalist interpretation of Locke's theory of money, and instead focus on the role that Locke's concern about the epistemic instability in conventional intersubjective agreements played in his defence of unalterable currency denominations.[10] In this account, Locke's monetary theory was animated by a conscious effort to provide the fragile mental construct that is money with a normative foundation to exclude currency from the range of issues included in the regular course of political debate. Arguably the most sophisticated version of this argument is Stefan Eich's recent offering in which he elegantly illustrates the political logic informing what he takes to be Locke's 'depoliticisation' of money. For Eich, Locke's solution to the problem of the 'malleable conventionality' of money was to protect the 'monetary contract' by sanctifying the fiat decision to link money to an initially arbitrary, but subsequently unalterable, quantity of silver.[11] The unifying thread linking the otherwise opposed naturalist and conventionalist interpretations, including Eich's decisionist model, is the fundamental assumption that Locke sought to make considerations about money operate in a depoliticised manner outside the parameters of normal political deliberation.

My approach builds upon the focus on Locke's epistemological concerns about the monetary compact, but I reject the claim that Locke believed establishing trust in money required accepting a fiat approach to monetary policy. Rather, taking Locke's concern for the political ramifications of the money supply as a given, I believe the more important question relates to Locke's expectations for prudential judgement about the distributive consequences of monetary policy, as distinct from the question of the depoliticisation of money. We shall see that Locke's theory of money is not radically depoliticised, and, indeed, I will argue that it complements his broader conception of liberal statecraft. My central claims are twofold. First, Locke did not seek to resolve the paradox of commodity money being both natural substance and contractual legal construct by eliminating or minimalising either element of the compound relation. Rather, throughout his economic and political writings Locke maintained a complex balance between nature and convention in his treatment of money.[12] Second, I challenge the common assumption about Locke's fears regarding the epistemic fragility of money, which rests on a misunderstanding of Locke's crucial concept of mixed modes, the epistemological category to which he assigns money. Commentators often get Locke backwards by not recognising that, for Locke, mixed modes are more intelligible than material substances. As such, we need to recontextualise Locke's theory of money in terms of his conception of practical reason,[13] in order to appreciate that it is not the epistemic fragility of normative concepts that drove Locke's reasoning about money, but rather his relative confidence about the conceptual durability and adaptability of complex legal and moral ideas.

If, as Michael Zuckert observes, Locke is arguably the first important political philosopher 'to define political economy as the central task of politics',[14] then it would seem natural to integrate Locke's argument about money into the broader conception of liberal statecraft he calls the 'great art of government'.[15] Locke's statecraft involves his commitment to the philosophical principle of individual natural rights combined with an approach to political and economic issues that prioritises prudential judgements derived from practical reason over and against mechanistic theoretical propositions and sweeping universal laws of human behaviour.[16] In contrast to the decisionist model, in which Locke held that money originated in political judgement and then subsequently foreclosed all future discursive possibilities about the currency, I view Locke's conception of money as a mixture of natural and conventional elements amenable to periodic political deliberation about the distributive consequences of monetary policy. Thus, I propose that Locke's long association with the origins of a natural science of economics distorts his understanding of the relation of politics and economics, and has obscured our sense of the complex normative features of Locke's theory of money in particular.[17] By challenging the idea of Locke as the apostle of sound money, I hope to recover access to the range of theoretical perspectives and practical possibilities for political action concerning money offered in Locke's liberal statecraft.

Before turning to Locke's monetary tracts, I provide some brief historical context for the English currency debates of the 1690s and then consider the role of money in Locke's more familiar political and philosophical writings. I will then turn to examining in some detail Locke's argument for the 'natural price of money' in *Some Considerations* and his case against currency devaluation in the later *Further Considerations*. I will argue that Locke's economic writings present a theory of money that, rather than serving simply

as a justification of sound money, combined features of an individualistic epistemology and distinctly political modes of prudential
reasoning characteristic of Locke's liberal statecraft as he sought
to protect the economic foundations of community in a normative
network of credit, trust, and social relations.

Economic Controversies in 1690's England

Locke's economic tracts are arguably the most policy-directed
writings in his entire *oeuvre* as they were composed in his official capacity as senior adviser to the Crown and member of the
newly formed Board of Trade.[18] Locke's fascination with interest
rates dated back to April 1668 when a Bill championed by Josiah
Child, Governor of the East India Company, proposed to lower
the legal rate of interest from 6 per cent to 4 per cent. Child
argued that this measure was necessary to restore English commercial supremacy over rival Dutch traders by imitating their policy of keeping interest rates low. Acting as Principal Secretary to
the Chancellor of the Exchequer Lord Shaftesbury, Locke wrote
a memo opposing Child's proposal. Locke's position on interest
rates prevailed in 1668, but the House of Commons reconsidered
lowering rates again in 1690, and it was in response to this later
effort that Locke revised and expanded his earlier pamphlet into
what became *Some Considerations*.

With respect to the question of re-minting and potentially devaluing England's silver currency, Locke advocated dramatic government action to confront an economic challenge that he believed
'threatened the very legitimacy of the English state'.[19] The Recoinage
Controversy of 1695 had its roots in problems dating back decades
in England. First, there was a shortage of silver in the country due
to the fact that for many years there had been a divergence in value
between English silver shillings, on the one hand, and the price of
silver bullion, on the other, such that silver bullion came to exceed
the value of silver coin markedly. This created an arbitrage opportunity to melt down English silver coins to convert into bullion for
export to foreign markets in order to obtain a higher return either to
buy gold guineas or to purchase more comparatively cheaper English silver coins. This produced a shortage of silver: the main source
of currency in England. The second problem was the phenomenon
known as 'clipping'. Once again, the discrepancy between the price
of silver coin and silver bullion was the culprit as it provided incentive to shave off or 'clip' some of the silver coins in order to collect

the shavings for melting down into valuable bullion. This meant that many, if not most, silver coins in circulation were in actuality lighter than the quantity of silver associated with the denomination.[20] The effect of clipping was to undermine public confidence in the real value of English coins and to encourage an international network of counterfeiters and smugglers.[21]

The need to reform the monetary system was given even greater urgency by the demands of the Nine Years War against France (1688–1697), as by the summer of 1695 the government of William III scrambled to raise loans desperately required to supply unpaid troops in the field in Flanders. This crisis mercilessly exposed the inadequacy in the English currency and credit system.[22] The Recoinage Debate must be understood in the context of the deliberate long-term policy to lay the foundation for what Brewer identifies as the 'fiscal–military state' that would propel Britain to imperial glory in the following century.[23] But while there was broad agreement in 1695 about the need to address the problems in the English monetary system with some form of recoinage, there was no consensus on the proper course of legislative action. Two main alternatives emerged: (1) re-minting and devaluation of all silver coins, or (2) re-minting them at the original valuation. The Secretary of the Treasury William Lowndes proposed a nominal devaluation of all silver currency by 20 per cent with compensation provided for all those who surrendered clipped coins.[24] In Lowndes' view, devaluation was the best way to ensure that recoining did not result in a radical reduction in the supply of coins. On the other side, in *Further Considerations* Locke argued that all the silver coins in circulation should be re-minted at the old weight and value using a more advanced technique called 'milling' that promised to make clipping more difficult in the future. For Locke, the only way to restore the proper relation of bullion to coin, and public confidence in the currency, was by restoring the original value of the denomination. In order to understand Locke's reasoning during the controversies of this period, we need to consider aspects of his theory of money presented in his familiar philosophical and political works.

A Philosophy of Money

The intellectual foundation of Locke's economic theory lies in his epistemology. According to Locke's 'Historical Plain Method' in the *Essay Concerning Human Understanding*, there are no innate practical or speculative ideas, and there are serious limits set on claims to knowledge within the 'compass of Humane Understanding' (E 4.21.1). The 'division of sciences' reflects three distinct categories: first, knowledge of the nature of things or substances; second, 'that which men ought to do as a rational and voluntary agent to attain happiness'; and, finally, 'the distinct ways and means by which the knowledge of these other sciences can be communicated' (E 4.21.1). The knowledge of things material and immaterial that have 'their Natures, Constitutions and Operations', Locke calls 'physike (φυςικ ή) or natural philosophy' (E 4.21.2). The 'skill of right applying our own powers and actions, for the attainment of things good and useful', Locke identifies as 'praktike (πρακτικ ή)'. The most considerable branch of this being ethics (E 4.21.3). The third kind of scientific knowledge Locke terms 'semiotike (ςημειωτικ ή) or the doctrine of signs', which is typically associated with logic 'the business whereof, is to consider the Nature of Signs, the Mind makes use of for the understanding of Things, or conveying its knowledge to others' (E 4.21.4).

The concept of money employed in Locke's economic writings spans all three of the divisions of science. First, Locke emphasised that silver coin has a substantial reality as a material thing, that is, a precious metal of finite quantity. While ideas are the building blocks of knowledge, Locke insists that 'our idea of substance' is 'obscure, or none at all' with respect to thinking about body (E 2.23.15). The deep opacity in our knowledge of substance derives from the fact that the 'real' essence of any substance is unavoidably elusive: 'as to real essences of Substances, we only suppose their being without knowing what they are' (E 3.6.6). In contrast to empirical observation governing understanding of substances, practical reason directed towards 'the attainment of things good and useful' (E 4.21.3) is characterised by what Locke terms 'mixed modes'. Mixed modes are consciously constructed by a combination of simple ideas made 'arbitrarily' by the mind 'without patterns, or reference to any real existence' (E 3.5.3), but rather by way of mental frameworks Locke calls 'archetypes' (E 4.4.8). Mixed modes comprise the 'greatest parts of the words made use of in Divinity, Ethics, Law and Politicks' (E 2.22.12). Locke concludes that the value of money is discernible precisely because it is a mixed mode derived from social convention and does not depend upon knowledge of any naturally existing thing (E 2.22.1). But gold and silver are also, of course, durable and scarce material substances that supply the quantifiable, measurable and portable objects that serve as the means for facilitating exchange. Commodity money is, then, both physical substance (silver and gold) and a moral mixed mode (valued currency).

Several commentators claim that Locke's reasoning with respect to money is driven by his deep anxiety about the inherent epistemic instability in mixed modes, especially as currency denominations are subject to the problem of disagreement about the meaning of language.[25] However, this line of argument risks losing some of the original texture of Locke's epistemology for he insisted in the *Essay* that substance is more difficult to understand than mixed modes. So little does material substance tell us about the intrinsic qualities of material reality that Locke compared the mysteries of physical body with the spiritual realm: 'the idea of corporeal substance in Matter is as remote from our Conceptions, and Apprehensions as that of Spiritual Substance' (E 2.23.5). The deep opacity in our knowledge of substance derives from the fact that the 'real' essence of any substance is unavoidably elusive: 'as to real essences of Substances, we only suppose their being without knowing what they are' (E 3.6.6). But Locke argues that mixed modes can be known precisely because they are entirely products of the mind, therefore, whereas natural philosophy can never reliably extend beyond the epistemological level of probability, Locke concludes that morality is 'amongst the sciences capable of demonstration' (E 4.3.18).[26] Thus, while money understood as substance (metal) is ultimately ineluctable, money conceived as a 'mixed mode' mental construct is comprehensible, normative and, in principle at least, instrumental to the promotion of human happiness.

While Locke certainly recognised that one of the great obstacles confronting human knowledge acquisition is the abuse of language and the difficulty related to settling upon stable publicly accepted definitions of terms (E 3.9–11), his political theory nonetheless presupposed a general human capacity to establish commodity currency exchange both in civil society and the foundational state of nature. In the philosophical anthropology underlying the state of nature in Locke's *Second Treatise of Government*, he explicitly linked money with the law of nature that is 'intelligible and plain' to any rational creature (II:12). Locke argues that in the early phase of social organisation no single individual could realistically acquire property to the injury of anyone else because it was not yet true that 'the desire of having more than men needed had altered the intrinsic value of things' (II:37). The alteration in the 'intrinsic value of things' is produced when 'by mutual consent' people agreed to place value on some 'lasting thing' such as a 'little piece of yellow metal' that could be used to exchange for the 'truly useful, but perishable' supports of life (II:37, 47). In his discussion of land, which he calls the 'chief matter of property', Locke contends that one acre of uncultivated land in pre-colonial America and another in monetarised England have 'the same natural intrinsic value', and yet one benefits humankind much more due to the productive capacities unleashed by money (II:32, 43). But whereas the concept of the 'intrinsic' and 'natural' value of land is tied to its productive capacity, these terms bear a different meaning with respect to money insofar as the natural and intrinsic value of money seems to be indelibly relational and context-specific. The 'little piece of yellow metal' has monetary value because individuals agree to ascribe to it value.

A central feature of Locke's historical treatment of the origin of money is his claim that international recognition of distinct legal borders presupposed agreement about the use of money. The importance of money to the process of community formation is undeniable for Locke as he insists that there are still parts of the world which lie 'waste' because the inhabitants thereof have not 'joined with the rest of mankind, in the consent of the use of their common money' (II:45). Indeed, Locke concludes that claimable wasteland 'can scarce happen amongst that part of mankind that have consented to the use of money' (II:45). Thus, the 'common consent' to distinct borders is coterminous with the 'common consent' (express or tacit) to the use of exchangeable 'common money' in the form of silver and gold. Money, then, was not present in the original 'great and natural community' of the human species, but rather only emerged in tandem with the 'positive agreements' through which people 'combine into smaller and divided associations' (II:128).

Locke declared that money is 'a barren thing and produces nothing but by compact'.[27] The natural *use* of money derives from fundamental agreement and consent, whereas the natural *value* of commodities necessary for life is presumably self-evident. The exchange value of money allows overcoming the natural problem of spoilage because with the 'invention of money' different degrees of industry become more rational. A cultivator has little incentive to expand production beyond subsistence unless there is some commonly recognised non-perishable commodity that can serve as money (II:48). All the world was originally uncultivated wasteland like pre-colonial America, for 'no such thing as money was anywhere known' (II:49). Locke thus recognised the historical and contingent character of money as monetarised and non-monetarised societies continued to co-exist, however problematically, even in his own time.

Perhaps the chief moral implication of the invention of money is the 'tacit and voluntary consent to inequality' by which 'men have agreed to disproportionate and unequal possession of the earth' (II:50). As several commentators have noted, the mechanism that effectively creates inequality in the pre-civil condition, that is, the invention of money, is dependent upon an extra-justificatory layer of consent.[28] But this initial consent or agreement, even if ambiguously both 'tacit and voluntary', includes the possibility that under conditions of civil government the normative meaning of money is transformed as it is assimilated into the comprehensive social compact that terminates the state of nature. Locke recognised the moral validity of pre- or extra-civil economic exchange involving 'promises and bargains for truck' between individuals in a non-monetarised condition such as two people on a desert island or a 'Swiss and an Indian, in the woods of America' (II:14). The natural law limits on acquisition apply in these situations precisely because these scenarios do not presuppose the existence of money.

But the consent to use money in civil society requires surrendering the natural liberty to use or not use money in exchange for the benefits provided by civil government. That is to say, exchange of money in the state of nature is directed by the natural law imperative of human preservation and, thus, while not requiring a surrender of natural liberty per se, is nonetheless subject to the 'inconveniences' of the state of nature that make economic activity unstable (II: 13). In civil society, however, individuals surrender their natural liberty in exchange for government-provided benefits, including a secure currency.[29] Civil society transforms money by making possible an enhanced conception of trust that provides a normative grounding for Locke's largely utilitarian justification for inequality in the increased economic production made feasible by the invention of money. Locke's account of money in the *Second Treatise* exposes the psychological infrastructure of a monetised society dependent upon the proper balance between the capacity of conventions to alter the 'intrinsic' value of things, and the need to generate sufficient trust among individuals to make a system of lending, borrowing, selling and buying possible.

The Natural Price of Money

In definitional terms, for Locke, money is both a physical substance and a mixed mode. It is both a quantifiable thing with certain discernible characteristics and, at the same time, money is a mental construct representing a fundamentally moral determination of the value of something with respect to human needs.[30] What, then, does 'nature' mean in the context of Locke's treatment of interest rates, or as he puts it 'the natural price of money'?

Initially in *Some Considerations*, Locke presented what is *natural* as signifying the limits of legislative control inasmuch as he concludes it is 'manifest' that the price of money cannot be 'regulated by law' (SC 211). Locke applied the same question to inheritance and reached the identical conclusion: 'it is impossible to make a law that shall hinder a man from giving away his money or estate on whom he pleases' (SC 211). This is a curious analogy for in the *First Treatise of Government* Locke acknowledged that the natural right of inheritance is in fact typically regulated by 'municipal laws' (I:91). What Locke appears to mean in the context of interest rates is, then, that the de facto rate of interest evades legislative control because 'no man borrows money, or pays use, out of mere pleasure' (SC 211). As such, given the necessitous character of lending and borrowing money, presumably it will not be easily discouraged by legal prohibition, if at all.

But how, then, are we to make sense of Locke's claim that people borrow money only out of necessity, when he argued in the *Second Treatise* that the invention of money presupposed that individuals desire having 'more than men needed'? (II:37). One possibility is that Locke intended to redefine necessity in terms of a relative or shifting standard of value such that money can change the intrinsic value of a thing only inasmuch as notions of what is useful for human life are not conceptually bound in essentialist or unchanging categories of the good.[31] But did Locke believe that the idea of intrinsic or natural value had no substantive content whatsoever?

Locke approached this question through the concept of the 'natural price' of money, which he defines as 'the rate of money which the present scarcity of it makes it naturally at, upon an equal distribution of it' (SC 216). The 'natural price' of money often militates against the policy of lowering interest rates because when the legal rate is too low, there is no real incentive to lend money as: 'For some years since, the scarcity of money having made it in England really worth more than [the official] six per cent' (SC 215). But if, as Locke claims, individuals borrow money out of necessity, then they will accept without objection loans at interest rates considerably higher than the artificially lower legal rate. Locke maintained that the natural price of money can be raised when the money supply is low in proportion to a country's trade, so that if £2 million were needed to carry on trade but only £1 million was actually available, then the natural price of money will be raised (SC 218). But the natural price of money is *sui generis* because money is a unique commodity that has a 'double value' insofar as it serves both for exchange of goods and as a potential source of yearly income. In the latter case, there must be income inequality with some people having surplus money that they can lend at interest and others having less than they require to satisfy their needs (SC 250). Locke hereby draws a parallel between lending money and renting property – both of which depend upon inequality – but he defends usury as being typically less exploitative then renting out land to tenants (SC 251).

Money is also a unique commodity because the normal market forces of supply and demand do not apply. For Locke, the pivotal concept relating to demand is 'vent' by which he meant not simply demand, but rather a complicated relationship of commodities with variable consumption and elastic demand: 'The vent is nothing else, but the passing of commodities from one owner to another in exchange . . . this vent is regulated, i.e., made quicker or slower, as greater or lesser quantities of any saleable commodity are removed out of the way . . . and no longer lie within the reach of exchange' (SC 258–9).[32] The concept of vent as it applies to money differs from other commodities insofar as because the desire of money is consistently almost everywhere the same, 'its vent varies very little, but as its greater scarcity enhances its price' (SC 255). The price of commodities naturally fluctuates, but demand for money will remain stable despite the quantity available. The quantity of money determines the price, but intrinsic value is determined by the amount of silver in weight and the price set to it on international exchanges. Intrinsic value, thus, does not mean unchanging worth, but rather 'the value of money . . . depends only on the plenty, or scarcity of money, in proportion to the plenty and scarcity' of the necessaries and conveniences of life (SC 244).[33] By this reasoning, the inflation in 1690's England compared with two centuries prior was due entirely to the increased supply of precious metals since European colonisation of North and South America began (SC 262–3).

Locke argues that lowering the legal rate of interest would have the effect of actually decreasing the money supply. It would be as if England hypothetically were suddenly to have only half as much money in circulation as seven years ago and yet had the same annual product of commodities, in which case 'it is certain that either half our rents should not be paid, half our commodities not vented, or half our labourers not employed' (SC 266). Locke's commitment to a quantity-based theory of money meant that despite the vital role of labour in accounting for the origins of private property, Locke did not subscribe to a strict labour theory of exchange value, for as Karen Iverson Vaughn describes his economic theory: 'labor creates value, but value is measured by the marketplace'.[34]

The 'intrinsic' value of money or any other commodity is not a deduction from a scientific law of nature. Rather, Locke emphasised that it is 'the universal consent of mankind' that has annexed value to silver and gold (SC 234). Insofar as Locke's theory of money presupposed a degree of naturalism, this extends only so far as there being actual specie or bullion to represent the 'pledge, which writing cannot supply the place of' (SC 234).[35] Locke insists that the 'universal consent' expressed in the agreement to value gold and silver in exchangeable form across monetarised countries represents the 'natural and current interest of money' in contrast to the 'legal and forced' standard proposed by those who seek to lower the rate rashly through legislation (SC 253). Here 'natural' and 'current' mean what is widely accepted or freely, almost spontaneously, agreed to, whereas 'legal' and 'forced' suggests no general societal agreement upon value beyond a specific claim of legislative competence. The 'natural price' of money is, then, a basis for generating the level of trust required for natural exchange and any system of credit and lending. Thus, 'natural' in this context, does not indicate an essential characteristic that transcends human volition, but, rather, Locke suggests something closer to what Hugo Grotius identified as *ius gentium* or law of nations embodied in customary norms and laws based upon a shared understanding of the value of silver and gold.[36] It is this shared understanding that makes trust in exchange relations possible.

Perhaps even more important than the practical objections to lower interest rates is Locke's moral criticism of the distributive consequences of lowering interest rates as he highlights the injustice of punishing those 'with estates in money' (whom he literally identifies as 'widows and orphans'!), who are much more vulnerable to losses on the return of interest on their savings in money than the landed gentry (SC 219). However, this emotional appeal to the plight of vulnerable people is balanced out somewhat by Locke's hard-headed assessment of how reduction in the money supply would impact the various socio-economic classes in England. Labourers who typically live 'from hand to mouth' (SC 236) would be the least affected because they have little cash on hand in any case.[37] It is the landholders and brokers who will feel the greatest impact because the former are dependent on rents that will drop in price and the latter need to have considerable stores of surplus funds available to conduct business. In contrast to modern political economy, Locke did not consider consumers as a distinct economic variable because 'there are so few consumers, who are not either labourers, brokers, or landholders, that they make a very inconsiderable part in the account' (SC 242).

The most important normative dimension of Locke's analysis, however, has to do with the relation between the civil state and the monetary infrastructure undergirding the system of credit. Locke asserts that one of the 'unavoidable consequences' of lowering interest rates will be to turn many thousands of English subjects into perjurers. If the reduction of coin in circulation will increase the natural price of money, then it is 'likely to cause great perjury in the nation' as illegal borrowing is a crime involving 'secret trusts and collusions of men' that can never be proven 'without their confession' (SC 213). The problem of criminalising perfectly rational and, in Locke's view harmless, behaviour goes beyond the scope even of economic relations for as Locke sees it: 'Faith and trust, especially in all occasions of attesting it, upon the solemn appeal to heaven by an oath, is the great bond of society' (SC 213). What is at issue, then, with respect to interest rates is nothing less than the moral preconditions of human sociability. Without public confidence in the veracity of oaths, witness and pledges 'it will be impossible for the society . . . to subsist' (SC 213). While Locke believed that establishing a healthy money supply is one of the basic purposes of civil government, he did not assume that the public good and private interest are simply identical. Lower interest rates may 'be a gain to the borrowing merchant', but do no good for the kingdom (SC 220). Indeed, Locke saw an important role for government to promote distributive justice by protecting the people most vulnerable to the adverse effects of lowering rates for 'common charity teaches that those should be most taken care of by the law, who are least capable of taking care of themselves' (SC 220). Locke's technical arguments with respect to interest rates, thus, acquired moral significance in terms of the public authority entrusted with the task of securing the economic infrastructure of civil society.

The Recoinage Controversy

Further Considerations (1695) published at the height of the recoinage debate commenced with an encapsulation of Locke's monetary theory: (1) 'silver is the instrument and measure of commerce in all the civilised and trading parts of the world'; (2) 'the intrinsic value of silver, considered as money, is that estimate which common consent has placed on it'; and (3) 'silver is the measure of commerce by its quantity, which is the measure also of its intrinsic value'.[38] As the commodity representative of every other commodity, money is in some sense 'equivalent to all other things' for 'as the wise man tells us, money answers all things' (FC 139).[39] With respect to 'intrinsic value', Locke typically meant the actual amount of silver in coins by weight, not the total amount of silver available in a given economy. However, in the context of the recoinage debate the concept of 'intrinsic' takes an additional, even more primary, meaning for Locke as it signifies an economic version of the logical principle of non-contradiction foundational for speculative philosophy: 'For an ounce of silver, whether pence, groats, or crown pieces . . . or in bullion, is, and always eternally will be, of equal value to any other ounce of silver' (SC 304–5). Thus, while the notional value of money may be determined by international markets, the substantive principle of value is not contingent upon the market or exchange for 'so much silver will always be worth . . . so much silver, given in exchange one another' (SC 318). The government, thus, cannot alter the actual value of silver, but may 'only alter the denomination' of coins (SC 305).

The problem with the devaluation proposal advanced by Lowndes had to do with the difficulty relating to the semiotic capacity for mixed modes to be represented by substances. For example, minting shilling pieces that are one-twentieth in weight lighter involves changing the denomination, not the value of silver. Locke concedes that 'raising' one form of specie is manageable (if problematic), but he insists devaluing all silver coin at once is potentially disastrous insofar as a general devaluation 'will rob all creditors of one-twentieth of debts' (SC 309). The effect of this policy in Locke's view is to affect a form of grand larceny that reaches into the pockets of many English subjects. In contrast, Locke advised that all of the light, clipped coins be restored to 'full weight' through a demonetisation process that is 'orderly and by degrees' (FC 418). Moreover, Locke insisted that the recoinage process must involve a universal recall, including not only clipped coins, but also all the 'unclipped' full weight coins (FC 415).

Locke believed that only the complete reminting of all silver coins could ensure that they were no longer exported to be melted into bullion abroad (SC 334). The option of devaluing gold in order to disincentivise hoarding and clipping silver was not a viable policy for Locke because 'gold is not the money of the world' as the agreement upon its use and exchange is not as 'universal', comprehensive and inclusive as silver (FC 423). Did Locke not see that recalling all silver coins would likely reduce the number of coins in circulation, and thus violate one of his own basic principles about the money supply?[40] The answer is both yes and no. Locke expected that recoining would release the many full-weight coins from 'Gresham's Hoard', that is, bring them back into circulation, thus, balancing out any potential reduction.[41] However, on a more fundamental level, Locke was aware of the real possibility of diminishing the money supply, but he concluded that there was a higher moral imperative to reaffirm the social agreement to the use of money.

In the *Second Treatise* Locke emphasised that the agreement to place value on a 'yellow piece of metal' allowed the non-perishable, precious metals to represent quantities of perishable goods necessary for life (II:50). However, in his monetary tracts the semiotic question of representation focused specifically on the issue of coins. Why do we need coins at all, if the quantity of silver 'makes the real value of it' (SC 311)? First, Locke acknowledged the practical inconvenience of requiring everyone to carry scales for every transaction. Coins, thus, do the service of signifying the quantity of precious metal. But this function does not resolve the basic question of what actually is being represented. Scales cannot distinguish between fine and mixed silver. Thus, the most important function of coins is to provide a publicly recognised measure of both the weight and the purity of the precious metal. This, of course, presupposed agreement upon the common guarantor of whom it may be said: 'the stamp was warranty of the public' (SC 312). Coin is metal transformed 'the public faith as security' (SC 312).

Locke reframed the technical questions surrounding the recoinage debate in distinctly normative terms, condemning coin-clipping as a 'robbery committed on the public' (SC 322). As such, the moral effect of devaluation would be to validate an untold number of criminal acts. In contrast to Lowndes, Locke refused to countenance any compensation for holders of clipped coins due to the fact that he believed they were complicit in this massive defrauding of the public inasmuch as they should have refused originally to accept these clipped coins in earlier transactions.[42] The only beneficiaries of devaluation would be the bankers and brokers whose arbitrage Locke believed was largely responsible for the currency crisis in the first place. As the major possessors of full weight coins hoarded up, they 'by the proposed change of our money, will be an increase of one fifth, added to their riches, paid out of the pockets of the rest of the nation' (FC 439). Locke was morally indignant at the prospect of what amounted to a speculator bail out that 'will only serve to defraud the king, and a great number of his subjects' (FC 479).

Public authority was central to Locke's thinking about recoinage precisely because money is so indelibly woven into the moral foundations of civil society. For Locke, a monetarised economic system is both a series of social networks of trust and credit, and an agreement on the meaning of symbols and representational devices.[43] The epistemic underpinnings of public discourse apply as much to money as to other moral, ethical and legal concerns for 'it is no wonder, if the price and value of things be confounded and uncertain, when the measure itself is lost' (FC 430). Civil government is meant to remedy the 'inconveniences' of the state of nature (II:13) in which all too often individuals are 'strangers or such as trust not one another' (FC 452). To Locke, restoring public confidence in the value of money required combatting two corrosive effects of clipping. First, it meant recognising that illicit clipping and legal devaluation both sanction important economic forces beyond the control of civil government.[44] Locke feared that the precedent of devaluation in 1696 would potentially encourage further reckless devaluations in the future. By contrast, recoinage at the original weight and value would establish an important principle that the state will not cede control of the money supply to irregular and illegal market forces that 'have taken off the authority of public stamp, and declared it not to be lawful money' (FC 414).

But perhaps an even more fundamental aim of Locke's plan for recoinage was to preserve the principle of the validity of contract. Lowndes' proposal for devaluation would reward a form of economic treason, and thus seems to condone the socially destructive idea that 'Men are absolved from performance of their legal contracts' (FC 415). Much as Locke's political theory was premised on the notion of free and equal individuals generating all of their civil obligations through consent, so too did he believe that the entire system of advanced economic exchange beyond the limited scope of natural barter depended upon legally enforceable contractual obligations. If people could not trust the government to honour its promise about the value of coins, how, Locke reasoned, could anyone trust the civil authority to enforce any other kind of contract? But Locke did not view the problem of devaluation solely in terms of violation of trust for he also insisted that there was no evidence that it would achieve what its proponents sought to do, namely, bring more silver coins into circulation. Ultimately, Locke was convinced that both the principle of trust and the practical operation of commodity demand and supply would confirm his normative premise about money.

Locke's Liberal Statecraft

Trust has long been viewed as a central feature of Locke's political and moral philosophy.[45] I have tried to recontextualise Locke's treatment of money in terms of an account of trust that presupposed a considerable degree of confidence about the epistemic basis of political and social conventions as they interrelate with economic usages pertaining to the price of money or the value of silver. In his political writings, Locke argued that while the power of government is delegated from the natural executive power of individuals, the end for which government is entrusted with this power is solely 'that men might have and secure their property' (II:11, 139). Locke identified 'bounds' that this trust places on government action, which if taken 'contrary to their trust' legitimises the dissolution of power back to 'the people [that] had put into their hands' this power in the first place (II:142, 221–2). But Locke insists that the revolutionary breakdown of trust is a relatively rare experience (II:224–6). Locke also located his treatment of money in the context of discourse about trust being the stabilising 'great bond of society' that makes a system of economic exchange possible (SC 213). But if trust in the institutional sense relates to a threshold with respect to assessing the violation or non-protection of rights, how can money similarly be understood in terms of rights?

Locke's account of money reveals the vital economic dimension of his often-neglected liberal statecraft.[46] In the *Second Treatise*, Locke alluded to 'the great art of government' that produces 'laws of liberty' designed to 'secure protection and encouragement of honest industry' (II:42). Locke's argument with respect both to interest rates and recoinage established the priority of laws and policies designed to protect networks of credit. Locke presented the seventeenth-century English community very much in terms of a group of competing, but interdependent, households that need to trust one another.[47] The maintenance of this system of trust is the primary object of Locke's statecraft, and the preconditions of trust are twofold: (1) preserving state control over the currency; and (2) upholding the principle of distributive justice.

The importance of state control over the currency is a function of the crucial role that consent to the use of money plays in Locke's account of the social compact. While money originates in the state of nature, it is transformed by the public commitment to certain benefits derived from the use of money in civil society. Clipping coins undermines this public commitment as it amounts to 'raising it [the value of a denomination] without public authority' (FC 417), and is in effect 'robbery committed to the public' (SC 322). Locke's statecraft is, then, directed in part to remedying deleterious economic forces that originate beyond the control of civil government.[48] In this sense, Locke's desire to restore systemic balance in the economy by reaffirming the legally established connection between silver content and specific denominations parallels his call in the *Second Treatise* for the exercise of prerogative power to restore a 'fair and equal' system of representation in a legislature that had become 'very unequal and disproportionate' due to gradual demographic changes (II:157-8).[49] In both cases, Locke's aim was to reaffirm the fundamental principle of consent underlying the political community. Similarly, much as a corrupt legislature cannot be expected to reform itself, so too Locke suggests that the civil state's role in securing legal currency is irreplaceable as is obvious from the inability of individuals *qua* individuals, or even as members of civil society, to solve the problem of coin-clipping without government intervention.[50] But is this an exercise of practical reason and statecraft or merely an attempt to restore in a mechanistic manner the conditions of the original monetary agreement arrived at by fiat?

The latter possibility disconnects money from Locke's statecraft by highlighting what is sometimes taken to be the arbitrary and rigid character of Locke's judgement about money, rather than the prudential dimensions I identify. Recontextualising Locke's monetary compact in terms of a modulation in his theory of consent, which is capable of being formative, legitimating and even constitutive, but does not require us to accept for money the supra-obligatory (dare I say sacrosanct) status Locke ascribed to the creation of a 'People' (II:89, 120, 222). Thus, while Locke may have sought to delegitimise certain kinds of discretionary political meddling in the currency, his statecraft presupposed that decisions about the range of matters that are exclusively beyond the normal political process are themselves subject to deliberation and revision. This is not to suggest that Locke would have rejected the idea of central bank independence, although he was famously rather ambivalent about the fledgling Bank of England.[51] And it is certainly true that a 'sound money' policy could serve as a prudential exhortation about the dangers of devaluation. However, the problem with associating Locke with a philosophical commitment to sacrosanct currency is that this, for all practical purposes, dissolves prudence, and, as history seems to confirm, tends to validate the incorporation of Locke's theory of money into a strict, quasi-scientific monetary doctrine antagonistic to his statecraft.

Clearly, Locke viewed recoinage in somewhat prohibitive terms with respect to government action, arguing that 'the quantity of silver established under the several denominations . . . should not be altered till there was an absolute necessity shown of such a change, which I think can never be' (FC 415), and that once the standard metallic alloy of coins has been settled, it 'should be inviolably and immutably kept to perpetuity' (SC 329). While these passages suggest that Locke sought in some sense to depoliticise money, it is important to distinguish between the uncompromising rhetoric of Locke's polemic and the decidedly utilitarian logic of his argument. First, despite his protestations of horror about the prospect of devaluation, Locke was well aware of the past practice of currency revaluations in England and elsewhere (FC 458–60). Locke even conceded that many English people had tacitly consented to a de facto devaluation of silver coin by factoring in the added cost of lighter coins into their exchanges, borrowing and debts (FC 469). Moreover, as Kleer demonstrates, Locke was aware that the purchasing power of English coin could change over time independently of its metallic content for 'there is no manner of settled proportion between the value of an ounce of silver, and any other commodity'.[52] Clearly, then, Locke recognised that his call for recoinage at original value was not the universal practice.

More importantly, Locke framed the issue of the epistemic stability of money within the context of his doctrine of the public good, which presupposed the value of prudential judgement. An unalterable monetary standard is not an axiom insofar as it is necessarily conditioned by the fundamental principle of the public good *'salus populi suprema lex'* (the safety of the people is the highest law) (II:158). The decisive problem with devaluation is the foreseeable consequences for 'the public will lose by it' (SC 329). Locke's presumption is that 'under the present denomination', England has 'had a greater increase, and larger continuance of plenty of money, than perhaps any other country can show' (FC 463). Thus, the metallic content of the denominations should not be altered unless there is an 'absolute necessity' for change (FC 415). But it is a matter of practical reason to decide whether this absolute necessity has arisen. One measure of this necessity can be seen in Locke's judgement that in England devaluation would injure creditors 'without any the least advantage to the public' (FC 416). It is likely that Locke did in fact see some advantages to Lowndes' devaluation scheme,[53] but he decided that on balance it was more important to reassert state control over the currency and to deter future coin-clipping. Arguably, then, Locke's polemical strategy was to combat Lowndes' plausible proposal by exaggerating the certainty of his own argument about the stability of the monetary standard.

Locke's rhetorical strategy was animated in part by the particular context of the unique historical conditions that made his recoinage plan dependent upon the improved milling techniques that promised to dramatically reduce clipping in the future. In the absence of improved milling techniques, would Lowndes' proposal have been more consistent with Locke's aim of restoring public trust in the money supply? Arguably this contingent fact would have made a considerable difference to Locke's calculations. Moreover, the specific conditions produced by extra-legal actions such as clipping and international arbitrage require that it was in the long-term interest to restore public confidence in the legal currency because failure to do so would 'destroy the public faith' in future acts of parliament relating to aspects of the economy beyond currency, including loans, public debt and banking (FC 417). Locke's public good imperative does not, then, foreclose the possibility that devaluation could be an apposite action in a different context, even if he presumes that in 1690's England such a policy would be seriously mistaken.

Locke's conception of trust in his monetary tracts also presupposed an underlying principle of distributive justice. He recognised that as a procedural and historical question, it was clearly within Parliament's purview both to set and to change currency denominations (FC 458–60). However, the political judgement about the substantive impact of government action would fall within the prudential orbit of Locke's thoughts on the distributive consequences of monetary policy. While most modern commentators on Locke's monetary tracts tend to ignore considerations of distributive justice in favour of focusing on his putative fixation on the unalterable metallic content of coins, for Locke and his contemporaries the question of who would bear the costs of devaluation was of equal or even more importance.[54] The fundamental

assumption underlying Locke's account of the distributive consequences of devaluation was that all legal contracts are executed in
silver by weight, not by denomination. Several implications flowed
from this premise.

First, he insisted that currency devaluation would 'rob all creditors of one-twentieth (or 5 per cent) of their debt' (SC 309). But
Locke was not simply defending the interests of the investor class
that would become central to the Financial Revolution in England.
He worried also about the impact of monetary policy on people sur-
viving on relatively fixed incomes (SC 219). Locke feared that devaluation in England would only reward the speculators 'who have
great sums of weight money . . . hoarded up by them' by increasing
their income by one-fifth 'paid out of the pockets of the rest of the
nation' (FC 439). Locke alerted that the great social danger in lowering interest rates would be to centralise economic control in the
hands of bankers and goldsmiths (SC 216), even as he warned that
this concentration of financial power would come at the expense of
institutions of civil society such as 'the Church, the Universities and
Hospitals' that would be injured by devaluation (FC 417).[55] Thus,
for Locke, the distributive consequences of monetary policy required
consideration about not only the potential impact on the poorer
classes, but also about the negative effects of cartelism and speculation on England's system of credit and civil society more broadly.

From Locke's perspective, Lowndes' devaluation plan failed to
protect rights because it did not take into account 'equity and consideration of the subjects' property' (FC 457) inasmuch as it placed
an unfair burden on ordinary people and those whom 'common
charity' teaches should most be provided for in law (SC 220), while
rewarding the speculators who were most responsible for the currency crisis in the first place. Locke insisted that the interests of
private individuals cannot be sacrificed with the 'least advantage to
the public' (FC 416). *Salus populi suprema lex* requires that while
Locke was committed to the individual right of self-preservation,
he was also, as Josephson describes, a political realist who incorporated the political community's 'native and original right' to
preserve itself into his consideration about justice (II:220).[56] What
is 'a gain to the borrowing merchant' may not be good for the
public (SC 220). Locke did not simply assume that there was no
conceivable context in which injury to one group could be justified
in terms of the 'advantage to the public'. Rather these judgements
about the subjects' property would require prudential judgement
suited to a liberal regime committed to individual natural rights.

On 2 January 1696 Parliament passed the Act for Remedying the Ill State of the Coin based in large part upon Locke's recommendation. Commentators are practically unanimous in their judgement that Locke's economic policy advice was mistaken, that Lowndes' devaluation plan was correct, and that the implementation of Locke's recoinage plan had a disastrous effect on England's economy as it produced an easily foreseeable dramatic reduction in the money supply in circulation with an even more predictable deflationary impact.[57] It is hard, then, to escape the conclusion that Locke's argument against currency devaluation was a remarkable philosophical misfire. However, simply dismissing Locke's foray into economic policy-making and ordering his legacy back to a contemplative ivory tower would be a serious error. For a start, we need to account for the historical fact that Locke's basic argument against devaluation would be taken by many for centuries as the philosophical inspiration for the gold standard, even though the putative father of 'sound money' expressed considerable ambivalence about the polemical nature of the monetary tracts, later citing them as works that 'are not those which I now relish, or that do, with Pleasure, employ my thoughts'.[58]

More importantly, however, Locke's monetary tracts reveal a dimension of his moral philosophy that is perhaps only partly visible in his more familiar political writings. Locke has been accused of advancing abstract theories of right at the expense of all but ignoring the practical art of governance.[59] Admittedly, in the *Second Treatise* Locke made only vague, but suggestive, references to the 'great art of government' that complements his natural rights philosophy. But while a full account of the priorities of the 'great art of government' is somewhat elusive in Locke's corpus, the identification of encouraging 'honest industry' as its end arguably highlights the centrality for political life of the issues, both economic and normative, that were the focus of his pamphlets on money. Arguably, the pattern set by Locke's emphasis on the fiduciary role of government regarding currency later helped to legitimate bank money and new credit instruments.[60] Locke's writings on money serve a significant role not only in situating the economic dimension of his teaching on trust, but also by limning the features of a conception of distributive justice in civil society that is compatible with the liberal principle of government devoted to the protection of individual natural rights. Perhaps it is only by way of integrating Locke's economic writings into his broader political philosophy that we can appreciate the full range of theoretical perspectives and practical possibilities for political involvement in the economy offered by Locke's liberal statecraft.

Notes

1. Hobbes 1994: 78, 89, 80.
2. Locke 2016 II:9, 11, 27.
3. Locke 2016 II:90, 134, 138–40.
4. See, e.g., Strauss 1953; Macpherson 1962; Hundert 1977; Appleby 1978: 236; Mitchell 1984. But there has also long been a smaller contrary school of thought that interprets Locke's account of property in communitarian terms (e.g., Dunn 1969; Tully 1980; Kramer 1997).
5. Kelly 1991: 3; Tully 1980: 149.
6. Letwin 1963: 176; Appleby 1976; Vaughn 1980: 115
7. See Macaulay 1866: 195–6; Feavearyear 1931: 135; Li 1963: vii. For the classic study of the Financial Revolution in England, see Dickson 1967.
8. E.g., Appleby 1976: 69.
9. Desan 2014: 368, 16–17.
10. E.g., Caffentzis 1989: 14; Carey 2014: 59–60; Casson 2011: 4–5, 254; Dawson 2007.
11. Eich 2020: 4.
12. Ince (2011: 29–33) also recognises the complex interplay of natural law 'universals' and contingent 'historical facts' in Locke's treatment of money in the *Second Treatise*, but Ince does not extend this insight into analysing Locke's monetary tracts.
13. For Locke's conception of practical reason, see Locke 1975: bk 4, ch. 21, s. 3. Hereafter in notes and text: E book.chapter.section.
14. Zuckert 1994: 272.
15. Locke 2016: s. 42. Hereafter in notes and text simply Treatise I or II and section.
16. See the definition of statesmanship in McNamara 1998: 5.
17. E.g., Letwin 1963: 176; Vaughn 1980: 115; Appleby 1976: 43.
18. See Laslett 1957: 370–402.
19. Pech 2007: 277.
20. Kelly 1991: 20–1.
21. Caffentzis 1989: 21.
22. Kelly 1991: 93; Li 1963:13; Eich 2020: 8.
23. Brewer 1988: 3.
24. Kelly 1991: 20–4.
25. Eich 2020: 18; Casson 2011: 6; Carey 2014: 74–5.
26. Of course, Locke famously demurred about his responsibility to provide such a demonstrative moral science (see E xx).
27. Locke 1991a: 250. Hereafter in notes and text SC and page number.
28. Zuckert 1994: 270; Josephson 2002: 188; Simmons 1992: 302–3.
29. Here I follow Mark Somos' (2019: 351) persuasive distinction between the operation of consent in natural liberty and civil liberty contexts.

30. Caffentzis 1989: 75–6.
31. But as Locke (1997: 340) explained in his essay 'Venditio', the natural value of a thing is not altered by changing its monetary price because a commodity now 'will not feed more men nor better feed them than it did last year' at a different price.
32. See Vaughn 1980: 25–6; Kelly 1988: 279.
33. Marx (1990: 185, 221) famously criticised Locke's 'confusion' in viewing the value of gold and silver purely in terms of quantity, and thus failing to distinguish between the value and 'specific value form' created by money.
34. Vaughn 1980: 32.
35. For Locke's concern about the unreliability of paper money at that time, see Dawson 2007: 288; Caffentzis 1989: 75–6.
36. Grotius 2005: 162–3.
37. Some commentators have taken these remarks to signify Locke's contempt for working-class people (e.g., Macpherson 1962: 216; Englert 2016: 564). However, this criticism misses the normative thrust of his objections to a policy Locke took to be injurious to the national economy as a whole.
38. Locke 1991b: 410–11. Hereafter in notes and text FC and page.
39. This allusion to King Solomon's words in Ecclesiastes 10:19 recurs several times in Locke's economic tracts. This is not the more familiar scriptural injunction against love of money as 'the root of all evil' that we know from 1 Timothy 6:10 or earlier in Ecclesiastes 5:10. It is not even in the spirit of the passage in Genesis 23:16 in which Abraham's careful counting out of the silver shekels to purchase Sarah's tomb was cited by Anglican clergy in the 1690s to warn against the sin of coin-clipping (Chown 1994: 62). Locke's preferred verse 'money answers all things' conveys the sense of money being a means by which people obtain their desire, but in the context of the broader message of the passage it also confirms the public character of money for it serves as a warning to rulers to be careful with public money for it answers all the political, economic and military needs that may arise in a dangerous world.
40. Vickers 1959: 70–1; Caffentzis 1989: 33.
41. Caffentzis 1989: 36.
42. Horsefield 1960: 58.
43. Muldrew 1998: 146–7.
44. Caffentzis 1989: 26.
45. See Dunn 1995: 91–9.
46. An important exception to this tendency to ignore Locke's statecraft is Josephson 2002.
47. Muldrew 1998: 124.
48. Caffentzis 1989: 26.
49. See Casson 2011: 245.

50. Nacol 2016: 67.
51. Woolhouse 2007: 333.
52. Kleer 2004: 544.
53. Carey 2014: 70.
54. For a good discussion of the important distributive justice dimensions of Locke's argument, see Kleer 2004: 545–6. On the contrary, Desan (2014: 358) argues that Locke was unconcerned by distributive consequences.
55. For Locke's distrust toward the banks, see Kelly 1991: 26; Pincus 2009: 46.
56. Josephson 2016: 19.
57. Appleby 1976: 56; Kelly 1991: 64–5, Horsefield 1960: 36; Casson 2011: 253, Chown 1994: 63; Schumpeter 1954: 28. But for a defence of Locke, see Kleer 2004.
58. Locke 1696 letter to William Molyneux cited in Li 1963: 104–5.
59. Pocock 1993: 394.
60. Desan 2014: 360–1.

Chapter 3

Interests and Rights in Bernard Mandeville's *Fable of the Bees* and Trenchard and Gordon's *Cato's Letters*

A standard reading of the movement of British political thought from the seventeenth century to the eighteenth century is that the main conceptual development in classical liberal political economy arose from the rejection of the somewhat vulgarised version of the English natural rights theories of Thomas Hobbes and John Locke by the luminaries of the Scottish Enlightenment, including David Hume, Frances Hutcheson and Adam Smith. According to this narrative, the crystallisation of the argument for commerce in eighteenth-century Britain presupposed the transformation from a political theory dominated by the discourse of pre-civil individual rights and a rationalist law of nature framework to a new political vernacular that emphasised natural moral sentiments and the concept of economic interests.[1] In this chapter, I propose an amendment to this familiar account, one that re-situates the genesis of the philosophical defence of commerce earlier historically than typically thought, in the context of the polemical responses to the challenges posed both to law and conventional morality by the Financial Revolution in early eighteenth-century England. By recontextualising the origins of modern thought on commerce in the light of the debate about the new financial structures and institutions that transformed English economic life in this period, I hope to illuminate the rich, but often neglected, site of theoretical reflection about the problems and possibilities of commerce afforded most directly by the controversy surrounding the South Sea Bubble of 1720.

My central argument is that it was in response to the challenges posed by the Financial Revolution in England in the opening decades of the eighteenth-century that we witness the first clear mutual appearance of both the familiar natural rights-based version of liberalism as well as a new kind of argument that would in time come to be associated with the 'harmony of interests' philosophy. I focus on the pivotal nexus between the interest-based argument for commerce in Bernard Mandeville's *Fable of the Bees* and the natural rights-based argument in *Cato's Letters* authored by John Trenchard and Thomas Gordon. These controversial works were partners in crime, as it were, sharing a fiery fate condemned to the flames as a public nuisance by the Middlesex Grand Jury in 1723, as well as being arguably the most theoretically sophisticated writings on commerce in England in the first decades of the eighteenth century. The main claims in this chapter are twofold: (1) that Mandeville's *Fable of the Bees* and Trenchard and Gordon's *Cato's Letters* signify two different, and distinctly liberal, conceptual responses to the economic transformations in this period; and (2) that it was the Dutch immigrant Mandeville – rather than the later Scottish thinkers – whose infamous maxim 'Private vices, Publick benefits' established the seeming paradox at the core of the interest-based defence of commerce. Admittedly, this approach may be controversial for several reasons.

First, the radical Whig offering *Cato's Letters* is hardly acknowledged by all as even being a liberal tract. Indeed, many commentators see it as an example of the classical republican paradigm deeply hostile to liberal ideas of commerce and individual rights. Second, while Mandeville's egoistic and hedonistic moral philosophy is widely held to be the epitome of what Hume labelled the 'selfish system',[2] his role in the development of the philosophical case for commerce is often obscured because he did not employ the discourse of natural rights typically thought to be constitutive of British liberal thought in the period prior to the Scottish Enlightenment. I will argue that Mandeville is a pivotal figure in the development of the modern spirit of commerce precisely because while he affirmed the principle of limited government and personal liberty, he did so in terms of a discourse of interests, rather than natural rights, that in important respects adumbrated the later revolution in moral philosophy normally associated with Hume's rejection of natural justice and contract theory, as well as Smith's natural harmony of interests.[3]

The historical context that illuminates the contours of my argument is, of course, the Financial Revolution in England. The period from 1690 to 1720 witnessed a dramatic transformation in English economic life through the establishment of public debt and the creation of the Bank of England in the 1690s, and later with the adoption of new forms of property and sophisticated financial combinations such as the East India and South Sea companies.[4] These joint-stock companies sold publicly traded shares and were governed by a corporate structure including a board of directors. Developments in commercial banking included the use of bills of exchange for financial transactions and the establishment of the institutional framework intended to promote a stable system of credit. Arguably, the first major shock to the new financial system was the South Sea Bubble of 1720 in which this politically well-connected company, which had assumed by law the national debt (providing holders of the debt South Sea shares at the same nominal value in exchange), triggered a massive speculative frenzy over the summer of 1720 which witnessed the value of company stock skyrocketing from £100 a share to over £1,000 a share.[5] When the bubble finally burst in late summer, it produced a financial crisis of bankruptcies and the risk of a nationwide credit freeze. In the aftermath of the scandal, Robert Walpole and the Court Whigs assumed the leadership role from which they would dominate English politics for the next several decades. In response to the public outcry, Walpole launched a parliamentary inquiry into political corruption in the awarding of the South Sea Company's privileges; established a programme of partial compensation for victims of the scheme; and stabilised the financial sector by engineering the reallocation of South Sea stock to the Bank of England and the East India Company.

The South Sea Scandal was both the first serious crisis of confidence in the new English financial system, as well as an important marker in the publishing history of Mandeville's *Fable of the Bees* and Trenchard and Gordon's *Cato's Letters*. Mandeville first published the *Fable* in 1714 to little notice as an encomium to commerce at a time of great economic expansion, while *Cato's Letters* began appearing in the weeks after the bubble burst and continuing from November 1720 to July 1723 in the *London Journal* and later in the *British Journal*. In the wake of the South Sea Scandal, Mandeville republished a much-expanded version of the *Fable* in 1723, provoking considerable controversy before completing an entirely new second volume in the edition of 1729. The *Fable* and *Cato's Letters* represent two distinct, but recognisably liberal responses to the raw nerves of the Financial Revolution exposed by the South Sea Scandal. To Mandeville, the intrinsic practical difficulties of moral rigorism are compounded by an accidental alliance of sorts with the dogmatic rights doctrine contained in *Cato's Letters*. Indeed, arguably the popularity of *Cato's Letters* in the early 1720s was one of the chief incentives for Mandeville to re-publish his expanded versions of the *Fable* in 1723 and 1729.[6] From the vantage point of the Court Whigs, with whom Mandeville sympathised, Cato's angry rhetoric about public vengeance and unalienable rights appeared as threatening to commercial society as the moral hectoring and pieties of traditional Christian and classical moral virtue. For their part, Trenchard and Gordon advanced what they took to be a moral corrective to the commercial ethos in England that had degenerated into endemic public corruption masked by the apparent Mandevillean delight in condoning private vices. In *Cato's Letters* we see the Opposition Whig attempt to save the Financial Revolution in England from its own toxic tendencies that threatened to render nugatory any genuine confidence and trust in fair dealing with others in the market.

The opening sections of this chapter outline the main features of the natural rights philosophy of *Cato's Letters*. I will demonstrate that Trenchard and Gordon were not, as some suggest, appealing to either classical republicanism or to traditional Christian ideas of virtue. Rather, the core of their moral vision was the Lockean idea of individual natural rights. I will also illustrate that Trenchard and Gordon maintained the complementarity between natural rights and commerce, even as they sought to inculcate an ethos of suspicion about political corruption among the citizenry and a spirit of vengeance against political and economic elites who perpetrate collusion to defraud the public. The following sections will turn to Mandeville's critique of moral virtue and the classical and Christian hostility to commerce. I will illuminate how Mandeville sought to replace the traditional idea of moral virtue with the morally neutral language of interests in order to generate a new understanding of the positive social effects of self-interest. I will then explore how Mandeville replaced the Lockean contractarian account of the origin of civil society with an exercise in speculative anthropology and proto-utilitarian philosophy. We will see that the permissive, non-judgemental ethos of a Mandevillean interest-based politics set a considerably different civic model than the spirited rights-based liberalism of Cato, even as they both championed commerce and quintessentially liberal ideas about personal liberty and limited government. I will conclude with some reflections about how the legacy of these polemical exchanges surrounding the South Sea Scandal adumbrated the conceptual cleavages between the natural rights-based and the harmony of interests-based versions of liberalism that would become central to the development of liberal commercial republican thought later in the eighteenth century and beyond.

Cato's Liberalism

The intellectual pedigree of *Cato's Letters* has been the subject of intense debate for decades. They have been identified with civic humanism,[7] the seventeenth-century English Commonwealthsmen,[8] and even as the classical republican foil to Mandeville's updated Epicurean philosophy of permissive hedonism.[9] However, there is also a considerable body of work that situates *Cato's Letters* in the orbit of early modern liberal thought inspired by John Locke,[10] or as an exotic hybrid of liberal and distinctly modern republican elements.[11] For our purposes, it is useful from the outset to recognise that the animating spirit of *Cato's Letters* is a form of ethical realism reminiscent of Machiavelli as Cato admits that he 'shall take the liberty of considering man as he is, since it is out of our power to give a model to have him new made by'.[12] Cato also mirrors Mandeville's famous scepticism about the venerable teaching regarding 'the intrinsic excellence of virtue', which he suggests greatly underestimates the importance of self-interest, as well as rewards and punishments, as motivations for good actions (CL 108:762). Cato adopts only ironically the demand that virtue must entail self-denial as he intones somewhat tongue-in-cheek that is it is reasonable to assume that 'virtue is its own reward' because 'it seldom meets with any other' (CL 61:420). Cato also embraced two of the key tenets of liberal moral philosophy championed by Hobbes and Locke through his rejection of the doctrine of free will (CL 110:774–5), and his repudiation of the Christian–Aristotelian premise that practical principles of moral knowledge are 'implanted in our Natures' by God (CL 109:767). For Cato, virtue and vice, as well as good and evil, are not a function of ontology, but rather are intelligible only 'in relation to men's action to one another' (CL 110:772).

The argument that virtue is conditioned by relative circumstances and the calculus of reward and punishment rather than 'intrinsic excellence' leads Cato to redefine virtue in a modern, non-classical way. This redefinition does not, however, culminate in the celebration of 'private vices' made famous by Mandeville. Instead, Cato redirects the ends of virtuous activity in the light of a mental framework available to practical reason that illuminates 'certain rules of mutual convenience or indulgence, conducive or necessary to the well-being of society' (CL 108:761). Most of these rules are 'obvious' because they are discernible in every individual's private desires (CL 108:761–2). But given the self-regarding character of human desire, virtue requires irreplaceable legal and political inducements to 'make it all men's interests to be honest' (CL 108:766). Cato's moral philosophy is, thus, at core Hobbesian, but it is modified from the original in important ways. Cato agrees with Hobbes that 'self-love is the strongest passion', which grounds the 'first law of nature, that of self-preservation' (CL 31:222; 33:239). But Cato's insistence on the priority of passions over reason does not result in the kind of preservationist reductionism that occurs with Hobbes, for Cato contends that the 'passion for liberty' is the 'parent of all virtues', being stronger even than the desire for self-preservation (CL 62:428–30). While Cato identified reason as primarily a deliberative faculty, this does not mean that Trenchard and Gordon interpreted liberty in terms of overcoming self-interest.[13] For Cato, love of liberty is perfectly compatible with a very pessimistic account of human nature. Indeed, Cato appealed to the authority of Mandeville's mentor Pierre Bayle to support his contention that human beings are 'not ruled by principle but by passion' (CL 44:298). In contrast to a 'solemn soothsayer, a poet or philosopher' who constantly praises the 'dignity of human nature' (likely an oblique reference to Mandeville's nemesis the Earl of Shaftesbury), the liberal individualist Cato is content with the formulation that human beings are naturally 'foolish, helpless, perfidious, impotent, easily misled and trepanned' (CL 105:742). The passion for liberty produces all the virtues only when the individual's interests are aligned with the capacity for action.

In keeping with Hobbes and Locke, Cato presupposed that passions operate mechanistically (CL 105:742).[14] Even if 'all nature is perpetual motion' possessing no stable essences, the principle of causation in nature is apprehensible to our senses through the laws of motion, albeit that these laws may in practice manifest in 'infinite ways' (CL 77:563). Central to this necessitarian account of nature is, of course, Cato's rejection of the idea of a providential God and of miracles (CL 77:562). In Cato's natural theology, one's confidence in the existence of certain fundamental laws of nature renders it impossible to reject the idea of 'Almighty God, who makes his sun to shine and his rain to fall upon the just and unjust' (CL 52:345). Needless to say, this conception of the divine offers little cosmic support for moral virtue.

Cato also viewed passions as a source of fundamental human equality. From the normative premise 'men are naturally equal', Cato drew the politico-juridical conclusion that 'none ever rose above the rest but by force or consent' (CL 45:306). Cato dismissed out of hand the 'wild notions of inequality' propounded by proponents of divine right monarchy such as Locke's opponent in the 1680s Robert Filmer and his supporters in the ranks of the Tory party in Cato's time (CL 45:307). Natural equality also informs Cato's practical objections to the classical ideal of virtue involving self-denial and rational control over the passions. The exemplars of this ideal for Cato were the Stoics who held 'many admirable and virtuous precepts', but whose 'absolute indifference' to pleasure and pain was too onerous to ever become a popular teaching (CL 105:743).

Cato assumes that neither religion nor official propaganda about the beauty of virtue can restrain the effects of self-interest: only with the 'security of laws' can human passions promise public benefits. Thus, Cato believed that intelligent structural design of government is an effective response to the inadequacy of the classical account of moral virtue. But Cato reached a strikingly Mandevillean conclusion about the political meaning of accepting the ethical argument that good and evil are primarily a matter of consequences, for as Cato admits 'nothing produces good in this world, but what may, and generally does, produce evil' (Cl 43:295). This conclusion brought Cato so far from the classical idea of virtue as good in itself that he was even prepared to endorse a kind of reverse Mandevillean trans-valuation of virtue by which 'ambition, avarice, revenge, are all so many virtues, when they aim at the general welfare' (CL 39:276).

The identification of *Cato's Letters* as an exemplar of classical republican moral philosophy is clearly problematic insofar as Cato bears the deep impress of the self-interested moral calculus pioneered in English liberalism by Hobbes and Locke. The other examples of Cato's modern liberal bona fides include his commitment to religious toleration (CL 80:585) and free speech (CL 15:110), as well as his critique, shared by Mandeville, of the misguided, counterproductive humanitarianism advanced by supporters of religious charity schools (who were also conveniently treasonous Jacobites!) (CL 133:919–24). What, then, are the main pieces of evidence cited to support the classical republican reading of *Cato's Letters*?

Commentators sometimes point to Cato's praise of ancient republican Rome and its celebrated hostility to luxury and commerce as proof of his classical commitments.[15] Cato certainly made several references to the glory of republican Rome, which he claims 'conquered by its virtue more than its arms' (CL 18:128). The public-spirited Roman citizen was driven by 'a passion to promote universal good, with personal pain, loss and peril' (CL 35:251). With the corruption of Roman patriotism into brutal, self-interested factions, Cato bewails, 'thus ended the greatest, the noblest state that ever adorned the worldly theatre' (CL 18:131).

It is important, however, to understand the context of Cato's scattered references to ancient Rome. For example, in Letter 18, which contains Cato's most extended discussion of Rome, the shadow of the South Sea Scandal looms large. Cato offers his account of Roman decline as an invitation for the English nation to examine itself to discover if 'we ourselves have none of these corruptions and abuses' that destroyed the Roman Republic (CL 18:131). Later Cato presented Rome as an object lesson of the potential dangers for English constitutional government produced by unregulated high finance: 'Is it a crime to be rich? Yes, certainly at the publick expense, or to the danger to the publick' (CL 35:254). In an unmistakable oblique reference to the South Sea Scandal, Cato condemned the 'sort of men' in Rome who promoted 'gainful and favourite speculations' that turn 'the world topsy-turvy' (CL 35:252). Even Cato's apparent praise of the egalitarian Roman Agrarian Laws was only applied very specifically to the Roman context. When pondering the question of whether England would be better governed as a republic or a monarchy, Cato concluded that the 'present distribution of property' in England (i.e., unequal holdings) made it preferable to continue with monarchy (CL 85:614).

Trenchard and Gordon were not hostile towards commerce or luxury per se, but rather expressed concern about the fraudulent manipulation of new forms of property and commercial enterprise that threatened to destroy the networks of trust and public credit vital to the flourishing of commercial society.[16] Cato freely admits that the desire to acquire is the 'grand design and business of all mankind', and that 'growing as rich as we can' within the limits of the public good is perfectly laudable (CL 87:626, 62: 432). In a marvellous metaphor, Cato characterised trade as 'a coy and humorous Dame' until she finds herself 'the best welcome and kindest reception' in a system of laws that secure property (CL 64:442). Cato excoriated corruption as fraud and bribery of public officials, not as the desire for luxury. Indeed, Cato extolled the general benefits accruing from trade in, and consumption of, luxury items: 'luxury of the rich becomes the bread of the poor' (CL 67:473).

The proliferation of trades designed to service the desires of the rich establishes a firm foundation for general economic prosperity and national strength. The trade in, and production of, things made desirable solely by 'custom and fancy' have the additional benefit of spurring 'invention and industry' (CL 67: 473) such that, with echoes of Mandeville, 'even the poor will have felicity arising from the superfluities of the rich' (CL 89:639). This is to say, the very subjects – moral virtue and luxury – often mistakenly identified as the fundamental differences between Cato and Mandeville are in reality elements of the nexus of ideas that united them in the greater orbit of early eighteenth-century English liberalism.

Cato's Politics of Rights

The normative ground of Trenchard and Gordon's argument for commerce was a philosophy of natural rights embedded in the concept of a state of nature exemplifying the juridico-theoretical concept famously illustrated in Locke's *Second Treatise*. Echoing Locke, Cato declares 'all men are born free' (CL 59:406). Cato also made the classic Lockean move of connecting the 'first law of nature', that of self-preservation, with a natural right to acquire property derived from 'the power which every man has over his own actions, and his right to enjoy the fruit of his labour, art and industry' (CL 33:239, 62: 427). Liberty is inseparable from the individual's self-ownership: 'Every man is sole lord and arbiter of his own private actions and property' (CL 427).[17] Arguably, Cato takes the logic of natural rights to a radical point beyond even what Locke explicitly endorsed when he directly stated that 'liberty is the unalienable right of all mankind' (CL 59:405). Locke certainly implied that the natural right to liberty (and property) exists outwith the human capacity to renounce or surrender completely, but he never actually used the phrase 'inalienable rights'.[18]

In this natural law framework, the purpose of government is primarily the protection of property, or as Cato phrases it 'to defend every man and his property from foreign and domestic injuries' (CL 62:427). But civil government's role in protecting property does not empower it to direct individuals' in 'their own affairs, in which no one is interested but themselves' (CL 62:428). As a general principle, Cato is happy to 'let people take care of themselves', at least with respect to matters that do not involve harming others (CL 62:428). But this insouciance about the effects of self-interest is always framed within the context of natural jurisprudence. In

Cato's gloss on familiar Lockean principles such as the derivation of the magistrate's power from the natural executive power of individuals, we see if anything an even more spirited defence of popular resistance to unjust civil authority than we expect from Locke. Government, Cato explains, is established only by the 'wisdom and force of mere men', and as such every individual 'must act according to the light and dictates of his own conscience' in deciding if government is abusing its power (CL 60:413). While Locke sought to inculcate a healthy suspicion of government among the citizenry, Cato took the emphasis on popular vigilance to a greater level and gave it a more concrete institutional focus through his advocacy of making 'the interests of the governors and of the governed the same' as much as possible through 'frequent fresh elections' and regular rotation in office (CL 60:417; 61:422–3).

Another important element of Cato's politics of rights is the prominent role of punishment. Retributive justice is a centrepiece of the Catonic polemic as his state of nature account is permeated with punitive images relating to the individual's natural right to 'repel injuries and to revenge them' (CL 11:87). The punishment power not only belongs to civil government, but also exists as a universal right 'inherent in private men' (CL 11:87). Where Cato breaks with the 'great philosopher' Hobbes (and follows Locke) is with respect to the question of whether the individual qua individual has a right by the law of nature to punish wrongdoers (CL 33:236). Cato's unique contribution to the Lockean modification of Hobbes' natural rights theory is the distinction drawn out in the *Letters* between crimes that arise from disobedience of positive law and crimes according to nature. Cato argues that the fundamental natural law maxim *salus populi suprema lex esto* can never be wholly encompassed by positive law. Just as the individual has an inherent power to punish wrongdoing in the state of nature by virtue of discretionary judgement, Cato maintains 'it is absurd to suppose that national legislatures, to whom every man's private power is committed, have not the same right, and ought not to exercise it upon proper occasions' (CL 11:87). Positive law cannot exhaust the possibility of identifying punishable crimes because there are villainous acts 'too monstrous for human foresight and prevention' (CL 11:88).

Clearly Cato's distinction between natural crimes and crimes according to the breach of law is framed in the context of the South Sea Scandal. Cato encouraged Parliament to punish harshly the South Sea directors and corrupt public officials regardless of the limitations of statute law. Cato insists that the goal of 'the art of governing' is to create institutions that prevent the gratification of 'private passion by publick means' (CL 39:276). These criminals who 'overturn trade and public credit' have committed a crime against the entire community that may not be sufficiently defined in law or assigned condign punishments (CL 12:94). By interpreting the malfeasance evident during the South Sea Bubble through a natural law prism, Cato discovers a potentially vast range of activities that are punishable by discretion of civil authorities, but that may not contravene any specific written law. In the context of the South Sea Scandal, Cato employed natural law theory as a means to grapple with the impact of the relatively new institutions and practices of the Financial Revolution, which were still largely unregulated and lacked clear sanctions for bad behaviour. Fraud, breach of trust and bribery are so obviously contrary to natural justice that even 'though national governments should never enact any positive laws' with known penalties to these vices in the new commercial context, government would yet 'have a right, and it would be their duty to punish those offences according to their discretion' (CL 11:87).

The target of Cato's remarks is most certainly the Walpole administration, which adopted a relatively moderate posture with respect to investigating the scandal and punishing the bad actors. This opposition critique of the Court Whigs employed vivid rhetoric of vengeance and righteous indignation, precisely the emotions we will see Mandeville was concerned to suppress in the *Fable*. Cato insists that 'nations should be quick in their resentments, and severe in their judgements', and in the context of the South Sea Scandal it is imperative to 'load every gallows in England with directors and stock jobbers' (CL 2:42). The 'scum of the Alley' used their 'prior intelligence, and knowledge of their own intentions' to raise and depress the national credit 'at their pleasure as they saw their advantage' (CL 20:144). While Cato viewed 'exemplary' punishments as a form of national self-defence to deter future crimes, it is important to recognise that this does not demonstrate a distrust or hostility to commerce per se, so much as indicate Cato's concerns about the harmful potentialities of the new financial instruments in the fledgling stock market.[19] Cato shuddered at the prospect of a corrupt financial elite marked by its own 'sort of cabalistic learning' plundering 'twenty millions of real property' from the 'honest and industrious' citizenry (CL 107:758; 6:58).[20] For the perpetrators of illicit gain, Cato recommends severe punishment and compensation to the victims (CL 3:45). With vengeance comes healing.

For Cato, the South Sea Scandal exposed two fundamental dangers confronting English commercial society. The first related to the structure of the joint-stock companies that sprang up like mushrooms across the City. In these companies the directors often have an interest separate from the shareholders as 'no one receives advantages . . . but the governors, directors' and agents who have built up vast fortunes, 'whilst the kingdom has been impoverished, and the company undone' (CL 90:647). Cato defends government regulation of the financial sector on the ground that it does not signify interfering with anyone's natural rights, but rather makes it possible that whatever unfair advantage 'to the detriment of others by ill laws may be taken by good ones' (CL 90:643). The second, and more serious, problem painfully exposed by the South Sea affair had to do with the system of public credit. Integral to the Financial Revolution was the idea of the national debt anchoring the wider network of credit that fuelled the emerging stock market. The collapse of the South Sea stock produced a crisis of confidence in the financial system as such with Cato bemoaning that 'credit [was] undone' by those South Sea director 'cannibals of credit' (CL 4:47; 5:51). The way to restore credit was to redefine the whole notion of public finance in order to promote 'mutual confidence' among lenders and debtors (CL 4:47) as opposed to the 'new-fangled and fantastical' investment model exemplified by the South Sea scheme, which was invented by John Law and imported to England from France (CL 107:757). This 'new sort of property' threatens to change 'honest commerce into bubbling', and render the system of lending 'precarious, uncertain and transitory' (CL 107:758). As such, Cato calls upon the 'Ministry' to regulate the market and devise more transparent methods to manage public credit (CL 107:760–1).

Mandeville's Critique of Moral Virtue

The genesis of the *Fable of the Bees* was the lengthy doggerel-verse style poem titled 'The Grumbling Hive: or Knaves turn'd Honest', published by Mandeville in 1705. Nearly a decade later in 1714 Mandeville repackaged this poem in a longer study including additional essays on the origin of moral virtue and a substantive commentary on the 'Grumbling Hive'. The central paradox of the *Fable* was presented in the subtitle 'Private Vices, Publick Benefits'. The 'Grumbling Hive' served as a literary illustration of the proposition that demonstrable social good can arise from the 'vilest and most hateful qualities' of bees, and, of course, human beings.[21] The poem tells the tale of how a dynamic, prosperous, freedom-loving hive suffered economic and political decline due to moral regeneration. In the flourishing hive millions of bees worked busily to satisfy their own 'lust and vanity' (F 1:18). These bees are not paragons of austere Calvinist virtue, but rather brazen patrons of corruption: 'there was not a Bee but that would, get more . . . than he should' (F 1:22). The sword of justice was not impartial as it checked only 'the desperate and the poor' (F 1:23). Far from generating distrust and social breakdown, the greedy, selfish bees all pursuing their own interest strengthened the polity: 'Such were the blessings of that State; Their crimes conspired to make them great' (F 1:24). With the advent of a moral reform movement in the hive, the newly chastened bees, now serious about virtue, precipitated a rapid decline in prosperity as luxury goods were banned to the great detriment of trade, and a whole host of occupations tied to trade and manufacture disappeared from the economy of the hive. Eventually, economic stagnation encouraged foreign attack, which was repulsed only with great loss of insect life. Reflecting on the sad fate of the moralistic hive, we realise that 'Fraud, luxury and Pride must live, while we the Benefits receive' (F 1:36).

The seriousness of the moral paradox at the heart of the *Fable* somewhat redeems Mandeville's palpable delight at provoking the righteous indignation of the better sort of reader, for he situated his own piece of whimsy in the very sanctum of modern ethical realism. Echoing Machiavelli, Hobbes – and as we have seen Cato – Mandeville complains that 'most writers are always telling men what they should be, and hardly trouble their heads with telling them what they really are' (F 1:39).[22] The concept Mandeville identified to encapsulate this tendency towards hyper-morality is *rigorism*. The intellectual provenance of the term lies in seventeenth-century French thinkers such as Saint-Evremond and Pierre Bayle, whose critique of austere Christian arguments against luxury greatly influenced Mandeville.[23] In the *Fable*, rigorism primarily means rational control over selfish passions by which 'Man, contrary to the impulse of Nature, should endeavour the benefit of others, or the conquest of his own Passions out of a Rational Ambition of being good' (F 1:48–9). The major psychological claim made by rigorists is that 'there could be no virtue without Self-denial' (F 1:323, 156).[24] Central to Mandeville's critique of moral virtue appears, then, to be an acceptance of the rigorist premise that virtue does indeed require self-denial.

Significantly, Mandeville did not deny the possibility of what he calls 'real Virtue', although he insists that it is much rarer than traditional proponents of moral virtue contend (F 2:336). In fact, he professed fairly conventional moral intuitions: 'I lay down as a first principle, that in all Societies, great or small, it is the Duty of every Member of it to be good, that Virtue ought to be encouraged, Vice discountenanced' (F 1:229). The author of the *Fable* even surprisingly insists that 'I have always without Hesitation prefer'd the Road that leads to Virtue' (F 1:231). How can we reconcile these statements with the apparent condemnation of moral rigorism throughout the *Fable*? One way to approach this question is to reconsider what exactly Mandeville is claiming on behalf of vice. He does not believe that all vices produce public benefits, but rather that demonstrable public good arises as a result of vice: 'no Society can be rais'd into such a rich and mighty Kingdom, or so rais'd, subsist in their Wealth and Power for any considerable Time, without the vices of Man' (F 1:229). Politically speaking, the problem of moral virtue is the unintended bad consequences of virtues such as moderation, frugality and austerity that can impair economic growth.

Mandeville's ethical realism required replacing the traditional idea of moral virtue with the morally neutral logic of interests in order to generate political effects contrary to what he took to be threats to the psychological mechanisms underlying commercial society. Among these was the moral critique of self-interest launched by the imposing figure of the 3rd Earl of Shaftesbury whose *Characteristicks of Men, Manners, Opinions, Times* was published in 1711 to considerable applause in English philosophical and literary circles. Shaftesbury's core teaching was that human beings possess a natural moral sense that directs us to a disinterested pursuit of public good with no prior consideration of one's own welfare or prior religious sentiment.[25] Shaftesbury's conclusion that human beings are naturally sociable and drawn by their natural affections towards satisfying a 'herding' appetite constituted an explicit rejection of Hobbes and La Rochefoucauld's argument that human beings act only out of self-interest.[26] In the essay 'A Search into the Nature of Society' added to the 1723 edition of the *Fable*, Mandeville declared that 'two Systems cannot be more opposite than his Lordship's [i.e., Shaftesbury] and mine' (F 1:324). While Mandeville expressed a certain affinity for the 'noble sentiments' in Shaftesbury's account of 'our exalted nature', he also predictably bemoaned the reality that these noble sentiments 'are not true' (F 1:324). The problem with Shaftesbury's teaching is that it encourages an illusory confidence in the capacity for moral virtue. In removing the element of self-denial so vital to the rigorists, Shaftesbury actually debases virtue by reducing it to a kind of unreflective instinct. While Mandeville identified 'real Virtue' as being too rare to be politically relevant, he dismissed the affective moral instinct promoted by Shaftesbury as too banal to ground any complex social behaviour.

What Shaftesbury and the rigorists had in common, of course, is the denial of the usefulness of vice. The limit case for Mandeville's moral vision is contained in the axiom that just as nothing is 'so entirely Evil, but that it may prove beneficial to some part or other of Creation', likewise nothing is so 'perfectly Good that it may not do injury to some part of society' (F 1:367). Mandeville's critique of moral virtue does not presuppose the Augustinian judgement that the rigoristic classical virtues of the Romans and Greeks were essentially splendid vices animated by pride. That is to say, Mandeville is not driven to defend vice out of a pessimistic vision of humanity's fallen nature.[27] Rather, his moral vision projected what he took to be the undeniable social and economic benefits of a materialistic, hedonic moral calculus. He insists that by praising the empirically measurable public benefits of vice, he does not thus 'bid Men be vicious' (F 1:231). Mandeville's point is that at a certain level of abstraction fully accessible perhaps only to 'the few', it becomes possible to recognise that self-interest not only reduces potential social ills, but also produces collateral benefits (F 1:231).

Mandeville's critique of rigorism also extends to the private sphere as he insists that even the 'road that leads to virtue' in primary associations like the family or personal friendship involve only the appearance of self-denial masking a complex interplay of self-interested desires. For example, Mandeville freely admits that 'all mothers naturally love their children', but he hastens to add that the passion grounding this natural emotion is 'self-love' (F 1:75). Even pity, 'the most gentle and least mischievous' passion, is still nonetheless a passion that may incline us towards charity for strangers, but also 'consults neither the publick interest nor our own Reason' (F 1:56). Pity, not to mention maternal love, 'may produce Evil as well as Good' (F 1: 56). In Mandeville's telling, the virtues of private life that hold together the primary associations of family and friends are in reality manifestations of inextinguishable self-love experienced more strongly the degree to which they are 'within the reach of our senses' (F 1: 76). Thus, self-interest and a hedonic calculus of pleasure and pain are as prevalent in personal relations as in public life.

For Mandeville, the logical priority of vice over virtue derives from the fundamental passions that ground human action. In contrast to Shaftesbury (and later Adam Smith), Mandeville insists that all passions are at core selfish. While self-love can be projected onto the concern for others, for example, one's children or an object of pity, self-love more typically has the effect of spurring competition and hostility among people: 'Self-love bids us to look on every Creature that seems satisfied as a Rival in Happiness' (F 1:139). Vice is the stabilising force in society because qualities of action and character traditionally associated with vice, especially vanity, pride and shame, are the effectual agents of social co-existence. In particular, shame and its reverse pride are the 'two Passions, in which the seeds of most Virtues are contained' (F 1:67). Both shame and pride are rooted in a kind of pleasure and pain produced by our natural 'desire to be thought well of' (F 1:63). While Mandeville argues that pride is 'so beneficial to society' that it turns out that the sense of shame is even more fundamental: 'It is incredible how necessary an Ingredient Shame is to make us sociable . . . no Society could be polished; if the Generality of Mankind were not subject to it' (F 1:68). The chief significance of shame is that it is the passion that comes closest to simulating moral virtues for it 'overrules our Reason, and requires so much Labour and Self-denial to be subdued' (F 1: 64). It is really only from an aversion to the pain caused by the feeling of shame that individuals will adhere to 'certain Rules to avoid those things that might bring this troublesome Sense of Shame' (F 1: 68). Societies will, of course, have different objects of shame depending on the customs and education of the time and place. Shame, then, provides the dependable, and culturally adaptive, tool for establishing certain range properties for civil conduct.

If shame grounds social existence in the negative sense of highlighting what individuals seek to avoid, pride and vanity represent the positive or constitutive dimension of self-love. Mandeville maintains that: 'Pride and Vanity have built more Hospitals than all the Virtues together' (F 1:261). The desire to be thought well of can be a powerful motivation for impressive acts of generosity. Pride and vanity are also the most characteristic 'vices' of commercial societies because they are particularly well attuned to the psychological desire for luxury. The merchant who imports luxury items undoubtedly is in 'many ways beneficial to the publick', while also being completely dependent upon 'the lavishness and drunkenness' of the people (F 1:85). Mandeville contends that the vain desire to be thought stylish that inspired 'the silly and capricious Invention of Hoop'd and Quilted Petticoats' has done more to promote national flourishing than any of the most exalted moral and religious doctrines (F 1:356). However, Mandeville's argument flirts with absurdity when he declares that 'everything is to be Luxury (as in strictness it ought) that is not immediately necessary to make Man subsist as he is a living Creature' (F 1:107). He admits that this definition of luxury as everything not absolutely necessary for survival is 'too rigorous', but given the subjective character of human desires, Mandeville challenges his critics to find a more suitable definition (F 1:107). Thus, Mandeville responded to the moral objection to luxury advanced by rigorists with an expansive, if not somewhat ironic, definition of it that produces a kind of *reductio ad absurdum* of rigorist logic that would reduce the virtuous society to one dedicated to the provision of only the most rudimentary biological necessities.

What can we draw by way of conclusion from Mandeville's critique of moral virtue? First, we see that the function of the central paradox of the *Fable* is to reinterpret virtue, but especially vice, in terms of consequences rather than motives for 'hateful qualities' that are absolutely necessary for making social co-existence possible (F 1:4). By highlighting his deep distrust of the motivations typically presumed to produce virtuous acts, similarly to Cato, Mandeville situated his treatment of morality in the context of the distinctively modern philosophical attack on the doctrine of free will.[28] The fundamental re-thinking of human agency proposed in the *Fable* also seems to align his conception of liberty with that of Hobbes who famously severed any consideration of freedom from virtue and vice.[29] For Hobbes, freedom is simply uninterrupted motion. Mandeville's healthy hive is a poetic representation of this Hobbesian premise, a frenzy of perpetual and constructive motion in which contentment is 'the Bane of Industry' (F 1:34). There is also a distinctly Lockean flavour to Mandeville's reflections on morality wherein the defining characteristic of freedom in the hive is the relentless pursuit of subjective desires that in Locke's words vary as much as 'Cheese or Lobsters'.[30] Mandeville's endorsement of the essentially contentless nature of human happiness makes him less a moral pessimist than an enthusiastic individualist. The major task remaining for us is to determine the extent to which Mandeville believed that the inexpungible, selfish passions can be managed with the aim of constructing a stable political order consistent with national prosperity and individual security.

The Politics of Interests

Mandeville's attack on rigorism was inspired by his belief that there was something disturbingly unnatural about the degree of self-denial and rational control of passion required according to classical and Christian accounts of moral virtue. His contrasting vision of ethical naturalism gave priority to self-regarding passions, but, unlike Hobbes, Locke and Cato, he did not situate those passions in a framework of natural rights. This is especially significant given Mandeville's treatment of the quintessentially liberal concept of the state of nature. He did not follow his liberal forbears in using the state of nature as a juridico-theoretic model to ground individual natural rights and the social contract. Rather, Mandeville's version of the state of nature is an elaborate specimen of speculative anthropology designed to account for the socialisation process by which the naturally selfish brutes of humanity's past gradually became civilised beings subject to law. The distinct political legacy of Mandeville's use of this anthropological state of nature was an approach to the study of government and society that emphasises interests rather than rights, and utility over ontology.

Mandeville's use of the state of nature motif changed over the course of the publishing history of the *Fable*. In the first edition in 1714 Mandeville described the state of nature as a condition in which human beings are 'neither Jews nor Christians; but mere Men ignorant of the true Deity', and of whom it can be said 'no Species of Animals is . . . less capable of agreeing long together in Multitudes than that of Man (F 1:40–1). Mandeville did not convey with this an Augustinian belief in humanity's inherent sinfulness, but rather this 'wild State of Nature' suggested an anthropology that hearkened back temporally to an early stage in human social and psychological development. Later in the essay 'A Search into the Nature of Society' added to the 1723 edition of the *Fable*, Mandeville amplified the anthropological dimension of his state of nature describing it in terms of the transition from a condition in which, foreshadowing Rousseau's *Discourse on the Origin of Inequality*, human desires and appetites were rudimentary and easily satisfied in the 'Savage State' through to our transformation into a 'Disciplin'd Creature' living in political communities. (F 1:346–7).[31]

However, it was only later in volume 2 of the *Fable* published in 1729 that Mandeville systematised his anthropology into an ambitious theory of the origins of civilisation, wherein he concluded that the transition from the 'Wild State of Nature' to the 'Disciplin'd

Creature' in civil society occurred over three stages. The first stage of social development arose in response to the 'common Danger presented to the human species by wild beasts' (F 2:230). This first stage of fear-induced, proto-Marxist *species being* gradually gave way to a second stage of development in which the 'danger Men are in from one another' compelled people to form distinct bands and companies with their own leaders (F 2:267).[32] The psychological impetus to this breakdown of universal species identification was the development of pride, vanity, unruly passions and 'the Discords occasioned by them' (F 2:267). It is in this second stage on the road to civilisation that we can identify the first appearance of basic rules with penalties forbidding 'killing and striking one another' and the 'taking away by force the Wives and Children of others in the same Community' (F 2:268). It was only after a long historical period in which human beings lived exclusively in this social condition marked by non-institutional authority and informal customs and rules that recognisable political societies finally came to be. Crucial to this third and final stage of development was 'the Invention of Letters' that allowed for the establishment of written laws without which true government is impossible (F 2:269). Civilisation is, then, the product of a vast historical process through the course of which human beings became creatures capable of social co-existence in large complex societies.

Mandeville's speculative anthropology clearly maps onto his account of human psychology. The ineradicable human passions that render moral rigorism so unrealistic also provide the psychic fuel of historical progress. The transition from the second to the third stage towards civilisation depended upon the development of ever more sophisticated and expansive desires and appetites: 'while Man advances in Knowledge . . . we must expect to see at the same time his Desires enlarg'd, his Appetites refin'd; and his Vices increased' (F 2:185). Mandeville's insistence that vice increases as society becomes more advanced indicates that the origin of vice is not simply passions, but rather vice is also the product of reason and cunning. Where, then, does Mandeville come down on the perennial philosophical question of whether or not human beings are naturally social? Mandeville's position does not correspond to a simple yes or no. On the one hand, he soundly rejected Hobbes' premise that 'Man is born unfit for Society' (F 2:177). But in rejecting Hobbes, Mandeville did not embrace the venerable Aristotelian idea of *zoon politikon* associated in early eighteenth-century England prominently with Mandeville's opponent Shaftesbury, who in the words of his spokesman Horatio in volume 2 of the *Fable* argued ideal-istically that there is 'in the Mind of Men a natural Affection, that prompts him to love his Species' (F 2:177).[33] Mandeville maintains that the fitness of human beings for society is real, 'but that it is hardly perceptible in Individuals, before great Numbers of them are join'd together, and artfully managed' (F 2:188). Sociability is, then, learned behaviour reinforced by custom and acquired habit: 'Man became sociable by living together in Society' (F 2:189).

Mandeville's state of nature does not play a normative role in grounding the social contract in the way we see in *Cato's Letters*. Where Trenchard and Gordon believed that the purpose of gov-ernment was unambiguously to protect individual rights, espe-cially property, for Mandeville the purpose of government is better expressed as promoting and extending human socialisation. Man-deville's anthropological account of the stadial character of civilisa-tion inclines towards the non-institutional, non-legalistic conception of the public reflected in his belief that the 'chief Organs and nicest Springs' of the body politic are not the 'hard Bones, strong Muscles and Nerves' of law and formal institutions, but rather the 'small trifling Films and little Pipes' that ground social intercourse among individuals (F 1:3).

It is the desires and appetites that draw people together, which Mandeville insists must be 'artfully managed' (F 2:189). Histori-cally lawgivers promoted socialisation by cleverly manipulating people's pride and exploiting their weakness to flattery. These wise rulers encouraged the belief that 'it was more Beneficial for every Body to conquer than indulge his Appetites, and much better to mind the Public than what seem'd his private Interest' (F 1:42). Unable to produce any direct and measurable reward for virtue, 'Moralists and Philosophers' propounded 'imaginary' rewards of psychic health and eternal life (F 1:42). These founding moralists appealed to a certain sense of human pride stimulated by notions of transcending physical desires. But in practice they discovered that flattery is 'the most powerful Argument that could be used to Human Creatures' (F 1:42–3). The flattery attached to public reward for self-sacrifice was the chief instrument to render 'Men useful to each other as well as tractable' to political indoctrination (F 1:47). Rigorism is, then, the 'noble lie' underlying the traditions of political life. While the promotion of moral virtue may require mass propaganda and political manipulation, the psychological resources that made this transformation possible are woven into the fabric of human nature.

Mandeville introduced two important additions to this treatment of virtue and human nature in the editions of the *Fable* published in the wake of the South Sea Scandal. The first was a distinction between 'Real, and Counterfeited Virtue' (F 1:230). Mandeville defined counterfeit virtue as the result of one passion counteracting another such as shame overcoming greed, rather than reason's triumph over passion. Mandeville did not, however, hereby buttress the epistemological claims of moral rigorism.[34] Rather, in keeping with the reorientation of his focus from motives to highlighting consequences, the major impact of the introduction of counterfeit virtue into the moral firmament of commercial England was to blur the distinction between virtue and vice. That is to say, in the aftermath of the tremendous financial shock that threatened to undermine the entire infrastructure of the new commercial economy, Mandeville revised major portions of the *Fable* to defend a generally more permissive posture towards moral judgement than was the case in his earlier account of the starkly rigoristic and austere conception of virtue. Counterfeit virtue, thus, represents part of Mandeville's multi-pronged effort to counteract both classical and Christin asceticism, on the one hand, and the punitive moralistic impulses of Catonic-style natural rights politics, on the other.

Another major addition to the *Fable* in the post-South Sea period was the discussion in volume 2 of 'self-love' and 'self-like' as the main triggers of the socialisation process. Self-love is the instinct in all animals that compels them to preserve themselves and their offspring (F 2:129). It is 'self-like' that makes social existence possible because it is the pleasure we take in our good estimation by others (F 2:130). Self-like is conceptually distinct from self-love inasmuch as the former is directly connected psychologically with pride as opposed to biological survival. Self-like also supplies motivation for social intercourse and polite speech as we listen to others in the hope of hearing ourselves praised. Self-love and self-like are not, however, simply socially constructive. In fact, Mandeville concedes that some self-regarding passions are so powerful that they require political leaders to adopt a rather permissive attitude towards law: 'The Passions of some people are too violent to be curbed by any Law of Precept; and it is Wisdom in all governments to bear with these lesser inconvenience to prevent greater' (F 1: 95).[35] But Mandeville's generally tolerant posture towards the range of human behaviour that can be effectively remedied by law and punishment is subject to an important caveat.

At one point in the *Fable*, Mandeville makes a rare reference to the law of nature 'by which every creature seeks to preserve itself' (F 1:200). He claims that the fear of death can be overcome in part by 'Lust', but more importantly the passion 'most effectual to overcoming it is Anger' (F 1:205). Anger is perhaps the political problem *par excellence* for Mandeville as it makes social intercourse difficult. The 'first care' of all governments must be to employ 'severe Punishments' to curb the destructive effects of anger (F 1:206). In this case, Mandeville shares Hobbes' assessment of the politically deleterious aspects of human psychology as he advocates the intelligent promotion of fear as a way to make human beings 'more orderly and governable' (F 1:204). Even with respect to the promotion of military courage, Mandeville cautions political leaders to inculcate a principle of 'Valour distinct from Anger' (F 1:208). Mandeville's estimation of the grave political problem posed by anger further highlights his difference from the spirit of resistance to, and moral revulsion at, public corruption in *Cato's Letters*.

Mandeville contends that 'the whole Art of governing' is 'built upon the Knowledge of human Nature' illuminated in the *Fable* (F 2:231). This understanding of human nature supports a political science that promotes the value of constitutional moderation above all. Moderate government in the Mandevillean mould is characterised by the 'Balance of Power', where 'no Man's Conscience [is] forc'd' and the sovereign power 'whether it be a Monarchy, a Commonwealth, or a Mixture of both' is so limited that 'no Luxury or other Vice is ever able to shake their Constitution' (F 1:117). There is clearly some truth to the observation that Mandeville's defence of luxury provides a justification for the technique of political 'influence' (or less charitably *corruption*) associated with the Court Whig philosophy of the Walpole administration.[36] Even while acknowledging in the years following the South Sea Scandal the need to 'defeat and prevent all the Machinations and Contrivances that Avarice and Envy may put upon Men to the detriment of his Neighbour' (F 2: 231), Mandeville was still inclined to view the socialization process in evolutionary terms rather than in a highly developed system of retributive justice.[37] Perhaps the best way, then, to characterise Mandeville's political art is that it limits the role for prudential leadership mainly towards protecting the commercial networks of trust that emerged historically through the evolutionary process.

Arguably, the most important element of Mandeville's account of the political art is its utilitarian spirit.[38] He presents politics not as

Cato's arena for a vigilant citizenry alert to the dangers threatening individual rights. Rather, for Mandeville, political life is defined by the cooperation and clash of various interests. Just as his critique of moral rigorism emphasised consequences over motives, so too with regard to politics 'when we pronounce Actions good or evil, we only regard the Hurt or Benefit the Society receives from them, and not the Person who commits them' (F 1:244). This does not mean that Mandeville failed to recognise the fundamental importance of some version of a right to private property: 'Let Property be inviolably secured, and Privileges equal to all Men' (F 1:184). But, crucially, Mandeville described property not in terms of natural rights, but rather as a function of its contribution to general happiness (F 1:57). Rather than attachment to transcendent natural law or natural rights principles, Mandeville insists that individuals are driven most obviously in the public sphere entirely by calculations of political and economic self-interest, and what seems 'to be the best to him' (F 2:178).

Mandeville's convictions about the experiential grounds of human judgement culminated in an early version of what would become known in later classical liberal thought as the *natural harmony of interests*. His 'private vices, public benefits' doctrine assumed the benevolent force of a supra-rational mechanism only hinted at by Locke's utilitarian justification of a monetarised system of private property based upon the benefit to all including the humble 'day labourer'.[39] Locke also vaguely implied the existence of something resembling the division of labour with his recognition of the value-added features of manufactured goods.[40] However, Mandeville took Locke's rough sketches and composed arguably the first well-developed account of the benefits of the division of labour, which, of course, would become the centrepiece of Adam Smith's political economy more than fifty years later.[41] Integral to his defence of luxury was Mandeville's assessment of the variety of tasks and skills employed to produce even the simplest trinket: 'What a Bustle is there to be made in several Parts of the World, before a fine Scarlet or crimson Cloth can be produced, what Multiplicity of Trades and Artificers must be employed' (F 1:356). Many tasks involved in production and manufacture would be 'impracticable, if it was not divided and subdivided into great variety of different Labours' (F 2:142). Mandeville's story of the crimson cloth foreshadowed Adam Smith's vignette about the technical marvels of a pin factory, which would, of course, become perhaps the most powerful metaphor for the genesis of the Industrial Revolution.[42]

There has long been considerable debate about Mandeville's economic philosophy. Some commentators, including the editor of the authoritative modern edition of the *Fable* Fredrick Kaye and influential economist Friedrich Hayek, lauded Mandeville as an early champion of laissez faire ideology and a forerunner of Adam Smith's fabled 'invisible hand'.[43] Others view Mandeville as a proponent of mercantilism and the range of government involvement in the economy that this approach entails.[44] We have seen that Mandeville believed the development of a relatively self-sustaining economic system to be the product of a lengthy social evolutionary process rather than the work of 'skilful politicians' intervening to set things right. It is only by virtue of the 'long Experience in Business' derived from 'several Ages' that 'the whole Machine' of economic life 'may be made to play of itself, with as little Skill, as is required to wind up a Clock' (F 2:322–3). While Mandeville's utilitarian tendencies perhaps militated against a rigid, doctrinaire commitment to laissez faire, it is arguably true that it is his confidence in the overarching harmony of interests, rather than political planning prone to extraneous and counter-productive moral considerations, that defines his major contribution to the history of economic thought.[45] As we will see in the following chapter, Adam Smith's invisible hand would wind up Mandeville's economic clock.

It is perhaps not surprising that Mandeville's initial response to the crimes alleged in the South Sea Scandal was distinctly blasé, including only a brief allusion to them in the context of his lengthy attack on charity schools (F 1:276). Even after the parliamentary inquiry into the corruption surrounding the South Sea Company, Mandeville's acceptance of the need for rules to govern large and complex associations was framed within a broader spirit of regulatory moderation and permissiveness that dampened the fires of retributive justice (F 2:321). On a practical level, Mandeville seemed to endorse the pragmatic, largely non-punitive, approach to crisis resolution perfected by the Walpole administration. Mandeville's Court Whig orientation translated philosophically into a multi-pronged critique of classical and Christian moral rigorism, the Shaftesburian doctrine of natural sociability, as well as the spirited natural rights arguments of the Opposition Whigs such as Trenchard and Gordon, whose morally charged rhetoric was also capable of dowsing the flames of the private vices required to produce public benefits.

The polemical response to the South Sea Scandal constituted a formative moment in the development of the argument for commerce in eighteenth-century England. The respective positions represented by the *Fable of the Bees* and *Cato's Letters* limned the contours of a complex debate that involved both interest-based and natural rights-based forms of discourse. While the radical Whig philosophy of *Cato's Letters* would be largely marginalised in England in the decades following the withering attack on natural rights philosophy by the Scottish political economists, Trenchard and Gordon would have a worthy successor later in the century in Thomas Paine, the figure who would radicalise Lockean natural rights theory in response to both the political tumults of the French Revolution and the ground-breaking political economy of the Physiocrats and Adam Smith. For his part, Mandeville's focus on the need to counter the prejudice against commerce fostered by classical and Christian virtue somewhat obscured his second-order concern to expose the potential danger posed to commerce by doctrinaire rights philosophy. In this respect, Mandeville pointed towards the Scottish Enlightenment, which would establish a form of 'moralised' Mandevilleanism[46] by superimposing a substantive normative dimension of other-regarding sentiments upon his basic intuition about the natural harmony of interests. It is in the light of this new philosophical dispensation, characterized by the dynamic friction between the opposing political vernacular of interests and rights born in the 1720s, that debates about the meaning of the Financial Revolution and its impact on international trade, public debt and national political institutions would continue well into the following century.

Notes

1. See, e.g., Hirschman 1977: 53–4; Myers 1983: 3–5; Dumont 1977: 76–7, Rotwein 1955: lxxxi; Dunn 1983: 121, 130–4; Pocock 1975: 497–8.
2. Hume 1961: 296.
3. Douglass (2020: 277, 293) also sees Mandeville in important respects pointing towards the Scottish Enlightenment. This is, of course, notwithstanding the critique of Mandeville levelled indirectly by Hume and quite explicitly by Smith, which tends to obscure the extent to which they were indebted to the author of the *Fable*. See Hume 2000: 193, 239, 370; Hume 1987: 280; Smith 1984: 308–12.
4. The classic study of the Financial Revolution is Dickson 1967.
5. Important studies of the South Sea Bubble include Cowles 1960; Carswell 1960; and more recently Balen 2003.
6. Gunn 1983: 106–7. Mitchell (2003: 304–5) provides evidence suggesting a possible collaboration between Mandeville and Gordon on

pieces published in the *British Journal* in 1723–1725. Despite the affinity these authors shared as supporters of personal liberty and commerce, nonetheless I maintain their modes of discourse and organising principles reflect different forms of the liberal defence of commerce.

7. Pocock 1975: 468, 507.
8. Robbins 1968: 15–25; Bailyn 1967: 34–5.
9. Horne 1978: x; Goldsmith 1985: 3, 103; Gunn 1983: 100–1, 106–8; Hundert 1994: 11.
10. Dworetz 1990: 85, 89; Hamowy 1990: 291–4; Rahe 1992: 532; Zuckert 1994: 300–2; Mitchell 2003: 294–6; Ward 2004: 288–94; Champion 2014: 132–5.
11. Burtt 1992: 154–7; Sullivan 2004: 229.
12. Trenchard and Gordon 1995, Letter 105, p. 744. Hereafter in notes and text simply CL Letter number:page number.
13. Hanvelt 2012: 90–2.
14. See Hobbes 1994: ch. 1, s. 4, pp. 6–7; Locke 1975: bk 2, chs 20–21.
15. E.g., Pocock 1975: 471–2, 491; Gunn 1983: 100–1; Hundert 1994: 11–12
16. Champion 2014: 134; Hamowy 1990: 281.
17. See also Locke 2016 II:27.
18. For Locke's reluctance to employ the discourse of inalienable rights, see Simmons 1983: 176, 185–6, 192. For Cato's importance in promoting inalienable rights, see Zuckert 1994: 303–4.
19. Champion 2014: 129; Hamowy 1990: 281.
20. Cf. Locke 2016 II:34. For a discussion of Cato's concerns about the long-term effects of high finance on property distribution, see Sparling 2013: 635.
21. Mandeville 1988: vol. 1, p. 4. Hereafter in notes and text simply F volume:page.
22. Compare with Machiavelli 1985: 61; Hobbes 1994: Introduction, s. 4, p. 5.
23. Horne 1978: 56.
24. For a good account of the role of self-denial in Mandeville's treatment of virtue, see Colman 1972: 131–3.
25. Shaftesbury 2001: vol. 2, pp. 18, 47, 100, 123–6.
26. Horne 1978: 34–5.
27. This is contrary to Burtt (1992: 128, 131) and Maxwell (1954: 249), who see Mandeville as fundamentally Augustinian.
28. Hobbes 1994: 24; Locke 1975: 240.
29. Hobbes 1994: 79.
30. Locke 1975: 269.
31. See Rousseau 1964: 114, 130–2. Of course, later no less a figure than Adam Smith would observe in his 1756 review of Rousseau's *Discourse on the Origins of Inequality* the Genevan's significant

philosophical indebtedness to Mandeville. For a good discussion of Mandeville's role as a philosophical connection between Rousseau and Smith, see Douglass 2017.

32. For *species being*, see Marx 1978: 33–46.
33. Horne 1978: 40
34. While Douglass (2020: 284–5) is correct to highlight the significance of Mandeville's revisions with respect to moral virtue in later editions of the *Fable*, I disagree that the upshot of Mandeville's rhetorical strategy was to intensify the commitment to rigorism in his account of virtue.
35. The specific context is Mandeville's discussion of prostitution.
36. Gunn 1983: 98; Dickinson 1975: 90; Hundert 1994: 9.
37. Goldsmith 1985: 51, 64; Hirschman 1977: 18.
38. For the utilitarian philosophy underlying Mandeville's theory of interests, see also Kaye 1924: lviii; Colman 1972: 136; Castiglione 1992: 159.
39. Locke 2016 II:41.
40. Locke 2016 II:42.
41. Hayek 1978: 249.
42. Smith 1981: 14–15.
43. See Kaye 1924: xcviii; Hayek 1978: 258–9; Dickinson 1975: 93.
44. See Viner 1958: 332–42; Rosenberg 1963: 184; Landreth 1975: 195; Castiglione 1992: 172–3. Castiglione (1992: 170) observes that no less than John Maynard Keynes viewed the *Fable* as a scathing satire of laissez faire.
45. Dumont (1977: 74–5) argues that Mandeville is in fact the first thinker to propound the natural harmony of interests doctrine.
46. See Castiglione 1983.

Chapter 4

Scottish Political Economy: David Hume and Adam Smith

In the period following the tumultuous 1720s, the United Kingdom experienced a time of extraordinary economic growth and
political success. By mid-century it became clear that the new
banking institutions and monetary instruments that ushered in the
Financial Revolution were part of a permanent transformation of
politics and economics in Britain. Similarly, in the middle decades
of the eighteenth century the British political class generally
coalesced around a hardened orthodox Whig interpretation of the
nation's constitutional system of balanced government. Well gone
now was the grand political and theological struggles of the previous century, as the fierce battles '*pro aris & foci*' were replaced
by Walpole's bland managerialism and Bolingbroke's perpetual
campaign against the administration.[1] In philosophical terms,
the highlight of British thought in this period was without doubt
the Scottish Enlightenment. The broad, path-breaking movement
that emerged from the great Scottish universities and the educated
classes on Britain's northern Celtic-fringe at this time included the
contributions of Francis Hutcheson and Thomas Reid in moral
philosophy and James Steuart and Adam Ferguson's works of
political economy, but arguably the most important figures of the
Scottish Enlightenment were the philosophic dynamic duo and
long-time friends, David Hume and Adam Smith.

Locating Hume and Smith in the tradition of classical liberalism perhaps requires some explanation inasmuch as the Scottish
Enlightenment is frequently associated with the communitarian
critique of the English natural rights philosophy we have encountered in Hobbes, Locke, and Trenchard and Gordon. Indeed,

Hume in particular was often identified as a political conservative, even a Tory on account of his rejection of the state of nature concept as an unhelpful fiction, his predisposition against rapid or violent political change and his condemnation of Wilkite radicalism.[2] However, I join those scholars who caution against the conservative characterisation of Hume.[3] Rather, I suggest that Hume's liberalism reflects the profound influence of Mandeville, and the interest-based, as opposed to rights-based, elements of the earlier liberal tradition. Politically Hume was not a Tory for throughout his career he supported the Glorious Revolution settlement and Protestant Succession without hesitation or any perceivable admixture of Jacobite sympathies. But he was no radical Whig either as he openly criticised Locke-inspired firebrands like Trenchard and Gordon for creating a 'party amongst us' whose political creed is that all human beings 'are born free and equal: Government and superiority can only be established by consent'.[4] Forbes' distinction between 'vulgar' and 'scientific' Whiggism is a useful schema for reconciling Hume's political and philosophical commitments with his deep disdain for partisanship.[5] The vulgar and scientific elements of Whiggism reflect the composite of theoretical materials co-existing, often uneasily, within the broad spectrum of mainstream mid-century British political thought: that is, the philosophically sceptical and culturally cosmopolitan dimension, as well as the more parochial political identifications. Perhaps the most distinctive feature of Hume's Whiggism was his abandonment of contract theory and natural rights philosophy in favour of a Mandevillean historical account of the origins of political society, and his thoroughgoing rejection of the starkly egoistic moral philosophy associated not only with Mandeville's theory of self-interest, but also with the natural rights doctrine of Hobbes and Locke.

While Hume expressed arguments that departed from standard liberal contractarianism, in other respects his commitment to fundamental classical liberal principles such as limited government, religious toleration, freedom of speech, private property and the advantages of commerce are unquestionable. In this chapter I will examine Hume's liberalism, paying particular attention to his defence of commerce. I will present Hume as a crucial figure in the process of what Dario Castiglione terms *moralising Mandeville*.[6] This will require investigation of the way in which Hume's epistemological scepticism and theory of the human passions correspond to Mandeville's instrumentalisation of reason in the fabled beekeeper's radical re-evaluation of the classical theory of moral virtue. However, I will also try to demonstrate how Hume consciously sought to moralise Mandeville through the introduction of certain natural sentiments of sympathy, and especially humanity, which permit an other-regarding viewpoint with considerable normative valence. Hume, thus, arguably offers an epistemologically more nuanced account of the moral basis of the public good than Mandeville, inasmuch as his political economy celebrates commerce and luxury without condoning vice. But more importantly, Hume's economic writings registered an important deepening of the Mandevillean idea of harmony interests with regard to trade, taxes and monetary policy, in combination with an argument for philosophical moderation designed to temper what he took to be the extreme tendencies of the prevailing economic ideologies of the time represented by mercantilism, on the one hand, and the French Physiocrats, on the other.

This treatment of the political economy of the Scottish Enlightenment will conclude with an examination of Adam Smith. I will argue that in Smith's thought we see both the extension and modification of the basic principles of Hume's epistemology into a sophisticated moral heuristic based on the perspective of the 'impartial spectator', and at the same time the hardening of the Mandevillean and Humean concept of the harmony of interests into the influential 'invisible hand' metaphor that Smith deployed to describe the operation of his 'system of natural liberty'. Central to Smith's conceptual achievement with the articulation of a system of natural liberty is his re-evaluation of the Lockean argument for labour as the source of private property. Smith's Locke-inspired division of labour theory fused elements of the natural rights tradition concerning property with a characteristically Mandevillean focus on the advantages of specialisation to produce an empirical argument for an interest-based form of liberal thought grounded upon the considerations of comparative utility. But before we can truly appreciate the theoretical ambitions of the political economy of the Scottish Enlightenment, we need to return, as they did, to the basics of human cognition.

Hume's Theory of the Passions

Hume's first major work *A Treatise of Human Nature* (1740) was not about politics or economics, at least directly, but instead was an examination of the epistemological basis of morality as deduced from the passions. Hume's famous scepticism in the *Treatise* produced a root- and-branch rejection of traditional accounts of causality based upon the philosophical maxim *that whatever begins to exist, must have a cause of existence*, the knowledge of which proposition was generally thought to be by means of intuition. However, Hume's epistemological scepticism did not result in intellectual paralysis, but rather shifted the grounds for moral, political and economic knowledge from 'abstract reasoning or reflection' solely to 'observation and experience' (T 1.3.1.50; 1.3.3.56). In terms of causality, this means that any conclusions we draw about cause and effect are actually judgements derived from the 'habit' of surveying certain objects or events conjoined in specific relations (T 1.3.11.86). This insight is the basis of Hume's doctrine of association, which would later become known more broadly as the epistemological school of *associationism*. In his later *An Enquiry Concerning the Principle of Morals* (or just *Second Enquiry*, 1751) Hume expanded on this account of how opinions are formed through habits originating in sensory impressions and appearances whereby the perception of an effect of one kind is followed by another 'whose appearance always conveys the thought of the other'.[7]

The major implication of Hume's sceptical epistemology was the elevation of the cognitive status of probability inasmuch as ideas such as belief in causation are incapable of epistemic validation, but are nonetheless necessary for practical life.[8] That is to say, probability can endorse the process by which habit becomes the basis for a certain imperfect, if invaluable, confidence in a mind-independent world subject to observable predictable patterns of the association of cause and effect (T 1.3.12.90; 1.3.15.116). Hume followed Mandeville's general diminution of reason, which he insisted 'is, and ought only to be slave of the passions' (T 2.3.3.266). The inability of reason to validate cognitively our moral experience was cited to justify Hume's aim of discrediting traditional rationalist moral philosophy that drew fundamental inferences from *a priori* logical or theological propositions.[9] Hume's alternative is, of course, a theory of knowledge empirically grounded that provides structure for an account of morality based upon sentiments and the affects. However, the structure of moral judgement is conditioned by the way in which perception of cause and effect is impacted by considerations of contiguity in time and space. Namely, objects and events that are close to us in time and space are 'conceived with a peculiar force and vivacity' (T 2.3.7.274). The difficulty this poses for determining rules of social behaviour is quite obvious inasmuch as our understanding of advantages learned by past experience runs contrary to the natural operation of the human mind (T 2.3.7.276). Thus, for experience to become meaningful social knowledge, it will typically require a gradual process of practice eventually hardening into convention.

Given Hume's epistemological scepticism, it is not surprising that he concurred with Mandeville's rejection of the rigoristic account of moral virtue, but significantly Hume's theory of the passions allowed for a reformed account of morality resting upon the distinction between natural and artificial virtues. For Hume, as for Hobbes and Locke, self-preservation is the primordial passion to which reason is subservient. In principle, this passion or 'love of life' is identical in humans and animals (T 1.3.16.118; 2.3.4.268). As such, virtue and vice are 'not discoverable merely be reason' (T 3.1.2.302). But while reason is instrumental, it is not nugatory, and therefore Hume insists it is possible to determine general rules for human behaviour despite reason being unable to independently validate moral judgement.

Thus, Hume's account of morality presents something of a paradox insofar as while he followed in large measure Hutcheson's repudiation of Mandeville's case against moral virtue, Hume at the same time adopted his own version of the 'selfish' system as a model for politics.[10] For example, recall Hume's famous claim that 'Politics may be reduced to a Science', by means of which knowledge it can be made 'the interest, even of bad men, to act for the public good' (E 15–16). In the essay 'Of the Independency of Parliament', Hume went even further in this Mandevillean direction by concluding that, constitutionally speaking, it is a generally valid rule of good government that 'every man ought to be supposed a knave, and to have no other end, in all his actions, than private interest' (E 42).[11] But did Hume also believe that economics can be reduced to a science? Before we can fully assess whether Hume did or did not concur with Mandeville's premise that all social and economic relations can be properly understood only by way of appreciating the knavish characteristics of self-interested actors, we need to delve more deeply into Hume's theory of justice.

Moralising Mandeville

Hume's theory of justice represents a locus in the intersection of his views on politics and economics. On one level, it confirmed his place in the classical liberal tradition inasmuch as he accepted the Lockean premise about the centrality of property for the origin of government. But Hume's liberalism is complicated as it combines both a historical and a normative account of the origin of property. In a break from Locke, he severed the concept of right, including the right to property, from the idea of nature per se. Justice is a virtue, but it is an artificial virtue: 'the sense of justice and injustice is not derived from nature, but arises artificially, tho' necessarily from education and human conventions' (T 3.2.1.311). Hume's evidence for the artificiality of justice is drawn from an anthropological methodology that demonstrates human beings' fundamental neediness, which forces us to seek society to survive (T 3.2.2.312). Pivotal to survival is the establishment of rules of property that emerge as conventions intended to 'bestow stability on the possession of external goods' (T 3.2.2.314). Only gradually over time do individuals become 'sensible of the infinite advantages' of these rules (T 3.2.2.314). This is, however, a complex and somewhat fraught process given what Hume believes about the contiguity problem of learning from past experience. He clearly assumes that reason, memory and imagination can combine in such a way as to make individuals aware of their interests. But Hume acknowledges the further problem of distinguishing and prioritising short- and long-term interests: 'There is no quality in human nature, which causes more fatal errors in our conduct, than that which leads us to prefer whatever is present' (T 3.2.8.345). The achievement of a socially stable property settlement would seem, then, to require that reason be more than a mere slave, or even simply auxiliary, to the passions.

In Hume's political thought the origin of government and the discovery or invention of rules of justice are conceptually intertwined and logically interdependent. The habit and experience that produces acceptance of the property settlement initiated a socio-historical process that culminated in the formation of political society. This conjecture requires not only that Hume reject outright the Hobbesian or Lockean conception of a pre-civil state of nature as an 'imaginary state', but also led Hume to dismiss the idea of a Rousseauian pristine golden age as an 'idle fiction' undeserving of any serious reflection (T 3.2.2.316–17, 321). In the essay 'Of the First Principles of Government', Hume concluded that it is on the basis of 'opinion only that government is founded' (E 32). In particular, it is opinions about interests and legal rights that assume special significance as the vital supports for civil institutions. Hume's assertion that obedience to law derives from a moral duty 'invented' to support justice has all the hallmarks of Mandeville's political anthropology, which we recall effectively stripped the idea of the public good of any sense of moral obligation on behalf of the individual. If justice has any greater normative meaning than simply a device by which 'skilful politicians endeavour'd to restrain the turbulent passions of men' (T 3.3.1.370), Hume would need to demonstrate that the seeds of justice and morality lie within an aspect of human nature not simply reducible to calculating self-interest.

Hume explicitly advanced his account of the origin of justice as a repudiation of the 'selfish system' of morality devised by Hobbes and Locke, and arguably extended by Mandeville (SE 296). But Hume's account of the role of the passions in morality also parallels the 'selfish system' in key respects. For instance, Hume insists that contrary to the classical and Christian view, vanity does not deserve harsh condemnation and should even be 'esteemed as a social passion' (T 3.2.2.316).[12] For Hume, the salutary consequences of a self-regarding passion like vanity lies in the capacity to encourage social feeling among individuals through concern for the judgements of others. Self-interest is the 'original motive to the establishment of justice' because the desire to acquire goods 'is insatiable, perpetual, universal, and directly destructive of society' (T 3.2.2.316). Hume's institutional solution to the problem of destructive self-interest is an example of the technique of psychological deflection familiar in the earlier liberal tradition: 'For whether the passion of self-interest be esteemed vicious or virtuous, 'tis all a case; since it alone restrains it' (T 3.2.2.316). Thus, one aspect of moralising Mandeville is Hume's call for intelligent constitutional design of checks and balances to restrain passion and to some extent depersonalise reason. However, his more fundamental correction of the 'selfish system' involved his rejection of Mandeville's contention that every passion is an egoistic 'modification of self-love' (SE 296). In the *Treatise*, Hume insisted that while it is rare to meet someone who is purely altruistic, 'yet 'tis as rare to meet with one, in whom all the kind affections, taken together, do not overbalance all the selfish' (T 3.2.2.313). Later in the *Second Enquiry* Hume appealed even more directly to accessible human experience as proof against the 'paradox' of radical egoistic moral philosophy: 'The most obvious objection to the selfish hypothesis, is, that . . . it is contrary to common feeling and our most unprejudiced notions' (SE 298).

The most important social virtues that Hume drew from the affects were sympathy and humanity. He admitted that even the passions that support justice and society are limited in scope for 'in general it may be affirm'd, that there is no such passion in human minds as the love of mankind' (T 3.2.1.309). Sympathy, though more limited than the love of humankind, has the benefit of making it possible to align individual tastes with public interest. Sympathy may be too weak to control self-regarding inclinations, but it does signify a natural propensity to feel concern for others as even 'when injustice is so distant from us, as no way to affect our interests, it still displeases us' (T 3.2.2.320). The source of the disinterested displeasure is the 'uneasiness' we experience by way of sympathy (T 3.2.2.320). Sympathy is largely a passive emotion, but Hume insists it is 'a very powerful principle of human nature' because it produces the sentiments that graft with the interests attached to all of the artificial virtues, including justice (T 3.3.1.369). Sympathy, however, does seem to depend upon some measure of proximity to allow for the perspective of the 'spectator' to develop, that is, the moral lens through which an agent assumes both objectivity and a genuine concern for others. As Hume acknowledges: 'We sympathise more with persons contiguous to us, than with persons remote from us: With our acquaintances, than with strangers: With our countrymen, than with foreigners' (T 3.3.1.371).

For its part, 'humanity' emerged as the most important social virtue in Hume's treatment of the moral cosmos.[13] Humanity bridges the contiguity gaps that restrict sympathy largely because the feeling underlying humanity is less passionate than sympathy. Humanity does not partake of the spectator, but is rather 'an internal sense or feeling, which nature has made universal in the whole species' (SE 173). Hume maintains that morality can be rendered an active principle only if there exists 'some sentiment common to all mankind' (SE 272). Humanity is more fundamental than sympathy because it is more universal or comprehensive and it is a product of felt experience not dependent on the proximity necessary for spectatorship. As Ryan Hanley, observes humanity is, for Hume, 'a decidedly cool unemotional preference for the well-being of others'.[14] How does Hume's idea of humanity compare with the concept of natural altruism advanced by Mandeville's nemesis Shaftesbury? Hume judged that Shaftesbury fell into the trap of confusing reason and sentiment, a problem which he claims bedevilled most of the ancient moral philosophers too. That is to say, Shaftesbury wanted moral virtue to derive from both reason and sentiment, or at least he sought to remove any serious conflict or tension between them (SE 171). Hume believed that the superiority of his account of humanity over Shaftesbury's natural altruism

derived from his grounding of social virtue in reliable human sentiments rather than Shaftesbury's dubious theory of practical reason.

For Hume, humanity is a characteristic of human nature that
signifies both an ethical disposition and a principle of intelligibil-
ity making it possible to identify moral distinctions between virtue
and vice. At one point in his discussion of natural virtue in the
Treatise Hume directly called out 'some philosophers' who claim
that all morality was invented by 'skilful politicians' (T 3.3.1.370).
This unmistakable reference to Mandeville exposes the vulnerable
underside of his confidence in the natural harmony of interests.
Hume declares that the practically universal recognition of natural
virtues such as 'meekness, beneficence, charity, generosity, clem-
ency, moderation [and] equity' demonstrate Mandeville's cynical
conclusions are 'not consistent with experience'. First, there are
virtues and vices that do not help or hurt the public, therefore, even
'skilful politicians' would have no motive to invent them. Second,
politicians could never produce a moral effect if there was not a
prior natural sentiment that predisposes people towards attributing
'approbation and blame' (T 3.3.1.370). In terms of government,
then, the combined force of artificial rules established to create justice and the existence of natural social passions of sympathy and
especially humanity produce a robust Humean account of the preconditions of a stable political order. But how did Hume believe
the interaction of nature and convention, so central to moralised
Mandevilleanism, operates in the economic realm?

The Defence of Commerce

Hume's most important contribution to the political economy of
the Scottish Enlightenment was a series of eight essays on topics
ranging from luxury, taxes, interest rates and the balance of trade
published in 1752 in a volume titled *Political Discourses*. These
essays were so popular that two more editions were released in
the following successive years.[15] It is perhaps indicative of Hume's
approach to economics that he included his major writings on the
subject in a volume devoted primarily to discussion of political topics. Economics was not an autonomous field for Hume. Indeed,
as Eugene Rotwein observes, Hume originally intended to explore
economic questions as part of the 'moral sciences' in an expanded
version of the *Treatise* that was never completed.[16] Hume's empiri-
cist epistemology and historical approach to the development of
morality does not lend itself to the discovery of a scientific natural

law of economics. Rather, the prevailing spirit of Hume's economic writings is one of moderation. It is well-known that one of the hallmarks of Hume's political thought and his attitude towards religion was his antipathy to partisanship and zealotry of any stripe.[17] His chief concern about partisanship was the extent to which it signified an unjustifiable attempt to make authoritative claims to knowledge unwarranted by the complex conditions presented to our faculty of judgement. As Hume was well aware, economic issues such as the national debt had been sources of political controversy practically since the outset of the Financial Revolution in England. But Hume was convinced that by mid-century the problem of economic partisanship had acquired a new and troubling level of intensity.

An introduction of sorts to Hume's political economy are his essays 'On Commerce' and 'Of Luxury', the latter's title changing to 'Of Refinement in the Arts' in the 1760 edition of the *Essays*. Hume supported commerce and followed Mandeville in defending luxury against the 'frenzies of enthusiasm' by Christian ascetics, whose austerity runs 'contrary to the more natural and usual course of things' (E 268, 259). Hume justified luxury not only as the object of relatively blameless human desires, but also due to the salutary consequences produced by commercial peoples who value the production of, and trade in, fine goods. Hume declares with Mandevillean aplomb that luxury contributes to 'the happiness of the state' (E 256). The 'natural bent of the mind' is to look beyond basic needs towards more refined sources of pleasure, and thus cultivating the taste for luxury encourages economic productivity as such (E 263, 256). Hume did not, however, shy away from the dubious moral effect of luxury, which he admits can unleash 'a spirit of avarice and industry', but in keeping with Mandeville he also insisted that even with increased individual greed, 'the harmony of the whole is still supported' (E 263). Hume's confidence in a harmony of interest speaks both to the happy intercourse of individual happiness and political strength for the more labour is employed beyond mere necessities, 'the more powerful is any state' (E 262). Whereas the ancients believed commerce undermined martial virtue, Hume insists that commercial success is easily converted into military power by modern nations like Britain. The desire for luxury also has the effect of stimulating socio-economic mobility as the lower classes feel the 'desire for a more splendid way of life', a condition which Hume contrasts favourably to what he takes to be the 'habit of indolency' characteristic of agricultural societies (E 261, 264).

In 'Of Refinement of the Arts', Hume highlights the way that commerce encourages natural social sentiments as people become more sociable due to the accumulated experience of mutually beneficial, and even pleasing, interactions (E 271). The progress in industry and knowledge generated by commercial exchange has a beneficial influence on the public good as the creation of a complex system of supply and demand produces 'a kind of storehouse of labour, which, in the exigencies of state, may be turned to the public service' (E 272). But Hume's confidence in the harmony of interest is tempered somewhat by his concern to maintain the very distinctions between virtue and vice that Mandeville trampled with such abandon. In fact, Hume unmistakably called out Mandeville as the prime example of the 'men of libertine principles' who 'bestow praises even on vicious luxury' (E 269). But what does Hume mean by 'vicious luxury'? Hume's argument about the potential negative effects of luxury is complicated to the point of being opaque.[18] While he insists that no gratification in itself, 'however sensual', should be esteemed vicious, Hume declares as a general principle that 'whenever luxury ceases to be innocent, it also ceases to be beneficial; and when carried to a degree too far, is a quality pernicious, though perhaps not the most pernicious, to society' (E 279, 269). This statement raises several questions that Hume leaves unanswered. Are there any luxuries that are inherently vicious? What would it mean to take certain luxuries too far? What standard of judgement would the moral philosopher have to employ to make such a judgement? Needless to say, it hardly helps that Hume appears to make an enormous concession to Mandeville by acknowledging that even vicious luxuries may not be the 'most pernicious' thing for a society, that is, the effort to ban vicious luxuries may produce even worse consequences. Nonetheless, while Hume seems to concur with Mandeville that even vice can have good effects (or at least suppressing vice can have bad effects), he still melodramatically proclaims, 'let us never pronounce vice itself in itself advantageous' (E 280).

With his defence of luxury, Hume's complex strategy for moralising Mandeville comes into focus. He aligned with Mandeville in defence of commerce against its traditional Christian and classical opponents. Moreover, Hume did not reject outright Mandeville's premise that selfish actions can contribute to the public good via a natural harmony of interests that has generally eluded most moral philosophers' perspectives. But Hume's major correction to Mandeville related to the Scotsman's judgement about the need to

maintain a typology of virtue and vice, albeit qualified by categories of what is natural and artificial, in order to account for the
authentic moral experience of individuals embedded in the concrete reality of social interactions. Hume's response, then, to the
purported ethical realism of Mandeville, and the progenitors of
the 'selfish system' Hobbes and Locke, is the discovery of a deeper
realism that purports to be both more high-minded and empirically
sound, and which makes sense of the practically universal experience of other-regarding passions such as sympathy, humanity and
benevolence.

Hume's Political Economy

The bulk of Hume's economic essays were devoted to discrete topics
in political economy such as the money supply, interest rates, trade
policy and the national debt. These essays can be divided into two
categories: one group intended to critique mercantilist ideas concerning trade and currency, and another group of essays on taxation and public debt targeting the French Physiocrats. It is perhaps
useful to think of Hume's opposition to these economic doctrines in
terms of intellectual dispositions he identified as 'superstition' and
'enthusiasm' (E 73–9).[19] By this rubric, mercantilists exemplify the
gloomy, cramped mental horizons of the superstitious with their
unhealthy fear of risk, their suspicions about remote and opaque
causes reducing all competition to a zero-sum game, and their
fetishistic worship of bullion.[20] By contrast, the Physiocrats with
their paradoxical supreme confidence both in the laissez faire principle and the enlightened, absolutist state, as well as their zealous
defence of the productive virtues of agriculture embody many of
the traits Hume associates with religious and political enthusiasts.

Hume's opening shot across the bow of mercantilism occurred
in the context of the centuries-long battle in England over the
money supply. In violation of one of the most cherished tenets of
the mercantilist creed, Hume insists that money has no place in the
'wheels of trade', and thus is not properly speaking one of the subjects of commerce (E 281). While he agreed with Locke that money
has 'chiefly a fictitious value', Hume rejected outright the quantity
theory of value because in his view 'the greater or lesser plenty of
money is of no consequence' (E 297). The primary flaw in mercantilist monetary thinking is mistaking a 'collateral effect for a cause'
by failing to recognise that the quantity of money available in the
economy is incidental (E 290). The most important factor affecting

economic strength 'really arises from the manners and customs of the people' (E 290). Hume seeks to expose the fallaciousness of the sound money doctrine by pointing to historical examples of when the 'greater plenty of money' actually proved a loss to a nation in its commerce with foreigners (E 283). The reason for this is the loss of competitive advantage due to the 'dearness of everything' that inevitably raises labour and production costs (E 284). Even this assessment is complicated, however, by Hume's judgement that despite the inflationary pressure caused by 'plenty' of money, an increased money supply can be a temporary stimulus to economic productivity and trade, especially in that moment between the increase in wages and the rise of prices in which a nation's purchasing power is enhanced albeit only temporarily (E 286).

Hume also challenged mercantilist orthodoxy over the issue of interest rates. He dismissed the monetarist doctrine that the rate of interest is set more or less by the quantity of coin accumulating in the country. Rather than the quantity of precious metals determining interest rates, it is a function of a more nuanced set of causal relations deriving from relative rates of supply and demand (E 296, 299). Hume's contention is that complex commercial societies characterised by refined tastes are better at distributing wealth relatively equitably throughout society than is true in simpler, agricultural economies. The key to preventing the concentration of wealth is to ensure the 'universal diffusion and circulation' of trade (E 293-4). An equitable distribution of wealth did not, of course, mean the elimination of inequality. Hume happily accepts the historical explanation for the origin of inequality in the stadial movement from the 'savage state of hunter gatherers' through to the advances driven by the concentration of socio-economic power in the hands of wealthy landowners (E 297-8). The factor that makes commercial society more equitable than agricultural society is the psychological impact of frugality. Landed wealth is not frugal because it spends what surplus it generates on luxury goods, and thus has no incentive to save. But Hume insists that it is an 'infallible consequence of all industrious professions, to beget frugality, and make the love of gain prevail over the love of pleasure' (E 301). In contrast to Mandeville, who largely dismissed frugality as morally dubious and economically counterproductive, Hume lauds the merchant class as 'one of the most useful races of men' precisely because of the commerce-inspired frugality that allows the moneyed interest to beget many lenders ready to employ their surplus income in a productive way (E 299, 300). Clearly, then, in Hume's rendering of the famed 'parsimony of the Scots',[21] one measure of the positive impact of luxury would need to be the extent to which consumption of luxury items did not prevent the merchant class from saving, lending and investing.

Hume's most important disagreement with the mercantilists related to the issue of trade. As is well-known, perhaps the most characteristic feature of mercantilist thought was the argument that international trade is a zero-sum game. While Hume accepted some limited utility in protective tariffs in certain specified circumstances, he extolled the mutual benefits of international trade and generally disapproved of tariffs even for a nation's staple commodities (E 324–7). Hume's optimism about the natural harmony of interests reached truly stirring (even immoderate!) proportions when he opined that not only is there a compelling collaborative interest among the various elements of the domestic economy, but he declared: 'Where an open communication is preserved among nations, it is impossible but the domestic industry of every one must receive an increase from the improvements of the others' (E 328). What explains Hume's, almost unHumean, idealism about the international harmony of commercial interests?

Hume's considerations on trade placed him in the middle of one of the major controversies among Scottish political economists in the period; namely, the 'Rich Country, Poor Country' debate about the relative advantages of wealthy and poor countries in trade.[22] Hume's 'Of the Jealousy of Trade' was the last economic essay added to his collected essays only in 1758 after years of engagement with critics of his earlier essays. The 'Jealousy of Trade' is notable for its striking cosmopolitan tone as he offers a foreshadowing of Kant's famous argument that the natural diversity of climate, customs and conditions compels nations to 'mutual intercourse and commerce'.[23] International trade does not deplete a nation's money supply because the economic productivity spurred by trade creates domestic investment opportunities that incentivise saving, lending and spending. But the most controversial aspect of the Rich Country, Poor Country debate had to do with the costs of labour. Hume maintained that so little does quantity of money serve national economic strength that in many cases the inflationary pressures would drive up labour costs and create a competitive disadvantage with poorer countries in which the desire for luxuries ignited by trade would spur their own domestic manufactures.[24] In a series of letters exchanged with James Oswald and Josiah Tucker, Hume confronted two principal objections to his optimistic rendering of the

Rich Country, Poor Country debate. First, there was the contention that increased money supply does not necessarily cause increased labour costs because plenty of money would still flow out of the country through the purchase of imports.[25] Second, some critics claimed that poor countries with cheap labour and materials will not always produce cheaper goods due to the advantages rich countries possess in terms of economy of scale.[26]

Hume's response to these objections was a vision of a kind of global partition of labour between rich and poor countries with their respective focus on skilled and unskilled labour. The effect of this international division of labour is a self-levelling mechanism in international markets which distributes to each country the amount of money proportional to trade.[27] With this argument, so reminiscent of the confident predictions of universally beneficent effects of economic globalisation in the 1990s, Hume set forth what Dennis Rasmussen calls a 'strikingly cosmopolitan' harmony of interests, which the Scotsman believed anxious and superstitious mercantilists failed to understand because it is a complex process that has indirect and remote causes not always immediately visible even to the experienced observer.[28] There was, of course, also a moderate dimension to Hume's economic cosmopolitanism. For instance, he did not advocate an automatic specie-flow distribution model on a global scale. Rather, he prioritised the more modest goal of trying to dispel fears that without capital controls all the money in a country would flee conditions produced by adverse balance of trade.[29] However, Hume's larger aim was to advance the principle that free trade allows countries to avoid economic decline due to loss of competitive advantage. He is confident that domestic producers can remain flexible enough to switch to new and innovative products if they lose the edge in other products.

But Hume is completely unsympathetic towards countries and industries that are not flexible, for in that case 'they ought to blame their own idleness, or bad government, not the industry of their neighbours' (E 330). Perhaps the full extent of Hume's confidence in the natural harmony of interests, not to mention his riposte to gloomy mercantilist assumptions about beggar-thy-neighbour economic doctrine, is crystallised in his 1758 letter to critic Josiah Tucker sent via the proxy Lord Kames in which Hume uncharacteristically appealed to 'the goodness of Providence' to vouchsafe that: 'It was surely never the intention of Providence, that any one nation should be a monopoliser of wealth ... Great empires, great cities, great commerce, all of them receive a check, not from accidental events, but necessary principles.'[30] Apparently even the great 'infidel' was not wholly lacking in faith in a higher power, at least with respect to global trade.[31]

Hume's critique of the Physiocrats dealt primarily with the issues of taxation and public debt.[32] These French political economists originated as critics of Colbert's mercantilist colonial system, and thus shared Hume's antipathy to that approach to trade and commerce. However, where the Physiocrats differed from Hume was mainly about the value of agriculture. Physiocrat thinkers such as François Quesnay, Victor Mirabeau and Anne-Robert Jacques Turgot emphasised the productive value of agricultural labour. Indeed, in contrast to Hume, they viewed agriculture as the sole source of wealth understood as *produit net*, or surplus above the necessary expense of production.[33] In this view, merchants and manufacturing were perhaps necessary, but effectively non-productive elements of the economy. And as the sole source of real wealth, agricultural land was the best, if not the only, practicable source of tax revenue for governments. Despite their commitment to the principle of private property and an attitude of laissez faire or government non-interference in the economy, the Physiocrats also perhaps paradoxically believed in the need for strong centralised government state apparatus to implement a rational economic plan shorn of all the antiquated and pernicious feudal relics that continued to make French agriculture backwards and inefficient. With their idealised account of the potential of French agriculture and unbounded faith in certain objective laws of economics discoverable by unassisted human reason, the Physiocrats were in Humean terms economic enthusiasts *par excellence*.

Take for instance the physiocrat argument that 'since all taxes, as they pretend, fall ultimately upon land, it were better to lay them originally there and abolish every duty upon consumption' (E 346). Hume rejected the physiocratic plan for a 'single-tax' model for several reasons. First, he favoured consumption taxes that prioritised luxuries and avoided burdensome taxes on staples: 'The best taxes are such as are levied upon consumptions, especially those of luxury; because such taxes are least felt by the people' (E 345). In Hume's opinion, the overly rigid and monistic single-tax idea failed to adhere to basic principles of distributive justice or to recognise that tax policy can be used prudentially to stimulate economic productivity, especially among the poor who in response to tax increases typically 'increase their industry, perform more work, and live as well as before without demanding more for their labour' (E 343).[34] In an exchange of letters with Turgot in 1766–1767, Hume further developed this critique of the single tax, and his defence of consumption duties, by arguing that the price of labour is not affected by taxation, but rather by the 'Quantity of Labour and the Quantity of Demand'.[35] Moreover, in contrast to physiocrat orthodoxy about agriculture being the sole source of real wealth, Hume speculates that the amount of revenue available from taxing the commercial class is 'much greater than that which arises from land'.[36]

Hume was also critical of what he took to be the centralising tendencies exemplified by the singular focus on the land tax. Quesnay, for instance, proposed that the monarch as representative of the French state is co-owner of all productive land in the realm, and thus taxes are levied only upon the portion of production legally owned by the sovereign.[37] Hume recoiled at what amounts to a 'legal despotism' that sought to create a centralised administration without any intermediate institutions.[38] For Hume, one of the great contributions that commerce made towards preserving liberty was its tendency to diffuse power among a multitude of competing, but also interdependent, interests. Arguably, it was in recognition of their role in fostering liberty that Hume denoted merchants among the 'most useful races of men' in contrast to the agricultural sector in which he believed a habit of indolence naturally prevails (E 300, 261). But even while the manufacturer would gladly put off the burden of any tax, Hume insists that the imposition of the tax burden solely upon the 'landed gentlemen' would be nothing less than arbitrary.

With respect to taxation, Hume rejected the simplistic, reductionist fiscal model of the Physiocrats in favour of a more balanced consumption-based approach that presupposed a fundamental harmony of interests between commerce and agriculture. However, on the issue of public debt Hume was much more sceptical about whether the institution of a national debt was truly in the public interest. The idea of public debt was celebrated by many French political economists in the mid-eighteenth century, but it had been a source of controversy in Britain prior even to the South Sea Scandal of the 1720s. Significantly, Hume's major objection to the public debt was, as Hirschman observes, fundamentally political, not per se economic.[39] Hume called it the 'new paradox' (E 352). He conceded that the one benefit of a system of public debt in countries like Britain, Holland or France is that it provides the merchant class with a ready supply of money 'that is continually multiplying in their hands, and produces sure again, besides the profit of their commerce' (E 353). But the disadvantages of public debt far outweigh any positives.

First, even the putative benefit of circulating money has a real down-side of producing inflationary pressure as paper drives out specie and raises the cost of everything, especially as the taxes required to pay the debt also tend to raise the price of labour and oppress the poor. In addition, the establishment of a financial system encourages 'the confluence of people and riches to the capitol', a concern dating back to Locke in the previous century (E 354). But the greatest danger Hume identified with public debt was increasing the influence of foreigners who control the nation's debt rendering the public 'tributary to them' and distorting the socio-economic equilibrium central to Hume's conception of the virtues of commercial society (E 335). While Hume largely agreed with fellow Scotsman James Steuart that economic expansion puts constraints on government power by strengthening the 'middle rank of men', Hume saw the public debt as a pernicious force working in the opposite direction.[40] This concern became an ever greater worry for Hume who added six new paragraphs to the 1764 edition of the essay 'Of Public Credit', the gist of which bewailed the 'unnatural state of society' in which 'the only persons, who possess any revenue beyond the immediate effects of their industry, are the stockholders' (E 357). Public debt corrodes the natural harmony of interests by undermining the customs and manners of the people who see the rewards flowing to bondholders 'who have no connexions with the state, who can enjoy their revenue in any part of the globe in which they choose to reside . . . and who will sink into the lethargy of a stupid and pampered luxury, without spirit' (E 357). The evil example of those who 'give great encouragement to an useless and unactive life' (E 355) saps the very life blood of a commercial people.

The dangers posed by the national debt are, according to Hume, existential. He deplored the manner in which British leaders since Walpole had employed debt financing as an alternative to politically unpopular property taxes. In this context, Hume's argument in 'Of Taxes' signifies more of a call to revise the English system from one based upon land tax to a consumption tax model, than it is an academic critique of the Physiocrats.[41] Hume was so alarmed at the danger of public debt that it even evokes an uncharacteristic appeal to the natural rights tradition of Locke and *Cato's Letters* as he declares: 'The right of self-preservation is unalienable in every individual, much more in every community' (E 362). Hume saw only two alternatives: either the 'natural death of public credit' that occurs when the political rulers of a nation renounce the debt during a crisis, or the 'violent death of our public credit' when the nation is so weakened and distracted by fiscal problems that it allows the rise of a hegemonic invader towards whom 'they themselves and their creditors lie both at the mercy of the conqueror' (E 363, 365). At the very least, the much-prized moderation of British politics will exist under perpetual threat of radicalisation as ambitious leaders set out 'visionary schemes' to discharge the debt (E 361).

It has long been recognised that Hume feared the negative effects that philosophic partisanship has on politics. We have seen that he also detected the pernicious and growing influence of philosophical partisanship with respect to economic theory. Hume was neither a pessimist nor an unbridled optimist about the prospects of human inquiry achieving a single, comprehensive economic doctrine. Rather, for Hume, responsible economic thinking requires recognition of the complex combination of passions, practical reason and observable historical phenomena that can point towards regular patterns of behaviour and practices. Did Hume believe economics, like politics, 'may be reduced to a science'? Arguably he did, but it is the kind of science grounded in probability that best serves human understanding as an antidote to both superstitious ignorance and enthusiastic extremism in the economic sphere. That is to say, Hume's economic science culminated in the argument for a natural, albeit not always self-correcting, harmony of interest revealed by reflection upon distant causes and compound effects. It would be left to Hume's friend and philosophical successor of sorts Adam Smith to deepen and formalise this aspect of Hume's interest-based liberal political economy.

Adam Smith Moralising Mandeville

In some respects, Adam Smith's identification as a classical liberal is much less controversial than is the case for David Hume. Though both are well-known as arguably the leading philosophical lights of the Scottish Enlightenment, Smith is even more clearly associated with classical liberal political economy both in the sense of presenting the psychology of 'modern economic man' *par excellence*, and in the way in which his palpable ambivalence towards politics is often interpreted to signify his intention to liberate economics from the moral and ethical constraints of traditional conceptions of government and distributive justice.[42] Certainly, Smith's liberal bona fides are indisputable insofar as he strongly defended the rule of law, limited government and the protection of private property. For our purposes, he is also important as the thinker who culminated the process of moralising Mandeville begun by Hume. That is to say, Smith crafted the theoretically sophisticated definition of liberty in terms of interests that provided the basis for the compelling metaphor of the 'invisible hand' of beneficent self-interest.

Smith famously described his 'system of natural liberty' as a condition that allowed 'every man to pursue his own interest his own way, upon the liberal plan of equality, liberty and justice'.[43] The normative premise of the system of natural liberty was a recognisably Mandevillian empirical argument for natural equality, as opposed to an ontology of rights. Smith relates that 'the difference of natural talents in different men is, in reality, much less than we are aware of'; indeed, the only significant differences between 'a philosopher and a common street porter' are those that derive from 'habit, custom and education', rather than nature (WN 28–9). The interest-based logic of Smith's famed 'invisible hand' metaphor seems in one sense to be a vivid representation of Mandeville's doctrine of private vices and public benefits. However, whereas Hume was willing, at least partly, to concede to Mandeville's critique of moral virtue by admitting the conventionality of justice and much of what normally passes for morality, Smith strove to more thoroughly moralise Mandeville's teaching by insisting upon a natural basis of justice and morality located in certain important natural human sentiments. In Smith's rendering of interest-based liberalism, Mandeville's celebration of spontaneity and self-interest need neither conclude in a complete collapse of the distinction between virtue and vice, nor the total conventionalisation of justice.

The key to understanding Smith's theoretical achievement in moralising Mandeville is to grasp his profound debt, and complex relation to, the thought of Hume. In many respects, Smith followed Hume's philosophical lead. Mandeville's argument about the subordination of reason found expression in Hume's insistence that 'Reason, is and ought only to be the slave of the passions' (T 2.3.3.266), much as Smith built his own system of natural liberty on the fundamental 'desire of bettering our condition' (WN 341, 345, 405, 540, 674). Hume's argument about the self-regarding core of morality including the social virtues is echoed in Smith's declaration that 'every man is, no doubt by nature, first and principally recommended to his own care'.[44] It is also not difficult to decipher the manner in which Smith adopted Hume's stadial history of economic development inspired by Mandeville's conjectural history of the origins of government and morality. Not only did Smith join Hume in rejecting the social contract theory of earlier liberals such as Hobbes and Locke in favour of a developmental model emphasising the role of custom, habit and obedience. He also singled out Hume for high praise as the only writer to recognise through his socio-historical analysis the massive, beneficent transformation brought about as 'commerce and manufactures gradually introduced order and good government, and with them, the liberty and security of individuals, among the inhabitants of the country, who had before lived in a continual state of war with their neighbours and of servile dependence upon their superiors' (WN 412).[45] Hume's argument for the salutary effects of commerce in the creation of social conditions conducive to peace, prosperity and legal security would become a prominent feature of Smith's empirically based case for laissez faire economics.

While in many respects Smith built upon the philosophical foundation supplied by Hume's modification of Mandeville's interest-based conception of liberalism, his most original contribution to the political economy of classical liberalism derived from his adaptation of certain Humean premises to both correct what he took to be problems with Hume's moral philosophy, and by extension to provide a more effective response to Mandeville's 'licentious system' (TMS 308). Central to Smith's correction of Hume is the issue of justice. Smith's argument with respect to justice contains two important, and related, dimensions: his attempt to articulate the natural basis of justice in contrast to Hume's stark conventionalism, and Smith's effort to reconcile a moral theory based on sentiments with an economic doctrine deduced from self-interest. First, with respect to the naturalness of justice, it is useful to recall Hume's argument that the conception of justice originated in certain conventions primarily relating to property that gradually developed historically into building blocks of society due to the benefits these conventions produce. Utility, thus, is central to Hume's understanding of justice.

Smith, however, grounds justice in the natural sentiment of 'resentment' (TMS 67–9).[46] Justice, as such, is distinct from beneficence inasmuch as the latter 'is always free', and therefore the want of it does not produce 'any mischief from which we can have occasion to defend ourselves' (TMS 79). One way to approach the different views Smith and Hume held about justice is to consider their distinct understanding of sympathy. As we recall, Hume saw sympathy as an other-regarding natural feeling that, while too weak to control our passions, nonetheless 'has sufficient influence to influence our taste, and give us the sentiments of approbation and blame' (T 3.22.321). Smith provides a more normatively substantive and expansive account of sympathy that is 'the source of our fellow feeling for the misery of others', and demonstrates human beings' natural sociability: 'How selfish soever men may be supposed, there are evidently some principles in his nature, which interest him in the fortune of others, though he derives nothing from it except the pleasure of seeing it' (TMS 9–10).[47]

For purposes of illuminating Smith's political economy, perhaps the main significance of his greater emphasis on natural sociability than Hume has to do with their different assumptions regarding property. Simply put, Smith viewed property as an integral part of personal freedom, and in this sense, property is more natural than is the case with the conventionalism of Hume. While Smith recognised that quarrels about property are a major source of conflict spurring the creation of any society's justice system, he did not, unlike Hume, see the idea of justice and property arising together logically or temporally.[48] For Smith, 'the sacred rights of private property' are not as dependent on considerations of utility as Hume maintained. Therefore, while Smith praised Hume as 'the agreeable and ingenious philosopher', who explained 'why utility pleases', it is also probably fair to conclude that Smith was at best only partly committed to the principle of utility as the source of moral judgement (TMS 179).[49]

The other aspect of Smith's moral philosophy that is crucial for understanding his political economy is what many scholars dub the 'Adam Smith problem' produced by the apparent difficulty in reconciling the moral philosophy of the *Theory of Moral Sentiments* with the apparent egoistic psychology of the *Wealth of Nations*. One way to reconcile these two strands of Smith's thought is to acknowledge that he neither viewed sympathy simply as benevolence, nor economic self-interest purely in terms of selfishness.[50] Arguably the key to reconciling the seemingly divergent tendencies in Smith's moral and economic theory lies in his famous invention of the 'impartial spectator'. The impartial spectator is built on a recognisably Humean foundation as a conceptual device that re-situates, if not necessarily depersonalises, considerations of justice such that 'by the imagination we place ourselves in [the] situation' of another, and in this way conceive of their emotional and physical state (TMS 8). By virtue of this imaginative projection, 'whatever is the passion which arises from any object in the person concerned, an analogous emotion springs up, at the thought of his situation, in the breast of every attentive spectator' (TMS 10). The disembodied moral experience of the spectator is powerful enough to 'humble the arrogance' of one's self-love, and it is perhaps only because of the imaginative faculty enabling spectatorship that Smith ultimately has confidence that an individual 'dares not look mankind in the face' and proclaim that one only acts according to the principle of self-interest (TMS 83). The impartial spectator is the imaginary bearer of the judgement of universal humanity that illuminates the path towards duty by promising the desired approbation of others.[51] The impartial spectator is not, however, a universal, natural standard of justice per se, for Smith maintains that the distinct properties of the spectator's moral perspective are historically and culturally relative.[52] In this respect, the moral conventions are a function of the natural mental faculties.

In addition to his disagreement with Hume about justice, another original contribution Smith made to the development of eighteenth-century interest-based liberalism had to do with his critique of Mandeville. Smith was both influenced by Mandeville and the same time strongly critical of the famous doctor.[53] Smith decried 'the licentious system' produced by Mandeville's doctrine of private vices and public benefits as both 'wholly pernicious', and yet bearing more than a passing resemblance to truth (TMS 308). 'The system of Dr. Mandeville' carried a certain plausibility, in Smith's view, because his Anglo-Dutch predecessor correctly surmised the importance of the 'love of praise and commendation', which Mandeville terms 'vanity' (TMS 308). However, Smith rejected Mandeville's conclusion that the power of 'self-love' makes it impossible that anyone can ever really prefer someone else's prosperity to his own (TMS 308). Smith not only admitted that the desire to be esteemed is capable of producing much good, he went further to argue that it is possible to have public virtue that is not simply selfish: 'the desire of doing what is honourable and noble, cannot with any propriety be called vanity' (TMS 309).[54] By insisting that 'the desire of acquiring honour and esteem by really deserving those sentiments' is not beyond the moral capacities of individuals, Smith renders it likely that 'all public spirit' is not reducible to a 'mere cheat and imposition upon mankind' (TMS 309). That is to say, Smith believed that the natural love of praise Mandeville dismissed as vanity could, if properly directed, produce a genuine love of true glory.

Smith is somewhat more sympathetic to Mandeville's claim that human actions necessarily fall short of the level of complete self-denial to which moral virtue has traditionally been thought to aspire. As Hanley observes, in this sense Smith rejected the 'benevolent' system of his teacher (and arch-critic of Mandeville) Frances Hutcheson, who maintained that 'disinterested benevolence' is characteristic of virtue (TMS 304–5).[55] But while it is true Smith believed complete self-denial is unnatural, he also criticised the 'ingenious sophistry' of Mandeville's definition of virtue in starkly ascetic, rigoristic terms (TMS 312). By interpreting virtue so narrowly and selectively, Mandeville renders the concept of virtue practically meaningless for the virtues 'do not require an entire insensibility to the objects of the passions which they mean to govern' (TMS 312). According to Mandeville's reasoning, even basic things are luxury such that 'there is vice even in the use of a clean sheet, or of a convenient habitation' (TMS 312). Similarly, Mandeville's 'great fallacy' is to represent every passion as wholly vicious in any degree and direction so that sexual desire in 'lawful union' is no different from the 'most hurtful gratification' (TMS 312).

It is not surprising, then, that Smith rejected Mandeville's claim that justice and moral virtue are simply contrivances designed by cynical political elites to facilitate social construction and cohesion. But in terms of the actual operation of self-interest in the economic context, Smith and Mandeville were in fundamental agreement. They both believed human nature was revealed by virtue of a certain spontaneity of activity as individuals sought to satisfy their desires. Smith also concurred with Mandeville's judgement about the positive effects of spontaneous self-interest: 'The restless Industry of Man to supply his Wants . . . have produced and brought to Perfection many useful Arts and Sciences.'[56] Smith offers a similar account of the way in which the mistaken belief that our desires can be fully satisfied is the 'deception which raises and keeps in continual motion the industry of mankind' (TMS 183). It was in the context of illustrating this grand deception that Smith presented the famous 'invisible hand' metaphor in the *Theory of Moral Sentiments* in which he claimed (rather optimistically) that in spite of the 'natural selfishness and rapacity' of the rich, they are led insensibly to the 'same distribution of the necessaries of life' as would be produced by an egalitarian allotment (TMS 184–5). The Mandevillean echoes about displaced intentionality are perhaps even clearer in Smith's later hyperrealist version of the 'invisible hand' metaphor in the *Wealth of Nations* in which he argues that the intangible forces that lead an individual 'to promote an end which was no part of his intention', actually serves the common good more effectively 'than when he really intends to promote it' (WN 456).

Smith also departed from Mandeville on the issue of trade and luxury, and he did so precisely because he believed the latter failed to understand the harmful effects of some forms of self-interest. In his *Lectures on Jurisprudence* from the 1760s Smith directly criticised Mandeville's assertion that 'nothing spent at home could diminish public or national opulence'.[57] Smith argued the fatal flaw in 'the foundation of Dr. Mandeville's system that private vices are public benefits' is his assumption that 'what is spent at home is all spent among ourselves' regardless of how frivolous the kind of consumption (LJ 393). Smith's stinging rebuke was that not all spending is conducive to producing wealth, and money spent encouraging a merchant to trade, or a farmer to improve the land is, the only manner in which money is truly put to 'service in industry and opulence' (LJ 394). Smith believed that Mandeville's argument for the benefits of moral vice did not properly account for the dynamic capacities of capital investment of productive labour as opposed to simple consumption and depletion of resources. That is to say, Smith accused the arch-realist Mandeville of being naive, and even too idealistic, about the beneficent effects of unregulated self-interest.

Smith's Political Economy

Arguably Smith's most important contribution to classical liberal political economy is, of course, his account of the division of labour. Whereas Hume's emphasis on the conventionality of property tended to diminish the value of labour, Smith reached back to Locke for inspiration. With clear parallels to Locke's seminal argument that private property originates in the ownership each individual has in the product of the labour of one's body (II:27), Smith extols: 'The property which every man has in his own labour, as it is the original foundation of all other property, so it is the most sacred and inviolable' (WN 138). Smith praised the laws of Britain for securing 'every man that he shall enjoy the fruits of his own labour' (WN 540). He did not, however, ground property rights in a Lockean labour theory of value per se, but rather by means of a spectator theory that emphasised the recognition of the pains that went into someone's labour and elicited the spectator's sympathy (TMS 84).[58] Despite Smith's Lockean appeal to labour as the source of property, his tendency to eschew the language of natural rights suggests his fundamental alignment with the interest-based liberalism of Mandeville and Hume.[59]

The connection between Smith and Mandeville on the division of labour is most apparent with respect to the concept of specialisation. While Locke introduced a rudimentary measure of the value-added by which 'bread is worth more than acorns, wine than water; and cloth or silk, than leaves, skins or moss' (II:42), Mandeville made specialisation of labour central to his economic theory. As he explained: 'There are many sets of hands in the nation, that not wanting proper materials', would be able in less than half a year to produce and fit out a mighty ship of the line, 'yet it is certain, that this task would be impracticable, if it was not divided and subdivided into a great variety of different labours' (F II:149). For Smith, the psychological characteristic that makes Mandeville's argument for specialisation so compelling is the uniquely human natural faculty of exchange: 'Nobody ever saw a dog make a fair and deliberate exchange of one bone for another with another dog' (WN 26). Smith's account of the division of labour thus depends on the rational faculty allowing barter and exchange by which emphasis Smith arguably provided a more intellectualised argument for commerce than did Hume and certainly Mandeville.[60] Smith reflects that 'the certainty of being able to exchange surplus produce of their labours in one trade induces them to separate themselves into different trades and apply their talents to one alone' (LJ 348).[61] A system of laws that encourages and reinforces this certainty about opportunities for exchange would, thus, be an important environmental factor in the establishment of commercial society.

To Smith, the discovery of the division of labour is the single most important historical cause of material flourishing. Famously, the *Wealth of Nations* practically begins with the statement: 'The greatest improvement in the productive powers of labour, and the greater part of the skill, dexterity, and judgement with which it is anywhere directed, or applied, seem to have been the effects of the division of labour' (WN 13). In the iconic example of the pin makers whose tasks are broken down into their simplest form, Smith drew on both the Lockean arguments about 'the proportional increase in the productive powers of labour', and similar observations about the enormous advantage in material well-being enjoyed by a European peasant in contrast to 'an African King' (WN 24).[62] Smith's insistence on the importance of spontaneity bears a Mandevillean flavour as he claims that the division of labour is 'not originally the effect of any human wisdom, which foresees and intends that general opulence to which it gives occasion' (WN 25). Also, in keeping with Mandeville, Smith admitted that where the psychological impulse towards benevolence may have only a tenuous impact on human behaviour, necessity supplies a more reliable motivation than appeals to altruism: 'He will be more likely to prevail if he can interest their self-love in his favour, and shew them that it is for their own advantage to do for him what he requires of them' (WN 26). Ironically, this appeal to necessity gave way to an argument for self-interest and private advantage, rather than a deeper recognition of shared necessity. The division of labour, thus, both reveals and conceals human nature.

Smith and Hume combined to give Scottish political economy an air of antipathy towards the cramped intellectual and moral premises of mercantilism. Smith was also very much Hume's supporter with respect to taxation, his concerns about national debt, and their shared conviction that wealthy nations can remain competitive in trade with poorer ones due to the lower costs of efficient production offsetting higher labour costs.[63] Despite these sources of continuity, it is difficult to situate Smith, as we did Hume, firmly in the spectrum of economic theory ranging from mercantilism, on the one hand, and the Physiocrats, on the other, as Smith clearly admired the Physiocrats, even if he disagreed with them in important ways. In the extended treatment of the chief physiocratic thinkers in the Book 4 of the *Wealth of Nations*, Smith extended high praise for Quesnay, that 'very ingenious and profound author', in particular for his efforts to create an economic system combining 'perfect liberty and perfect equality' (WN 672, 674).[64] For Smith, the chief strength of physiocratic thinking was that they correctly understood that the wealth of nations lies not in inconsumable riches of money, but rather in the amount of consumable goods annually produced by the labour of society and channelled into a system of generalised self-interest. However, their 'capital error' was that the physiocratic idea of free trade rested upon a regime of 'legal despotism' that was both 'partial and oppressive' (WN 674). In contrast to Smith's 'system of natural liberty', which presupposed a minimal level of government involvement in the economy, the Physiocrats believed only massive government regulation of economic life could paradoxically supply the conditions for perfect liberty necessary to encourage maximum levels of production (WN 678). Moreover, the Physiocrat fixation on agriculture blinded them to the enormous contribution that what they would see as non-productive activities such as commerce and manufacturing actually make towards the development of national wealth.

Another important landmark to help locate Smith's political economy is the work of his compatriot, the Jacobite exile James Steuart, whose enormous 1767 *An Enquiry into the Principles of Political Economy* presented a comprehensive theory of the field distinct from both mercantilism and the physiocrat doctrine. Steuart defined the primary task of political economy as being 'to secure a certain fund of subsistence for all the inhabitants, to obviate every circumstance which may render it precarious; to provide everything necessary for supplying the wants of the society, and to employ the inhabitants'.[65] The most obvious difference between Steuart and Smith is the former's argument for the centrality of the role of the 'statesman', for it is the wisdom that the supreme authority of government exerts in planning and establishing the system of modern economy that has proved to be 'the most effectual bridle ever was invented against the folly of despotism'.[66] For his part, Smith largely dismissed Steuart's state-oriented account of political economy for reasons similar to his disagreement with the Physiocrats; namely, in both instances they failed to recognise the advantages that the spontaneous operation of self-interest produces in a system of natural liberty. Indeed, Smith's antipathy towards monopolies and joint-stock companies derived from his judgement that they stultify genuine competition and promote irresponsible risk.[67] Whereas Hume was notoriously insouciant about the informal techniques of power and 'influence' that greased the political wheels of the Augustan period, Smith was less Hume or Mandeville, and more Trenchard and Gordon, at least with respect to the problem of corruption.

Hirschman reminded us long ago about Smith's 'ambivalence toward nascent capitalism'.[68] This ambiguous founder of capitalism was well aware of the paradox of progress whereby increased wealth in society leads almost inexorably to greater socio-economic inequality. One of Smith's most notorious statements in the *Wealth of Nations* seems to run counter to the harmony of interests: 'Civil Government, as far as it is instituted for the security of property, is in reality instituted for the defence of the rich against the poor, or of those who have some property against those who have none at all' (WN 715). But it is important to recognise the context here is Smith's account of the progress of economic development through stages from primitive shepherding through to complex, commercial society. The fundamental moral premise of Smith's stadial economic history is the assumption that the harmful effects of material inequality in advanced commercial societies are offset by the measurable improvement of the conditions of the greater part of the labouring class. In this way, the interest of all is in principle harmonious with the self-interest of each.

But Smith also drew attention to the profound social problems produced by the tendency of the ever-more refined division of labour to cause the degeneration of the intellectual and moral development of the working class, as well as a decline of the martial spirit necessary for national defence (WN 781–82, 784–6). In this respect, Smith expressed concerns about the division of labour similar to those of his fellow Scotsman Adam Ferguson's *Essay on the History of Civil Society* (1767).[69] However, while Smith was not generally optimistic about the positive force of political change, he did display some confidence that the paradox of the division of labour – that it unleashes the productive powers of labour, even as it produces moral and intellectual degradation among the workers – could be remedied through a commitment to enhanced public education. Of course, this would require appealing to the self-interest of the ruling class by convincing them that 'the safety of government depends very much upon the favourable judgement which the people may form of its conduct' (WN 788). The capacity to form such a collective favourable judgement presupposed, in Smith's view, a certain level of general public enlightenment. Thus, even granting the paradigmatic significance of the 'invisible hand' in Smith's system of natural liberty, this did not preclude the need for a Smithian theory of the state albeit one limited to providing national defence, the administration of justice and certain kinds of public works.

Smith's 'system of natural liberty' is not the 'state of nature' associated with the natural rights philosophy of Hobbes and Locke; that is, a theoretical device deduced from human psychology and developed to provide an account both of the origins of civil society and of individual moral obligations. Smith's system of natural liberty is primarily historical, as opposed to rational universalism, and, indeed, as several commentators have observed, Smith made no serious effort to provide a theoretical foundation for this economic system.[70] In contrast to the deontological version of natural rights liberalism, Smith was content to defend the free market primarily on grounds of comparative utility – that freedom better produces individual and communal prosperity than any present alternative. The remarkable extent to which historical and cultural relativism was combined with an egoistic psychology in the interest-based liberalism of Mandeville and Hume is thus brought to a kind of culmination by Smith. It is possible that Smith's proposed, but never published, master work on 'law and government' according to the principles of natural jurisprudence may have provided a clearer sense of Smith's belief on the possibility of integrating politics and ethics within the context of the natural rights tradition.[71] However, the fact that he never deemed his thoughts on this topic worthy of publication perhaps speaks volumes about the growing gulf between natural rights-based liberalism and its interest-based liberal sibling in the course of the eighteenth century.

Notes

1. Hume 1987: 31. Hereafter in notes and text E and page number. For Bolingbroke's attacks on Walpole's style of politics, see Sparling 2019: ch. 5.
2. Thomas Jefferson famously despised Hume, viewing him as an incorrigible political conservative (see Wilson 1989).
3. See Forbes 1975: 135; Rasmussen 2017: 13–14; McArthur 2007: 13; Stewart 1963: 191; Sabl 2012: 1–2. Wei (2017: 168) argues that Hume became more conservative later in life. Hardin (2007: 3–5, 26) maintains that Hume was neither conservative nor liberal, but rather a proto-social scientist.
4. Hume 2000: Bk 3, pt 2, s. 8, p. 347. Hereafter in notes and text T book.part.section.page.
5. Forbes 1975: 140.
6. Castiglione 1983.
7. Hume 1961: 77. Hereafter in notes and text SE and page number.
8. Hanley 2011: 212.
9. Hanley 2011: 211.
10. Church 2007: 169–70.
11. Baier (2010: 41, 48) suggests that Hume may have learned about the 'oblique' channelling of self-interest from Mandeville.
12. For the striking parallel between Hume and Benjamin Franklin with respect to the positive effects of vanity, see Franklin 1996: 2.
13. In the following discussion of 'humanity' I am indebted to Hanley 2011: 214ff and McArthur 2007: 17–21.
14. Hanley 2011: 221–3. See SE 225–6.
15. Hume 1987: xiii.
16. Rotwein 1955: xvi.
17. See, for instance, his condemnation of both the Leveller and the Puritan radicals of the English Civil War era (SE 193; E 27, 45, 68–71).

18. Danford (1990: 154) accuses Hume of being 'almost devious' in his studied vagueness about vicious luxury.
19. For a good discussion of the role of 'enthusiasm' and 'superstition' as interpretive devices in Hume, see Haakonssen 1993: 182–4, 198, 206.
20. For Hume's approach to risk, see Nacol 2016: 90–3; Rotwein 1955: xliii.
21. Blyth 2012: 110–11.
22. Here I follow Istvan Hont's excellent treatment of the 'Rich Country, Poor Country' debate (see Hont 1983: 271–315).
23. E 329; compare with Kant 1991: 50–1, 114.
24. Hont 1983: 273.
25. Rotwein 1955: 191.
26. Rotwein 1955: 195.
27. E 328; Hont 1983: 282.
28. Rasmussen 2017: 59.
29. Rotwein 1955: 199.
30. Rotwein 1955: 201.
31. For Hume's reputation as a notorious unbeliever, see Rasmussen 2017.
32. It should be noted that while Hume published most of his essays on economics several years prior to the publication of the most influential Physiocrats, I follow Miller (1981: 131) in presupposing that Hume had access to, and was engaging with, pamphlets outlining characteristically physiocrat ideas that circulated in Paris in the 1740s and 1750s. Later in a letter from 1769 Hume expressed his contempt for Physiocrats branding them 'the set of men the most chimerical and arrogant that now exist' (Skinner 1993: 247).
33. Seligman 1921: 125.
34. Miller 1981: 131.
35. Rotwein 1955: 208.
36. Rotwein 1955: 209.
37. Dumont 1977: 42.
38. Outram 2013: 44.
39. Hirschman 1977: 76. For the important role of political debate about the national debt in the process of state formation in this period, see Stasavage 2011.
40. Hirschman 1977: 82; Robertson 1983: 154–5.
41. Wei (2017: 93–7) and Sabl (2012: 192–9) persuasively argue that Hume traced the problems of supply and tax revenue well back in English history to the period before the English Civil War (see also Hume 1983: vol. 4, pp. 159 and 295).
42. See Myers 1983: 120; Hirschman 1977: 107–10. Cropsey famously described Smith's legacy as producing the 'deflection of political philosophy towards economics' (2001: 120). For a very different

interpretation that identifies Smith with the attempt to fuse classical and Christian ideals of virtue, see Hanley 2009.

43. Smith 1981: 664. Hereafter in notes and text WN and page number.
44. Smith 1984: 82. Hereafter in notes and text TMS and page number.
45. Rasmussen 2017: 120, also highlights the importance of this passage.
46. For the importance of resentment in Smith, see Schwarze 2020: 98–128.
47. For the differences between Hume and Smith with regard to justice, see Haakonssen 1981: 45; Rasmussen 2013: 122.
48. Fleischaker 2004: 175.
49. McNamara (1998: 44) calls Smith a 'reluctant utilitarian'.
50. Griswold 1999: 260.
51. Cropsey 2001: 163.
52. See TMS 159 and 205–06. For the cultural and historical relativism underlying Smith's impartial spectator, see Rasmussen 2013: 122–4. For a good discussion of Smith's critique of deontological arguments more generally, see Hanley 2009: 72–8.
53. For Mandeville's influence on Smith, see Winch 1992: 102ff; Winch 1978: 80; Douglass 2017.
54. Winch 1992: 103; Berry 1992: 80–2.
55. Hanley 2009: 151.
56. Mandeville 1988: 2:132.
57. Smith 1978: 393. Hereafter in notes and text LJ and page number.
58. Haakonssen 1981: 107.
59. Dumont rather implausibly claims that Smith's argument for the connection between labour and property actually rests upon a Lockean natural law theory, but Smith refrained from clarifying his natural law orientation out of a desire not to contradict his friend David Hume (Dumont 1977: 190).
60. Rothschild and Sen 2006: 322–4.
61. Compare with Mandeville 1988: 2:335–6, 421.
62. For Locke, famously the comparison was to a 'King' among the indigenous people of North America (Locke 2016 II:41).
63. Hont 1983: 299.
64. For Smith's admiration of the Physiocrats, see Winch 1992: 97; Haakonssen 2006: 2.
65. Steuart 2020: 20.
66. Steuart 2020: 249.
67. Nacol 2016: 106–10.
68. Hirschman 1977: 105.
69. Hont 1983: 295.
70. Rasmussen 2013: 120–1; Rothschild and Sen 2006: 363.
71. For some of the conjecture about the significance of Smith's missing work on natural law, see Rasmussen 2013: 124; Griswold 1999: 256–8; Fleischaker 2004: 147.

Chapter 5

The Political Economy of Thomas Paine

Thomas Paine is one of the most intriguing figures among late eighteenth-century English radical thinkers. While he has long been celebrated or condemned, depending on one's political persuasion, for his model of the intellectual *engagé* in both the American and French revolutions, in more recent times there has been renewed interest in Paine as a serious political theorist in the Anglo-American tradition.[1] In particular, Paine's innovative analysis of the relation of politics and economics, that is, his political economy, has been subject to considerable debate among scholars. Some commentators see Paine as the bourgeois radical champion of laissez faire individualism and the minimalist 'night watchman' conception of government.[2] Others identify Paine as an intellectual forerunner of working-class radicalism and the social welfare state.[3] Paine's thought has thus become a kind of Rohrschach test for how students of classical liberalism interpret the economic dimensions of the American and French Revolution-era theorising about the state.

However, this debate about Paine's political economy typically mischaracterises his thought because commentators often fail to recognise the significance of the change over time in Paine's reflections on the economic foundations of government. In this chapter I will argue that Paine's theory of the state transformed over several decades from a minimalist conception of government consistent with the laissez faire approach of Adam Smith's harmony of interests to an idea of the 'positive' state including among its responsibilities a broad range of social welfare policies. We must be careful, of course, to avoid anachronistic terms and references.

Thus, while Paine did not understand the 'positive state' precisely in terms articulated by later thinkers, especially twentieth-century progressives and social democrats, it is nonetheless arguably significant that Paine advanced major ideas on the government's role in providing social programmes that anticipated the welfare state. Particularly striking is Paine's Physiocrat-influenced recommendation in his last major work *Agrarian Justice* (1795) for the creation of a 'National Fund' designed to indemnify economically disadvantaged (i.e., landless) individuals for the loss of their common birth right to the natural property of the Earth.

This shift from a conceptual model of the state based upon the natural harmony of economic interests to one characterised by the imperative to remedy the problem of a rigid unequal class system was not, however, the result of Paine abandoning or changing his fundamental political principles. Rather, the transformation in Paine's idea of the state and political economy was the product of his career-long reflections upon what he took to be the egalitarian implications of natural rights philosophy. In his considerations about the meaning of the French Revolution, Paine adapted in important ways the Lockean theory of property rights he inherited from the English radical Whig tradition by introducing significant spatial and temporal limits on the moral claims of property ownership. Paine's later desire to articulate a new natural rights political economy was given acute urgency by his perceived need to respond to the penetrating critique of natural rights theory by his erstwhile friend Edmund Burke. While Burke shared several intellectual commitments with the interest-based version of Scottish political thought, such as a preference for balanced constitutionalism and a temperamental disposition favouring political moderation, arguably his critique of the rights doctrine cast Burke beyond the mental horizons of liberalism per se, making him, as Isaac Kramnick describes, 'the enduring philosopher of conservatism'.[4] With Paine and Burke, much more so than with Locke and Hume, for instance, the disagreements on political and economic principles no longer seem to be *en famille*.

This chapter will proceed in three sections. Section one examines Paine's thinking about politics and economics in the 1770s and 1780s prior to the French Revolution. In this section I highlight the minimalist conception of government and the natural harmony of interests that are the dominant theme of Paine's classic *Common Sense* (1776), as well as his vision of the night watchman state dedicated almost entirely to preserving the sanctity of contracts in his later 'Dissertations on Government, the Affairs of the Bank, and Paper Money' (1786). The following section examines how Paine's conception of the social responsibilities of government began to expand, as witness in his defence of the French Revolution in the *Rights of Man* against the scathing attack on political radicalism by the conservative Edmund Burke. This will involve analysing Paine's theory of natural rights with particular attention paid to the first adumbrations of his argument for the temporal dimension of natural rights philosophy, which requires both an account of intergenerational justice and a detailed proposal in *Rights of Man Part II* for social welfare programmes covering a wide range of 'poor relief' measures that Paine insists are 'not of the nature of a charity, but of a right'.[5]

The third section considers in some detail Paine's most radical redistributionist proposal, the 'National Fund' in *Agrarian Justice*. I will argue that this system of estate taxes on landed wealth created in order to fund a schedule of direct payments to economically disadvantaged individuals rests upon Paine's distinction between 'natural' property and 'artificial' property, a distinction that radicalised his earlier ideas about intergenerational justice by reframing these thoughts in terms of a broader critique of 'civilization' as the cause of poverty and inequality. Paine's later political economy thus initiated a repudiation of the Scottish political economists' stadial history of progress that reached a crescendo with a sweeping condemnation of the entire property settlement at the very foundation of European civilisation. This redefinition of landed property in terms of a positive natural commons also required Paine to revise the Lockean theory of acquisition based upon labour. *Agrarian Justice*, then, represents the culmination of Paine's thinking on natural rights in an early version of the welfare state.

Common Sense and the Night Watchman State

Tom Paine's call for American independence in *Common Sense* was published in January 1776 at a critical moment in the Anglo-American imperial dispute that climaxed six months later with the *Declaration of Independence*. It was both a highly influential political *piece d'occasion* in the imperial controversies of the period, and at the same time a sophisticated work of political theory in its own right. Indeed, before even speaking about 'the present state of American affairs', Paine introduced his call for independence with an extended treatment of the nature of government in general, and the serious defects of the celebrated British Constitution in particular.[6] The central premise of Paine's political theory in *Common Sense* is a version of natural rights philosophy originating in John Locke. Paine contrasts Locke's account of the origins of government and society to 'some writers' (most likely Thomas Hobbes) who 'have so confounded society with government, as to leave little or no distinction between them' (CS 66). Whereas the Hobbesian version of natural rights theory presupposed that there could be no justice, and even no society at all, without the sovereign's governing sword and laws, Paine followed Locke by insisting that society and government 'are not only different, but have different origins' (CS 66).[7] Society is the sphere of voluntary human interaction that covers economic, social and familial intercourse directed primarily by natural individual desires and interests. Government, on the other hand, is emphatically artificial, 'produced by our wickedness', and designed to restrain 'our vices' (CS 66). Society binds a community together through promoting happiness and uniting affections, while government 'creates distinctions' based upon individual legal claims. In sum, society is 'a patron' and government is 'a punisher' (CS 66).

While Paine insists that society is 'always a blessing' and government at best 'a necessary evil', the unifying principle connecting his conception of society and government is that these distinct conditions reflect two aspects of the economic foundations of political society (CS 66). Paine's account of the origin of government in *Common Sense* adopts a fundamentally Lockean understanding of property as he followed Locke in affirming that a system of voluntary exchange of goods, and even currency, does not require the coercive power of the state. With this rejection of Hobbes' stark conventionalism, Paine subscribed to one of Locke's core political beliefs that 'a country without government' is better off than a people oppressed by a tyrannical government of which it can be said 'we furnish the means by which we suffer' (CS 66).[8] A society can exist in lieu of government. Government is a product of consent designed to remedy the failings of moral virtue as even the 'blessings' of society are eventually endangered by the relaxation of the sense of 'duty and attachment' individuals have to each other (CS 67). It is only when the 'impulses of conscience' are no longer 'irresistibly obeyed' that individuals are compelled 'to surrender up part of [their] property to furnish means for protection of the rest' (CS 67). For Paine, as for Locke,[9] the primary purpose of government is to protect property.

Paine's account of the origins of government in *Common Sense* is also Lockean in the sense that it presupposed the idea of an original negative commons, that is to say, by nature no part of the Earth belongs to any one individual exclusively of the rest of humankind.[10] Paine illustrated this point by employing the case of European settlers in colonial America as a kind of proxy for Locke's theoretical state of nature. The original negative commons in Locke's state of nature meant that acquiring property required labour and did not need the consent of the rest of the human race to justify private property in the original common. For Paine, if we 'suppose a small number of persons settled in some sequestered part of the earth' (CS 67), then it is apparent that the settlers' first concerns would be about acquiring property to satisfy their wants and needs. But the intrinsic limits of human labour drive individuals unavoidably into society: 'The strength of one man is so unequal to his wants, and his mind so unfitted for perpetual solitude, that he is soon obliged to seek acquaintance and relief of another, who in his turn requires the same' (CS 67). The economic and emotional necessity that compels individuals to leave the 'state of natural liberty' is consistent, Paine claims, with a natural harmony of interests similar to Adam Smith's account of the 'invisible hand' voluntary principles of the free market.[11] As Paine describes it, in the pre-civil condition 'the reciprocal blessings' of society would render obligations of law and government unnecessary 'while they remained perfectly just to each other' (CS 67).

The origin of government for Paine is, thus, neither by divine right nor by an elaborate multi-stage social compact, but rather government emerges as a contrivance or 'a mode rendered necessary by the inability of moral virtue to govern the world' (CS 68). Government in its essence is as limited in scope as society is comprehensive in the range of economic and social activities it includes. The first governments were emphatically minimalist: 'Some convenient tree will afford them a State-House . . . In this first parliament every man, by natural right, will have a seat' (CS 67–8). The original legislation would be no more than 'regulations' enforced purely by public esteem (CS 68). While Paine's conception of society in *Common Sense* presupposed something much like the natural harmony of interests, it is nonetheless important to recall that this natural harmony rests upon individual interests deriving in the Lockean sense from the product of individual labour.[12] The Lockean natural rights philosophy grounds property rights in individual labour, but also, as Paine demonstrates, allows for a range of economic activities – what Locke calls 'promises and bargains for truck' – that do not depend on the institution of civil government, but rather presuppose the rational capacity 'for truth and keeping of faith' among people.[13] Insofar as government is a 'necessary evil', it at least has one virtue derived from the simplicity of its proper goal: namely, government's sole purpose is to protect the rights of personal security and property.

Paine's celebration of the voluntarist principles of society and the resulting minimalist account of the purpose and role of government reflects aspects of his thinking relating both to his philosophical reflections on natural rights and to the specific context of the American colonies in 1776. In philosophical terms, Paine seems to have been persuaded in 1776 that the logical implication of Lockean natural rights was the very limited role of government as strictly protector of property rights. This was both a rejection of the Hobbesian omnicompetent state and, at the same time, an affirmation of the voluntary nature of economic activities that flourish in the realm of civil society. In the American context, Paine's minimalist account of government served the cause of independence by discrediting the authority of the imperial government in London through diminishing the moral significance of government per se. The polemical effect of Paine's conceptual bifurcation of government and society was to reinforce the idea for his American readers that there is already an American society that exists independently of Britain and its government.[14] In 1776 America was, in Paine's view, for all intents and purposes a society or collection of interconnected societies in want of a government, and thus society is the principle to which he has recourse in explaining the devolution of political power within the British Empire.

But how did Paine in this early phase of his career envision the role of government in an independent, post-revolutionary American society? Apart from the state's role as a representational device designed to protect the rights of the people, in *Common Sense* Paine provided little indication of how he anticipated government would interact with society in the newly independent American states. Arguably, his first major treatment of the economic dimensions of the liberal state emerged in his 1786 'Dissertations on Government, the Affairs of the Bank, and Paper Money'. The context of this writing is the controversy in Pennsylvania over the charter of the Bank of North America. Deeply indebted farmers sought to increase the circulation of paper money and to repeal the charter of this privately owned bank, which threatened to refuse to accept paper money. Philadelphia merchants and artisans, fearful of inflation, resisted the issuing of paper money and fought vigorously against the repeal of the bank's charter. Paine joined the fray with aplomb in support of the bank and the merchants. He did so due to his faith in limiting the state's role in economics primarily to ensuring the sanctity of contract. In 'Dissertations on Government' the question of consent that had been rather muted in *Common Sense* assumed enormous significance. The fundamental role of government is to secure performance of contracts generated by the economic activities of civil society. Contracts between individuals can be altered only when unforeseen circumstances arise that require modification of the contract on terms reached 'by the mutual consent and agreement of the parties'.[1] Underlying this discussion is Paine's conception of government directed towards the protection of property rights and vested interests arising from contractual agreement.

Perhaps the most striking aspect of Paine's treatment of contract in 'Dissertations on Government' is the limits he believed that contractual obligation places on the activities of government. The logical premise of Paine's night watchman state is that the state itself must honour all of its public contracts and legal obligations. In practical terms, this means that a contract to which the state is itself a party is just as legally binding as a contract 'made between two private individuals' (DGP 172). The 'glory of a republic' is that in the event of a legal dispute, 'the greatness of one party cannot give it a superiority or advantage over the other' (DGP 172). The due process rights involved in any dispute between an individual and the state requires that the matter be 'decided upon, by the laws of the land, in a court of justice and trial by jury' (DGP 172). In the context of the controversy surrounding the Bank of North America, Paine argues that repealing the bank's charter and issuing paper currency would be illegitimate acts of political interference in the free market that violate the due process rights of individual merchants and investors in society.

It is in the course of defending the sanctity of contract that the early Paine advanced his most theoretically sophisticated account of the proper scope and powers of the state. The 'true principle of republican government', Paine claims is that 'a lawful contract or agreement, sealed and ratified, cannot be affected or altered by an act made afterwards' (DGP 172). But why does government not have a morally and logically prior right to invalidate contracts that a majority believe injured the public good? Paine contends that the natural rights philosophy embodied in republican government stipulates that 'in a republic it is the harmony of its parts that constitutes their several and mutual good' (DGP 172). The overriding public good is inseparable from the sanctity of contract inasmuch as it is the confidence and trust reinforced by law that guarantees the harmony of individual interests in society. For any government to violate or disrespect contractual obligation would put it in contradiction to the essential purpose of government in the first place. Paine also presented the state as a public entity distinct from the government per se. The principals, or 'real parties' in any public contract, Paine determines are 'the state and the persons contracted with' (DGP 173). The presiding government or 'assembly' is never a party to a contract agreed to by a previous assembly, but rather it is simply 'an agent in behalf of the state' through which securing 'the performance of the contract, according to the conditions of it, devolves on succeeding assemblies, not as principals but as agents' (DGP 173). Insofar as the state in its role as contract guarantor *par excellence* is a superintending principal distinct from and above government, then Paine concludes if one assembly tried to absolve the state from its legal obligations this would be equivalent to 'the servant attempting to free his master' (DGP 173). So fundamental does Paine see the sanctity of contract that were we to mistakenly accept the principle that governments can free themselves of obligations acquired by previous governments, then in effect 'every new election would be a new revolution' (DGP 1174).

Not surprisingly Paine extended this same logic to the question of replacing gold and silver coins, the value of which are determined in markets by the quantities available, with paper money. For Paine, the effect of introducing paper money is to arbitrarily through government action renegotiate the terms of every loan and contract in the country: 'When an assembly undertake to issue paper as money, the whole system of safety and certainty is overturned, and property set afloat' (DGP 193). The normative thrust of Paine's criticism of paper currency derives from his interpretation of its meaning in terms of the sanctity of contract. The minimalist night watchman that Paine assumed in 1786 to be the logical and only morally justifiable form of government on natural rights grounds was defined in large part by its responsibility to leave the primary forces in the society to non-state actors and free markets.

Social Welfare and *The Rights of Man*

Paine's most extensive philosophical examination of the origin and meaning of natural rights is contained in his two part *The Rights of Man* (1791, 1792). This landmark work is notable not only insofar as it illuminates Paine's political theory, but also due to the remarkable context in which it was written. Composed during the first two years of the French Revolution, the *Rights of Man* constitutes Paine's considered reaction to the dramatic political events in one of the European great powers. The French experience of revolution differed from the earlier American Revolution primarily due to the much greater extent of social, economic and political inequality that prevailed in *ancien régime* France than Paine had encountered at least among the English settlers in the American colonies. That is to say, the idea of revolution in France compelled Paine to reflect upon the importance of equality in his natural rights philosophy with renewed urgency. The *Rights of Man* also emerged from a stimulating intellectual milieu in Paris during the same period in the late 1780s when his friend and fellow Francophile Thomas Jefferson first developed his influential theory of generational justice.[16] Paine's later work was deeply impacted by Jefferson's call for the need to rethink the important temporal dimension in natural rights theory and of property rights in particular.

However, the most direct impetus for Paine's writing at this time was his desire to respond to his former friend Edmund Burke's scathing attacks on the French Revolution. It was as a rejoinder to Burke's historically based conception of government and rights that Paine developed arguably his most rigorous account of the natural grounds of both individual rights and legitimate government. Burke was less interested in discovering the theoretical grounds for the right of property than he was keen to affirm the social and political meaning of property as a vital element in the complex, hierarchical organic whole that is society.[17] Old money in the form of a traditional landholding class is, in Burke's view, 'sluggish, inert and timid' compared with the rising educated and entrepreneurial professional class.[18] But as 'the power of perpetuating our property in our families' is one of the socially stabilising factors that 'tend most to the preservation of society itself', it is a matter of great political significance that any balanced constitution imitate Britain by preserving and empowering a 'House of Peers . . . composed of hereditary property and hereditary distinction'.[19] Paine's redistributionist proposals in the *Rights of Man*, but especially in *Agrarian Justice*, would be diametrically opposed to Burke's conservative account of property and society.

In his American Revolution-era writings Paine presupposed a fundamentally Lockean conception of individual natural rights that he believed required a minimalist state dedicated to the preservation of property and the sanctity of contract. However, in the later *Rights of Man* Paine emphasised the normative principle of natural equality, which he proposes has both a logical-secular meaning and a theological basis. In response to Burke's argument that political rights derive from conventions that harden over time, Paine countered that if one attempts to trace the origin of rights back 'by precedents drawn from antiquity', then the effort is doomed to result in futile infinite regression for each generation in the past had ancients of their own, just 'as we shall also be ancients in our turn' (RM 215). Given the impossibility of discovering through historical examination when the 'rights of man' assumed reality, then the logical default is that these rights must be natural, for 'here our inquiries find a resting place, and our reason finds a home' (RM 215). Not only does history lead us into a theoretical cul-de-sac in the search for the origin of rights, the mere attempt to ground rights in history smacks of blasphemy as Paine insists that: 'The Mosaic account of Creation, whether taken as divine authority, or merely historical, is full to this point, the unity or equality of men . . . so far from being a modern doctrine, is the oldest upon record' (RM 216).

Even as Paine insists that reason and revelation confirm natural equality, this proposition does not completely respond to Burke, whose complaints about natural rights philosophy had less to do with the existence of natural rights, than it did with Burke's rejection of the moral significance of this primordial equality in civil society at present. Are these natural rights relevant today when compared with the substantive legal rights of actual Frenchmen or Englishmen? The heart of the dispute between Paine and Burke thus revolved around the question of the relation between natural rights and civil rights. Paine insisted that natural rights constitute the logical and moral 'foundations of all civil rights' in any polity (RM 217). In contrast, Burke dismissed 'metaphysic rights' as politically irrelevant until 'emerging into common life, like rays of light which pierce into a dense medium', these laws of nature 'undergo such a variety of refractions and reflections, that it becomes absurd to talk of them as if they continued in the simplicity of their original direction'.[20] The natural right to property is so highly conditioned by society in Burke's mind that it is only 'the rights of men under governments', that is, in particular communities, that produce 'advantages'.[21] For Paine, on the other hand, the causal connection between natural and civil rights is direct. Natural rights 'appertain to man in right of his existence' (RM 217). There are thus two kinds of natural rights, one relating to intellectual activity or 'rights of the mind', and the other pertaining to external actions that aim towards an individual's 'own comfort and happiness', but which are not injurious to the natural rights of others (RM 217). Civil rights, then, are simply the social manifestation of these natural rights – both intellectual and active – that pertain to the individual 'in right of his being a member of society' (RM 217). In contrast to the striking conventionalism of Burke, Paine affirms that civil rights derive their primary moral force from an intelligible and recognisable natural foundation.

Perhaps the clearest indication of the moral priority of nature in Paine's conception of rights is his insistence that certain natural rights are retained entirely even under civil government, while other natural rights are not retained in full, but are in part surrendered to government. The main difference between those natural rights that are retained in civil society and those that are not lies in the individual's power to execute that right as an individual. Thus, the 'rights of mind' relating to religious belief or to philosophical inquiry are retained in full because the individual is perfectly capable of forming judgements on his or her own. But the individual right to judge in one's own cause in a dispute with others is surrendered to civil government, at least with respect to actions, because the individual is unable, or at least much less able, to protect one's self and one's property without the support of 'the common stock of society' (RM 218). In keeping with the Lockean premise of his natural rights doctrine, Paine concluded that while civil power is constituted as the aggregate class of natural rights, this does not mean that the aggregate power of natural rights can be applied to justify the invasion of natural rights retained by individuals (RM 218). For Paine, as for Locke, surrendering part of the individual's natural right in order to empower government can be justified only if the end of government action is protection of those rights.

A second major difference between Burke and Paine arose in the context of intergenerational relations. Burke's historicised conception of rights presupposed that the fundamental experience of rights possession is as the beneficiary of an 'entailed inheritance'.[22] By way of a favourable comparison between the historic rights concept in England's Glorious Revolution, and the more radical theoretical natural rights philosophy of the French Revolution, Burke declared: 'We wished at the period of the [Glorious] Revolution, and do now wish, to derive all we possess as an inheritance from our forefathers.'[23] For Burke, not only does the idea of English political rights derive intellectual inspiration from 'our forefathers', but also their

moral obligations are historically entailed unto the present generation: 'All the reformations we have hitherto made have proceeded
upon the principle of reverence to antiquity.'[24] Burke's political
creed amounts to the dictum that no one alive today is responsible
for the rights and freedoms that the present generation enjoy.

Needless to say, Paine dismissed Burke's argument for inherited
rights as being profoundly opposed to reason: 'Time, and change
of circumstances and opinion, have the same progressive effect in
rendering modes of government obsolete, as they have upon customs and manners' (RM 262). Indeed, Paine claims that in the
Age of Enlightenment: 'Government is but now beginning to be
known' (RM 305). He is confident, however, that one thing that is
now beginning to be much better understood than in the past is the
moral obligations among generations. In this respect, Paine echoed
his friend Thomas Jefferson's conclusion in the latter's famous 1789
letter to James Madison that the answer to the 'question whether
one generation of men has a right to bind another', is that it is 'self-
evident' that 'the earth belongs in usufruct to the living: that the dead
have neither powers nor rights over it'.[25] Paine drew from this premise his own radical conclusion that as for 'every child born' today,
'the world is as new to him as to the first man that existed' (RM
216). Being born equally into society, every individual gains entry
into the harmony of interests as the 'common interest regulates their
concerns, and forms their laws' (RM 266). Paine's account of the
economic foundations of political society is practically unchanged
between *Common Sense* and the *Rights of Man* fifteen years later.
What is new, however, is Paine's focus on the problem of economic
inequality in the latter. In contrast to the consensual and cooperative
economic activities that occur under the 'great laws of society', Paine
now highlighted the problem of inequality, which he attributed to
the 'excess and inequality of taxation' caused by governments (RM
269). So badly has unwise tax policy distorted the natural harmony
of economic interests in society that 'a great mass of the community are thrown thereby into poverty and discontent' (RM 269).
Government, then, is not just the 'necessary evil' described in *Common Sense*, but becomes in the context of *ancien régime* France a
positive evil as the prime cause of economic inequality.

In order to understand Paine's claim that extreme economic
inequality is an artificially produced condition that has become
a malignant inheritance in present times, it is helpful to consider
Paine's account of intergenerational justice in his 'Dissertation
on First Principles of Government' from early 1795. In this tract,

Paine modified the Lockean natural rights argument of his earlier works by redefining contractualism in a new spatio-temporal frame of reference. In particular, Paine re-framed 'a nation' as a multi-generational collective in which generally speaking the 'minority in years [under 21] are the majority in numbers'.[26] In this 'ever running flood of generations' no part is superior to another, but the real normative thrust of Paine's argument derives from a sense of futurity, for 'the rights of minors are as sacred as the rights of the aged' (FPG 456). This conception of intergenerational justice posed a serious challenge to any rights theory that sought to promote the sanctity of contract. Paine doubted whether the vested interests of one generation can bind future generations. With clear resemblance to Jefferson's rhetoric about the earth belonging in usufruct to the living, Paine concludes that the present generations in any nation are 'but tenants for life in the great freehold of rights' (FPG 457). Perhaps Paine's most radical deduction from this principle of natural equality is what he took to be the economic implications of his temporal conception of rights, which casts doubt on the entire property settlement that entrenches inequality in the present: 'Who are the persons that have a right to establish this inequality? Will the rich exclude themselves? No. Will the poor exclude themselves? No. By what right then can any be excluded?' (FPG 459).

The introduction of a temporal dimension to Paine's rights theory supplied additional moral force to his argument for a refined focus on equality. But Paine did not believe natural rights required perfect equality. Rather, he acknowledged: 'That property will ever be unequal is certain. Industry, superiority of talents, dexterity of management . . . will ever produce that effect' (FPG 462). What the temporal aspect of his rights theory did entail, however, was a significant social welfare responsibility for 'the protection of a man's person is more sacred than the protection of property' (FPG 462). But if, as Paine claims, in a multi-generational society 'rights become duties by reciprocity' (FPG 461), what are the responsibilities of government with respect to reducing the economic inequality produced by government itself? In the closing section of *Rights of Man Part II* Paine proposed a series of reforms that would serve the double purpose of: (1) ending the government policies and practices that produced extreme inequality in the first place; and (2) providing some measure of immediate poor relief. Reformed governments must restore equity to the revenue-raising system by introducing progressive taxation and eliminating the historic 'poor rates' so as to shift the tax burden from the lower and middle classes to the more affluent segments of society. Paine also demanded dramatic cuts in military spending and the elimination of patronage positions littered with corrupt 'placemen' (RM 342). While seeking to 'lessen the burden of taxes', Paine nevertheless, in contrast to Hume and Smith, lauds the salutary effects of maintaining a manageable national debt, even as he insisted on finding new ways to finance the state that do not risk exacerbating inequality (RM 327).

Arguably Paine's most radical proposals relate to his plans for poor relief. These measures included direct annual payments to the elderly, a government donation of twenty shillings upon the occasion of each wedding and new birth, government subsidies to support the education of poor children and certain funeral expenses, and, finally, the establishment of workhouses in London that would effectively guarantee full employment in the English capital (RM 350). What is striking about Paine's proposals for poor relief is not just their radical expansion beyond prevailing ideas about economic inequality at the time. Rather, what is most remarkable about Paine's anti-poverty proposals is that he interpreted these policies as being 'not of the nature of a charity, but of a right' (RM 337). The *Rights of Man* contains redistributionist policy proposals that seem to contradict Paine's earlier account of the minimalist night watchman state. While in 1792 Paine identified government taxation as a source of economic inequality – something we might expect from his earlier work – it is nonetheless surprising to read the extensive role he assigned to government spending programmes as the means to reduce poverty. Poverty is a feature of intergenerational justice that Paine believed direct government action could ameliorate or even remedy. The message then coming out of the *Rights of Man Part II* is that economic inequality is a problem that revolutionary governments need to address, at least in the transitional phase, towards the establishment of the natural rights republic.

Agrarian Justice and the Positive State

Paine's last major work, *Agrarian Justice*, was written during the winter of 1795–6. This is a remarkable work for a number of reasons. First, it signifies a radical extension of the social welfare themes of the *Rights of Man*. However, now Paine's chief antagonist is no longer the British conservative Burke, but rather the radical French revolutionary Gracchus Babeuf who conspired to produce a popular revolt against the government of the Directory in 1795.[27] Paine's audience for this tract is nonetheless somewhat ambiguous inasmuch as while he insists that 'the plan contained in this work is not adapted for any particular country alone', Paine entrusted his 'little work' to the 'safeguard' of the Legislative and Executive Directory of the French Republic, and employed budgetary figures from England to illustrate his plan (AJ 471, 480–2). Paine's fundamental argument is that the system of landed property in economically advanced countries has deprived the vast majority of inhabitants of their 'natural inheritance' to the common property of the nation. The novel revenue source Paine introduces as the mechanism to indemnify the victims of landed property is a 'National Fund' supplied by a 'ground rent' system of estate taxes on landed holdings. The theoretical grounding of the National Fund reflects two major influences. First, Paine drew from Physiocrat thinkers the basic idea that the agricultural land in a nation actually belongs to the state.[28] The estate tax, then, is essentially a policy designed to operationalise state reclamation of its due, albeit upon the titular owner's demise rather than annually. Second, the National Fund reflects the way in which Paine's evolving understanding of the spatio-temporal limits on individual property rights compelled him to modify some of the fundamental assumptions of Locke's natural rights theory.

Ironically, Paine practically begins *Agrarian Justice* with a reference in the 'Preface' not to the proto-communist Babeuf, but rather to the more traditional Anglican Bishop Watson of Llandaff who had published a sermon stating that God in 'His Wisdom and Goodness' made both the rich and the poor (AJ 474). It is the sentiment expressed in this sermon that prompted Paine to reflect upon the putative naturalness of property and economic inequality. There are, Paine concludes, two kinds of property: (1) 'natural property', or that which comes from the 'Creator of the Universe' such as earth, air and water; and (2) 'artificial property', which is the 'invention of men' (AJ 472). This is the first time in Paine's major writings that he made this distinction. In a departure from Lockean orthodoxy, Paine categorised the kind of property produced by labour as 'artificial', whereas 'natural property' represents what he earlier identified as the original natural commons. Paine dismissed the question of establishing equality with respect to 'acquired' property due to the fact that this would require that 'all should have contributed in the same proportion, which can never be the case' (AJ 472). The focus, then, of *Agrarian Justice* is on the question of the nature of the original commons. In his earlier writings, Paine followed Locke in ascribing a negative quality to the original commons such that no individual had by nature any greater claim on natural goods than anyone else: no one by nature owned anything in the external world. However, in *Agrarian Justice* Paine's argument about natural property shifted towards an original positive commons such that everyone by nature *does indeed* have a claim to part of the original commons: 'Every individual in the world is born therein with legitimate claims on a certain kind of property, or its equivalent' (AJ 472).

Paine's focus on the idea of equality derived from a conception of positive original commons transformed his analysis of political life. The dichotomy between society and government that had been so prominent in Paine's early writings is now replaced with the bifurcation involving 'civilisation' and 'nature'. Traditionally, the objection to the idea of positive original commons, made, for example, by Locke, was that it seems to produce the moral requirement that the entire human race must consent in order for any individual to acquire property rights in any particular thing.[29] But Paine's adoption of the positive original commons model in *Agrarian Justice* reframed the issue of consent: why would anyone consent to their own permanent dispossession of that to which they enjoy a natural right with everyone else? In a stunning inversion of the stadial history of Hume and Smith, *civilisation* is the term Paine used to identify the socio-economic condition in which the majority of people no longer have access to this natural property, especially the earth or land, that originally belonged to all. The main purpose of Paine's 'reformed legislation' is 'to preserve the benefits of what is called civilised life, and to remedy at the same time the evil which it has produced' (AJ 474). Perhaps surprisingly, given his previous unabashed enthusiasm for progress in *Rights of Man*, Paine now declares that the question of whether civilisation has contributed to or injured general human happiness is one 'that may be strongly contested' (AJ 474), presumably between the Rousseauian, for whom the putative benefits of civilisation are highly problematic, and the Lockean, for whom the presumptive evils of civilisation are hard to perceive.[30]

The central feature of Paine's critique of civilisation is the moral problem of poverty. Paine asserts that poverty is 'a thing created by that which is called civilised life. It exists not in the natural state' (AJ 475). The cause of poverty is inequality. Unlike the basic equality enjoyed by those such as the 'Indians of North America' who live in the 'natural and primitive state of man', civilised life is characterised by dazzling 'splendid appearances', as well as shocking 'extremes of wretchedness' (AJ 474). Paine does not deny that the 'natural state is without those advantages which flow from agriculture, arts, science and manufactures' (AJ 475). Given this admission, why does Paine not endorse the argument of John Locke and Adam Smith, who claimed that despite the relative inequality in advanced economies it was better in material terms to be in the poorest class in Europe than to be a king in pre-colonial America or Africa?[31] For Paine, the human misery caused by poverty reflects an important psychological injury that seems to arise precisely because the inequality is relative. The class divisions in civilised countries with this comparative dimension have such a scarring effect on the development of human personality that Paine insists the life of 'an Indian is a continual holiday, compared with the poor in Europe' (AJ 475). Thus, civilisation stands accused of producing conditions for millions of people 'in every country in Europe' that means they are 'far worse' off than if they had been born before civilisation began (AJ 475).

Civilisation is a paradox for Paine. On the one hand, a return to the natural condition is both impossible and undesirable because 'man in a natural state, subsisting by hunting, requires ten times the quantity of land to range over to procure himself, than would support him in a civilised state, where the earth is cultivated' (AJ 475). Thus, in heavily populated civilised lands only one-tenth of the inhabitants would survive the return to nature. But, on the other hand, civilisation reflects the temporal dimension of Paine's evolving conception of natural rights in a particularly negative sense in that poverty acquires generational status 'like dead and living bodies chained together' in historical conditions in which the poor are like an 'hereditary race' (AJ 482, 484). Neither the benefits nor the evils of civilisation can be determined on purely utilitarian grounds precisely because the principle of a positive original commons provides a moral standard by which to judge private acquisition.

One of the examples of the joint-ownership character of natural property is, according to Paine, the universal right of access to water in common wells in Arabia. The earth no less than water was also originally 'the common property of the human race', for by nature 'it was not admitted that land could be claimed as property' (AJ 476). Natural reason also tells us that every individual is by nature a 'joint-life proprietor with the rest in the property of the soil and in all its natural production, vegetables and animals' (AJ 476). How then did the idea of landed property and the subsequent massive economic inequality arise? The original source of this inequality is, of course, labour, which Paine concludes is the source of the improvement made to the earth through cultivation. More precisely, for Paine the source of landed wealth derives from the fact that 'it is impossible to separate the improvement made by cultivation from the earth itself' (AJ 476). Paine's sense of the spatio-temporal limits on natural rights compels him to reject the right of first occupant because a given labourer 'had no right to locate as his property in perpetuity any part of it' (AJ 476). There was no idea of landed property prior to agriculture as hunters and herdsmen such as the Old Testament patriarchs Abraham, Isaac and Jacob were not land-owners (AJ 476). Ownership of land became possible only when the value of the improvement created by labour so far exceeded the value of the earth at that time 'as to absorb it' (AJ 477).

Is Paine not admitting, á la Locke, that labour creates the value that adds something to a common resource, which thereafter pro-duces a morally acceptable claim to private ownership?[32] There is clearly some truth to this notion insofar as Paine calculates that cultivation has increased the value of the earth 'tenfold' (AJ 477). But this figure is considerably less than the thousand-fold increase in value produced by labour in Locke's assessment.[33] Determining Paine's real judgement about the value of labour is also compli-cated by his assertion that it is perhaps 'impossible to proportion exactly the price of labour to the profits it produces', even as he acknowledged that the 'accumulation of personal property is in many instances the effect of paying too little for the labour that produced it' (AJ 485).

The ambiguity in Paine's evaluation of the value of labour reflects a deepening of his commitment to the idea of usufruct in *Agrarian Justice*. The significance of labour as the source of private right is rendered tenuous, or at least limited, by the perpetual moral sig-nificance of the positive original commons. This is not to mention that most landowners in Paine's time did not acquire their right by labour, but by inheritance. At any rate, at no time did, or logi-cally ever could, individuals have consented to the abandonment of their common right to 'natural property', especially the earth. The undeniable advantages produced by cultivation do not outweigh the fact that the 'landed monopoly' characteristic of civilisation 'has produced the greatest evil' (AJ 477). The great problem of economic inequality comes down to the apparent inseparability of the improvements made by cultivation from the value of the earth itself, which situation sets up the contest of rights claims between 'the common right of all' that became 'confounded into the cul-tivated right of the individual' (AJ 477). Labour, then, does not entail the extinguishment of the 'common right of all', but it does in Paine's view generate a temporally subsequent individual right to the 'acquired' property produced by labour. Paine concludes that the co-existence of these 'distinct species of rights' is permanent 'so long as the earth endures' (AJ 477). The attempt to reconcile these 'distinct species of rights' drove Paine's radical proposals in *Agrarian Justice* as he tried to devise a plan that would compensate, or even provide reparations to, the millions of landless poor in Europe who had been effectively dispossessed of their common right, while simultaneously respecting the legal rights of those individuals who had acquired property through labour or by inheritance.

Paine's proposed 'National Fund' in *Agrarian Justice* represents a departure from his earlier treatment of social welfare in *Rights of Man Part II* on a number of counts. The National Fund is a new way to finance the social welfare system that does not rely on progressive taxation and spending cuts but, rather, is supplied almost exclusively by a sizeable estate tax levied on the inheritors of landed property. While Paine reiterated that justice for the dispossessed is a matter of 'right, not a charity' (AJ 477), in *Agrarian Justice* this right is grounded in an historical claim to reparations for damages done, rather than directly from an equal natural right to self-preservation. Every proprietor 'owes to the community a ground rent . . . for the land which he holds' (AJ 476). The moral obligation imposed on the direct beneficiaries of land ownership presupposes the continuing protection of their property rights by the community. As such, Paine insists that 'agrarian justice' is not animated by the same principle as the ancient Roman 'agrarian laws' that proposed to establish equal allotments of property holdings. The estate tax plan operates on the assumption that the dispossessed majority of the population can be indemnified for their loss 'by subtracting from property a portion equal in value to the natural inheritance it has absorbed' (AJ 478). Notably, Paine highlights the potentially far-reaching egalitarian implications of his National Fund, which he insists will provide direct benefits to compensate individuals 'for the loss of his or her natural inheritance' (AJ 478).[34]

The National Fund plan is elegant in its simplicity. The inheritors of every landed estate will pay a 10 per cent tax on the value of the estate upon the death of the owner, and more than 10 per cent if the owner dies without any direct heirs or close family. Based on 1796 English fiscal year figures, Paine calculated that this estate tax would generate £5.6 million per annum. The primary beneficiaries of the National Fund would be disabled people 'totally incapable of earning a livelihood' and those over the age of fifty, who would receive

£10 annually (AJ 481–2). In keeping with the proposals in *Rights of Man Part II* to provide a one-time marriage and baby bonus, in *Agrarian Justice* Paine declares that the National Fund 'will furnish the rising generation with means to prevent their becoming poor' by providing a £15 start-up fund for each newly married couple (AJ 483). Paine judges that payment to the 'rising generation' is a strategic social investment in the community: 'When a young couple begin [in] the world, the difference is exceedingly great whether they begin with nothing or with fifteen pounds apiece' (AJ 483). Paine stipulates that the benefits must be universal in order to avoid creating invidious distinctions. The overall purpose of the National Fund is unambiguously redistributionist as Paine predicts that in every thirty-year generational cycle, the entire 'capital of a nation, or a sum equal thereto, will revolve once' (AJ 479).

Some commentators interpret Paine's proposals in *Agrarian Justice* as a function of his bourgeois radicalism, that is to say, he viewed social welfare programmes as a prudential measure designed to protect the system of private property against plebeian revolution from below.[35] There is some truth to the observation that Paine framed even his most radical proposals in terms of a kind of moderation. For example, Paine predicted that the National Fund would alleviate poverty over 'successive generations without diminishing or deranging the property of the present possessors' (AJ 478). Indeed, he insisted that great economic inequality was not the fault of 'the present possessors' of landed wealth, but 'the fault is in the system' (AJ 478). Moreover, in contrast to the proto-communist Babeuf, Paine presented his proposals as a means to protect the rights of 'all those who have been thrown out of their natural inheritance', as well as 'equally defend the right of the possessor to the part which is his' (AJ 477). However, it is important to acknowledge that Paine viewed even this balanced approach to property rights as likely not practicable until there has been 'a revolution in the system of government' (AJ 477). Rather than a prudential public policy intended to defuse class antagonisms, Paine viewed the National Fund reparations scheme in terms of a conception of distributive justice: 'that not a man or woman born in the Republic but shall inherit some means of beginning the world, and see before them the certainty of escaping the miseries that . . . accompany old age' (AJ 487). Paine's assumption was that the social welfare imperative in *Agrarian Justice* was a function of revolutionary 'national justice', which will find advocates 'in the heart of all nations' (AJ 484, 487).

Why did Paine believe that it was the state's responsibility to indemnify individuals dispossessed by the historical development of landed property? On one level, Paine's argument seems to be a practical one; namely, that no system of philanthropic charities would be capable of alleviating mass poverty and chronic inequality. Only the revolutionary republic possesses the institutional structures and administrative expertise to tackle this gargantuan task: 'It is only by organising civilisation upon such principles as to act like a system of pulleys that the whole weight of misery can be removed' (AJ 483). Unlike charity, political justice is non-voluntary as it does not depend upon the 'choice of detached individuals' (AJ 483). The National Fund plan should be seen as 'growing spontaneously' out of revolutionary principles and must be national in scope (AJ 483).

The other reason Paine provides for the state's unique role as guarantor of social welfare and redistribution of wealth relates to the way in which the state represents society. The theoretical importance of the representative function of the state is that it grounds Paine's claim that individuals generate a social debt due to enjoyment of the benefits of their rights: 'It is as impossible for any individual to acquire personal property without the aid of society, as it is for him to make land originally' (AJ 485). Paine's assumption of natural sociability – a feature of his thought since *Common Sense* – now provides the moral justification for redistributionist policies that would have been unimaginable in Paine's earlier works: 'all accumulation . . . of personal property; beyond what a man's own hands produce, is derived to him by living in society' (AJ 485). Paine's positive state in *Agrarian Justice* becomes the 'treasurer to guard' the individual's property in an economic system that aspires to 'make property productive of a national blessing, extending to every individual' (AJ 486). It is now the state rather than a pre-political idyllic condition of 'society' that promotes, and even imposes, the harmony of interests: 'when the more a man acquires, the better it shall be for the general mass' (AJ 486). *Agrarian Justice* arguably represents the theoretical culmination of Paine's political economy in a conception of the state that gradually developed from a commitment to the sanctity of contract to the principle of massive redistribution of wealth, and from a concept of natural rights that emphasised the moral priority of consent to a vision of substantive economic rights.

This chapter aimed to demonstrate that Thomas Paine's account of the relation between politics and economics underwent a significant transformation throughout his career. He went from being an advocate of a minimalist night watchman state and laissez faire individualism to becoming a champion of the positive state committed to the principles of social welfare. But this transformation was not a product of Paine abandoning or radically altering his core philosophical commitments. Rather, the development of his thoughts on government emerged from his reflections upon the moral meaning and political and economic implications of natural rights theory. Paine's political economy illustrates the degree to which concepts such as natural rights, private property and contract were historically fluid and contested ideas as he reinterpreted the Lockean notion of property rights through spatial and temporal limits on the concept of private ownership. Paine thus introduced the principle of positive original common – the normative claim that natural property, including land, belongs to the entire national, if not human, community – into the post-French Revolution account of 'national justice'. In the process, Paine's later work not only, as we shall see in the following chapter, adumbrated the liberal normative economics of the nineteenth-century utilitarian 'philosophical radicals', but also in important ways was a theoretical anticipation of the modern welfare state.

Notes

1. See, e.g., Lamb 2015; Claeys 2003; Fruchtman 2009.
2. See Dorfman 1938: 386; Foner 1976: 146; Foot and Kramnick 1987: 26–27; Nelson 2006: 290; Kaye 2006: 136; Thompson 2007: 145, 159–60.
3. Christian 1973: 367–8; Seaman 1988: 122; Zuckert 2013: 252–3; Fatovic 2015: 221–60.
4. Quoted in O'Neill 2007: 1.
5. Paine 1987a: 337. Hereafter in notes and text RM and page number.
6. Paine 1987b: 79. Hereafter in notes and text CS and page number.
7. Compare Hobbes 1994: ch. 13, ss. 5–8, pp. 75–8 and Locke 2016 II:13, 19, 21.
8. Compare with Locke 2016, II:90–1.
9. Locke 2016 II:87, 124.
10. Locke 2016, II:25–8.
11. Smith 1981: 456. Several commentators have observed Paine's indebtedness to Smith (e.g., Fleischaker 2004: 198, Foner 1977: 153–6; Fruchtman 1993: 102; Jones 2004: 41). For readings of Paine that are more sceptical of the connection to Smith, see Claeys 2003: 97–8; Lamb 2015: 114–15. I maintain that Paine's political economy shifted gradually from a laissez faire doctrine akin to Smith's eventually towards a positive, welfare state.

12. Canavan 1987: 681; Ward 2004: 378.
13. Locke 2016 II:14.
14. Ward 2004: 379; Foner 1976: 92.
15. Paine 1987c: 172. Hereafter in notes and text DGP and page number. Paine insists that legal bankruptcy is not a 'dissolution of contract' (DGP 171).
16. For a good discussion of the mutual influences Paine and Jefferson had on each other in Paris in the late 1780s, see Philp 2013: 144.
17. Canavan 1995: 51. Canavan sees Burke's political economy as fairly mercantilist (1995: 119). For the contrary view that sees Burke as a proponent of Smith's idea of commercial liberty, see Collins 2017.
18. Burke 1987: 55.
19. Burke 1987: 55.
20. Burke 1987: 65–6.
21. Burke 1987: 66.
22. Burke 1987: 37.
23. Burke 1987: 35.
24. Burke 1987: 35.
25. Jefferson 1950: 392.
26. Paine 1987d: 455. Hereafter in notes and text FPG and page number.
27. Paine 1987e: 472. Hereafter in notes and text AJ and page number.
28. See Seligman 1921: 125–42.
29. Locke famously argued that: 'If such a consent as that was necessary, man had starved, notwithstanding the plenty God had given him" (Locke 2016, II:28).
30. Fatovic (2015: 237, 247) and Fruchtman (2009: 123) argue persuasively that Rousseau's critique of civilisation in the *Second Discourse on the Origins of Inequality* influenced Paine's argument in *Agrarian Justice*.
31. Locke 2016 II:41; Smith 1981: 24.
32. For a thoughtful treatment of the potential distinction Paine makes between the creation of value by labour and the increase in value, see Lamb 2015: 129–33.
33. Locke 2016 II:40.
34. This is perhaps an uncharacteristic expression of concern for sexual equality on Paine's part (but compare with CS 72).
35. Seaman 1988: 133; Dorfman 1938: 382–3; Kaye 2006: 136.

Chapter 6

John Stuart Mill and the Stationary State

John Stuart Mill is often seen as an important figure in the transition from the classical liberalism of the seventeenth and eighteenth centuries to the more egalitarian, social welfare form of liberalism that emerged in response to the effects of the Industrial Revolution later in twentieth-century Britain.[1] For our purposes, however, it is perhaps more significant to highlight Mill's role as a kind of culmination of classical liberal political economy. In Mill's political and economic writings, we see both direct linkages back to the rights and interest-based conceptual nerve centre of classical liberalism, as well as a fuller development of the early liberal response to socialism and communism we first encountered in Paine's *Agrarian Justice*. Mill is also arguably the last British thinker to offer a comprehensive philosophy including rigorous and systematic reflections on politics, ethics, morality, aesthetics, economics, logic and culture. An unparalleled intellectual provocateur, Mill was the epitome of the philosopher *engagé* who spent many decades publicly commenting on political and philosophical controversies in a variety of journals and newspapers, and even served a three-year term in Parliament as the MP for Westminster.

Today Mill is probably best known as the author of *On Liberty* (1859), one of the seminal texts in the liberal tradition of free speech, personal autonomy and pluralism. However, in his time Mill was at least as famous for his writings on political economy, especially his massive *Principles of Political Economy* (1848), which passed through more than a half dozen editions in Mill's lifetime and became established as the classic textbook of British political economy for decades until the appearance of Alfred Marshall's 1890

Principles of Economics.[2] The principle of individual freedom as the requirement for the full development of human character underlies Mill's political economy as fully as it does every other aspect of his thought.[3] It is perhaps hardly surprising that the same thinker who proclaimed in *On Liberty* that 'over himself, over his own body and mind, the individual is sovereign', would have professed earlier in his economic writings that 'there is a part of the life of every person who has come to years of discretion within which the individuality of that person ought to reign uncontrolled either by any other individual or by the public collectively'.[4] In terms of political economy, the most important aspect of his commitment to individual freedom is Mill's application of this logic with apparent full force to the economic realm as he famously declaimed: 'Laisser faire, in short, should be the general practice, every departure from it, unless required by some great good, is a certain evil' (CW 3:938, 945). As we shall see, Mill believed clarifying and negotiating the relation between the idea of the moral primacy of the individual, on the one hand, and his conviction that historical progress is drawing human beings into ever greater and more complex forms of social organisation, on the other (for Mill, the two pre-eminent normative truths discovered in late modernity), was the central task of political economy.

The connection between his defence of liberty and his reflections on political economy helps us to locate Mill in the broader tradition of classical liberalism. Mill's utilitarian philosophy clearly rejected the discourse of natural rights, but his endorsement of the doctrine of interest was not simply a restatement of what came before. Much as what Mill called Jeremy Bentham's 'philosophy of interests' expanded upon the idea of utility latent in the Scottish Enlightenment thinkers such as Hume and Smith, similarly did Mill modify, or to his mind 'humanise', Bentham's version of utility by removing what he took to be its reductionist and excessively materialist tendencies.[5] Mill's emphasis on individuality and human dignity not only brought utilitarian theory closer to the deontological claims of the natural rights tradition, but we shall see that Mill's political economy culminated in an account of a liberal best regime of sorts adapted from the concept of the 'stationary state' inherited from the classical political economy of Adam Smith, Thomas Malthus and David Ricardo.

Mill's brief, but puzzling, passage about the stationary state in Book 4 of the *Principles* has confounded commentators for nearly two centuries. In this remarkable sketch, Mill reflected upon the concept of the zero-economic growth 'stationary state' – the dreaded bane of classical political economy since Adam Smith – and reinterpreted it in laudatory terms as what one observer has called a 'liberal utopia'.[6] Commentators are divided, however, as to the central principle animating Mill's case for the stationary state, with it being seen variously as part of an argument for an ancient Aristotelian idea of happiness,[7] for civic republicanism,[8] for a version of proto-socialism,[9] as a rejection of socialism on behalf of economic liberty,[10] and as a revision of Ricardian economic theory.[11] I offer an alternative reading of Mill's stationary state, one that emphasises his intention to establish a normative economics that promotes liberal pluralism insofar as the stationary state represents the absorption of abstract individual rights into the concrete interests of a community animated by a spirit of cultural progress. Herein lies the central paradox of Mill's political economy as he highlights the tension between the goal of cultivating individual thoughts, beliefs and thoughts, on the one hand, and the seemingly inexorable course of historical progress, on the other, which is characterised by the ever-increasing capacity for social cooperation.

The ambiguity in Mill's approach to economics lies in the fundamentally normative bent of his analysis as he sought to establish a model of political economy inspired by a vision of intellectual and moral progress, rather than the psychological and cultural addiction to endlessly increasing productive capacities. Even as he critiqued socialism, Mill sought to correct the laissez faire doctrine by illuminating the positive role the state can have in creating the conditions allowing for a harmony of interests in the economic sphere.[12] In Mill's rendering, the zero-growth economy of the stationary state signified a liberal cultural ideal that facilitates a transformative stage in the development of the human capacity for public spirit. This is an historical process which Mill suggests transcends the consuming ideological quarrels of the period, pointing hopefully towards vistas of political economy beyond the rigid formulas of either capitalism or socialism. In this way, Mill's political economy illuminated the material conditions for a non-economic, and decisively moral, end or *telos* for what he termed the 'Art of Life' that makes it theoretically possible to reconcile the normative claims of the autonomous individual with the permanent interests of humanity as a progressive being.

In order to fully appreciate the range and depth of Mill's political economy, as well as situate his economic thought in the classical liberal tradition more generally, we will begin with a brief examination of Mill's formative intellectual influences. We will then turn to Mill's economic writings themselves and examine the main features of his critique of socialism, as well as his argument for the importance of, but also limitations on, the doctrine of laissez faire. This chapter will conclude with a consideration of Mill's remarkable postulation of the stationary state as it provided the framework for his reinterpretation of liberal political economy in terms of distributive justice and the moral and intellectual improvement of the working classes.

Utility and Classical Political Economy

Before we turn to Mill's economic writings, it is important to familiarise ourselves with the complex intellectual context of the period. As is well known, the formative philosophical influence on John Stuart Mill was the utilitarian philosophy established by Jeremy Bentham and promoted by his father and Bentham's close friend James Mill. Bentham and James Mill were the driving forces behind the school of 'philosophical radicalism' that provided John Mill's primary political education. According to Bentham, political and economic institutions should be designed such that self-interested individuals have sufficient motivations to act so as to maximise general happiness, understood as the sum of individual happiness.[13] Bentham thus transformed utility from an instrumental principle of legitimacy contrasted to consent and rights claims, as was characteristic of Hume, for instance, into a substantive end determined by the greatest happiness for the greatest number with happiness measured by excess pleasure over pain.[14] But in terms of economics, Bentham was in basic agreement with Hume regarding the conventional basis of property rights, and a general presumption in favour of free markets and the benefits of luxury.[15]

John Mill characterised Bentham's version of utilitarianism as an 'interest philosophy' (CW 8:890). The epistemological foundation of this interest-based liberal politics was the philosophy of mind termed *associationism*. As we saw in Chapter 4, associationism traces its roots back to Hume's *Treatise of Human Nature* (1739) in which he claimed that ideas are formed when sense perceptions are combined in the mind according to mechanical laws analogous to the laws of physics.[16] For Bentham, interest-based politics is a function of his philosophy of intellectual hedonism. Whereas the earlier form of interest-based liberalism in Hume and Smith typically sought to discover some innate psychological propensity towards benevolent concern for others, Bentham and his followers deployed associationism as a means to formulate a mechanical system for generating concern for the common good artificially.[17] It was James Mill who provided Benthamite 'philosophical radicalism' with much of its democratic aura by championing majority-rule democracy and populist parliamentary reforms as the logical outcome of this hedonistic psychology. In James Mill's democratised interest philosophy, good government depends upon the identity of interest between the governing body and the community at large.[18]

The other formative influence on John Mill's political economy was, of course, the venerable tradition of classical political economy tracing back through David Ricardo, Thomas Malthus and Adam Smith. Smith was the towering figure of classical political economy who cast an enormous shadow over his successors in the field of economics. In addition to his foundational theories of the wages fund and of the natural price, Smith also gave his imprimatur to the laissez faire doctrine with its hostility to monopolies and protectionism. In terms of political economy, perhaps Smith's most enduring legacy was the fundamental observation that for a society to be considered affluent, it required that the labouring classes be prosperous.[19] In addition to the process of economic growth or contraction that logically characterises progressive and regressive nations, Smith also posited the possibility of what he termed a 'stationary state', defined by zero-economic growth and stagnant wages and prices.[20] For Smith, the stationary state *par excellence* was China, a nation in which 'the funds destined for the maintenance of labour' (the basis for his theory of the wage fund) remained stable despite population increase, and thus wages were perpetually kept low.[21] Whereas life in the progressive state is good for the 'great body of the people' who enjoy high wages, Smith concluded that life is 'hard in the stationary, and miserable in the declining state'.[22]

While the stationary state was clearly not a desirable condition for Smith, it would be Thomas Malthus who endowed it with the dreadful image that came to characterise the concept for decades thereafter. In his landmark study *An Essay on the Principle of Population* (1798), Malthus criticised Smith for failing to recognise that not every increase in revenue improves the lot of the labouring classes.[23] For Malthus, the key factor is population or, more specifically, the spectre of overpopulation when the poorer classes most vulnerable to shortages and the resulting high prices of the 'necessaries and conveniences of life', suffer as 'population and food, increased in different ratios'.[24] Malthus imbibed the physiocratic fixation on agricultural production, but he projected a more pessimistic account of population increase and the strain it puts on a nation's resources. In the Malthusian perspective, the stationary state is a cypher, always on the verge of slipping into economic decline due to the pressures of overpopulation, for the greatest obstacle to improving the material conditions of society is 'the perpetual tendency in the race of man to increase beyond the means of subsistence'.[25]

Arguably the most formative influence on John Mill's political economy was that of his father's close friend David Ricardo. Ricardo's *The Principles of Political Economy and Taxation* (1817) formulated reductive economic laws based upon both the Benthamite conception of egoistic human psychology and the Malthusian premise of the evils of overpopulation. Ricardo famously critiqued Smith's theory of rents and values. However, he accepted the Smithian principle that there is a natural tendency for wages and profits to fall as labour becomes more plentiful. While Ricardo opposed any government attempt to set wages outside the 'fair and free competition of the market', he did advocate laws discouraging 'early and improvident marriages' that contribute to overpopulation.[26] Even if Ricardo was not as pessimistic about the concept of the stationary state as Malthus, he nonetheless characterised it as an unpleasant situation always prone to deterioration of the 'general condition' for the labouring classes.[27] Ricardo accepted the basic principle encapsulated in Say's Law (invented by French economist Jean-Baptiste Say) that production is the key to economic growth. Thus, for Ricardo the only remedies to the problem of the stationary state were the stark choice between either 'a reduction of people or a more rapid accumulation of capital through improved technology and increased production'.[28] In the tradition of classical political economy prior to John Mill, standing still economically speaking held little or no attraction, and indeed a degree of repulsion.

John Mill's intellectual development drew heavily from both the tradition of Bentham's philosophical radicalism and from classical political economy, but the trajectory of his theoretical ambitions extended the concept of utility and liberal political economy into new and original modes of thought. While a decided ambivalence towards the idea of natural rights remained a characteristic of Mill's thought throughout his career, his approach to the determination of interests also departed seriously from Bentham's original model. In the course of recovering from his well-documented psychological and emotional breakdown in his early twenties, Mill came to view the Benthamite version of rationalism as too dismissive towards the role of sentiments in forming moral judgements. In his *Autobiography*, Mill confessed that he gradually realised the considerable degree of truth in the position of critics of utilitarianism, who charged that the calculating individual imagined by Bentham was a 'mere reasoning machine', the creation of a stark account of human nature that dramatically 'undervalues feeling' (CW 1:111, 113). Mill associated Bentham's version of utility with the crude reductionist model of philosophy characteristic of the 'Geometrical or Abstract Method' pioneered by Thomas Hobbes (CW 8:889). For Mill, the hedonic formulation of Bentham and Hobbes revealed the limits of any philosophy grounded upon a narrow vision of self-interest. By contrast, in his *System of Logic* (1843) Mill proposed his own 'Concrete Deductive Method' as a superior approach to determining interests, an approach that attends to the 'internal culture of the individual' (CW 8:889; CW 1:147). Mill's 'concrete deductive method' was deeply influenced by his French contemporary Auguste Comte's sociology, which incorporated history, religion and culture into empirical laws of society (CW 8:895–8). In Mill's refined version of utilitarianism, this more expansive and sophisticated methodology allowed for distinguishing between higher and lower pleasures, and for promoting the elevation of people's moral and aesthetic sensibilities as a public good.

John Mill's break from classical political economy was perhaps less personal than his critique of Bentham's philosophical radicalism. He confided that his father James had intended that his son would someday 'correct' the economic theories of Adam Smith in the light of the work of Ricardo, but Mill's reworking of classical political economy would eventually extend well beyond a mere restatement of the Ricardian model.[29] In a manner similar to his repudiation of Bentham, Mill related in the *Autobiography* that he came to share the view of the critics of classical political economy, who rejected the 'hard-hearted' economic analysis and anti-population doctrines 'repulsive to the natural feelings of mankind' (CW 1:113). The 'concrete deductive method' as applied to political economy meant defining it sociologically and recognising that the production and distribution of wealth operate as a 'result of a plurality of motives' (CW 5:902). As we shall see, the normative basis of Mill's political economy distinguished it from his predecessors. The non-reductive study of economics Mill proposes presupposed an end or *telos* defined in terms of art rather than science (CW 8:949). Mill, thus, accepted that the empirical laws of society govern political economy too, especially as the Comtean scientific understanding of history illuminates 'the progressive development of the species and its works' (CW 8:916).

Mill's assumption is that progress means the elevation of the mental faculties over the bodily functions, as well as, more problematically, the social primacy of the masses over the individual. The pursuit of truth is the main determining cause of social progress (CW 8:924, 920). However, for Mill, the scientific method of historical analysis must stand in service of an art capable of discerning the proper end of progress. In the *System of Logic*, Mill defined this 'art of life' as comprising 'three departments', including morality (right), prudence (expedience) and aesthetics (the beautiful or noble). He insisted that the *art of living* is at present undergoing the historical process of being created and developed in real time. But he also nonetheless likens this inchoate *eudaemonic* ideal to the kind of 'Doctrine of Ends' or 'principles of practical reason' typically associated with the 'German metaphysicians' (CW 8:949–50). For Mill, these 'laws of sociology' provide the basis for a new human science to which he gives the name 'Ethology, or the Science of Character', which he claims corresponds to the 'art of education in the widest sense of the term, including the formation of national or collective character, as well as individual' (CW 8:869). This gestating art of life and ethological science of character not only promises to provide moral 'first principles of conduct', but also rules of social development that are conducive to the 'happiness of mankind' (CW 8:951). In what follows we will examine in detail Mill's political economy in the light of his commitment to a teleological art of life and science of character; that is, a moral end framed in terms of what in *On Liberty* Mill would famously identify as 'the permanent interests of man [as] progressive being' (CW 18:224).

The Problem of Socialism

In contrast to his previous major effort *The System of Logic*, upon which Mill laboured periodically for more than a decade, *The Principles of Political Economy* was completed at a comparative lightning pace in the period from the autumn of 1845 to the end of 1847. This was an auspicious time in European history for several reasons. First, the backdrop to Mill's composition of the *Principles* was the massive, seemingly inexorable humanitarian crisis that transpired on England's doorstep during the Irish Famine of 1846–1849. The consecutive failures of the potato crop set in motion a disastrous chain of events in Catholic rural Ireland that appeared like a spectral image striding cruelly from the pages of Malthus' work on population and scarcity. Mill was sensitive early on to the scale of the crisis, which would result in the death and emigration of millions of Irish people, as he expressed his concern about the situation in Ireland and the problems of the Irish cottier system in a series of articles that appeared in the Whig *Morning Chronicle* starting in early 1846.[30] The second important element in the historical context of the original publication of Mill's *Principles* was the class conflict generated by the Industrial Revolution, which would result soon after in both the liberal revolutions that swept across the continent in the summer of 1848 and in the crystallisation of the various socialist and worker's groups in Europe into a coherent movement with the publication by Karl Marx and Friedrich Engels of the *Communist Manifesto*. The need to respond to the ecological and humanitarian disaster in Ireland and the apparent rise of socialism as a major ideological rival to classical liberal political economy would fuel much of the moral urgency for Mill's intervention into the field of economics.

Before we examine Mill's treatment of socialism in the *Principles* and the later posthumously published *Chapters on Socialism* (1879), it is useful to recall some of the main elements of Mill's account of property. Mill's thoughts on the origin of the concept of private property are more reminiscent of Hobbes than Hume or Bentham, insofar as he located it in the need to 'repress violence' caused by conflict over resources, rather than any presumed social apprehension of the utility of establishing the mine–thine distinction.[31] In the opening chapter of Book Two of the *Principles* titled 'Of Property', Mill emphasised a certain provisional quality embedded in the concept of private property as he insists that 'the principle of private property has never yet had a fair trial in any country, and less so, perhaps, in this country [England] than in some others' (CW 2:207). However, Mill also highlighted the unique historical conditions produced by the Industrial Revolution, conditions that make 'reconsideration of all first principles' of economics practically inevitable given that more than at any former period in history 'the suffering portion of the community have a voice in this discussion' (CW 2:202). For Mill, re-examining first economic principles primarily required revisiting the fundamental question of the relation between production and the distribution of wealth.

Mill's account of the sharp conceptual distinction between production and distribution is a hallmark of his political economy, and is unique among his predecessors, including Ricardo.³² Whereas production has 'necessary conditions' that 'partake of the character of physical truths', distribution of wealth and resources is a matter of 'human institution solely' (CW 2:199, 21). That is to say, increased production of a given quantity of a resource is possible only through 'knowledge of laws of nature' that allow for improvements to technology; but distribution of produced goods is governed by 'rules determined by the consent of society', or those who dispose of active force (CW 2:199–200). However, in his preliminary remarks to the *Principles*, Mill qualified the volitional dimension of distribution somewhat by recognising it as a 'partly human institution' because how institutions work in different contexts is dependent upon the various modes of conduct a society may choose to adopt (CW 2:21). His reconsideration of the relation between production and distribution would also impact Mill's position on another tenet of classical political economy; namely, the theory of value and price pioneered by Adam Smith. In contrast to the 'confusing' ambiguity in Smith's account of value, Mill insists that 'value has nothing to do with' distribution alone and not at all with production (CW 3:456). Apart from making the technical point that while a general rise in prices is possible, a general rise in value is not because it is relative to exchange, Mill's more important observation with respect to value and distribution is to correct what he took to be the fallacy 'too common in political economy, of not distinguishing between necessities arising from the nature of things, and those created by social arrangement' (CW 3:455).

Mill approached the question of socialism through the paradigmatic relation of production and distribution. But his position with respect to socialism is certainly complex. Indeed, he has been denounced as a committed socialist by neo-classical political economists such as Friedrich Hayek and Ludwig von Mises, or as the victim of the supposedly corrupting influence of his partner Harriet Taylor.³³ I believe the characterisation of Mill as a socialist is mistaken for as I shall demonstrate, he recognised too many serious problems with it ever to endorse socialism *tout court*. Perhaps the real significance of Mill's respectful considerations about socialism is that they illustrate the extent of his break from the old Benthamite school of philosophical radicalism. In his *Autobiography*, Mill confided that in his twenties: 'I was more a democrat, but not the least a Socialist', because he accepted private property as the '*dernier mot*' of legislation' (CW 1:239). However, over the course of the 1840s Mill confesses that 'he and Harriett' became 'much less democrats' as 'our ideal of ultimate improvement went far beyond Democracy, and would class us decidedly under the general designation of Socialists' (CW 1:239). How did Mill understand socialism? In the *Principles* he defined socialism not in terms of the abolition of private property, but rather as 'any system which requires that the land and the instruments of production should be the property not of individuals, but of communities or associations, or of the government' (CW 2:203).[34] However, Mill's major reference point for socialism was not Karl Marx, but rather French collectivist thinkers such as the Comte de Saint-Simon, Louis Blanc and Charles Fourier, as well as the Welshman Robert Owen. These were the 'utopian' socialists Marx facetiously dismissed as 'duodecima editions of the New Jerusalem'.[35]

Mill did not endorse socialism. For all intents and purposes, he remained convinced throughout his life of the importance of private property, although, reminiscent of Paine, he was considerably more ambivalent about inheritance.[36] But, in the contest of ideas between capitalism and socialism, Mill intimated that he believed there was much at present that is still 'an undecided question' (CW 2:205). However, it is also misleading to characterise Mill, as some have done, as an aristocratic liberal.[37] Mill's attraction to certain aspects of socialist collectivism was due to their potential service to the goal of extending the principles of democracy, rather than any nostalgia for an aristocratic past. For instance, Mill saw in the socialism of Saint-Simon and Fourier an albeit flawed reflection of a concept of distributive justice built upon the idea of equality of opportunity and a deep antipathy to the 'great social evil' of a parasitic non-labouring class (CW 3:758). Mill accepted Adam Smith's basic premise that no society can be truly happy if the greater part of its people is poor and miserable.[38] He also identified the central paradox of his age, to which the rise of socialism is partly explicable, as deriving from the social fact that even as the industrial system produced structures of dependence and a massive concentration of wealth, it also featured the unmistakable increase in the power of the working classes.[39] That is to say, socialists correctly identify the contrary interests at play in the modern economy, but arguably the most promising element of socialism, in Mill's view, was its recognition of the possibility of social progress, in particular the expectation that, while self-interest will continue to predominate human social psychology for the foreseeable future, the great mass of human beings is capable of greater public spirit than ever known previously.[40] Modern history, then, is in itself potentially a progressive force making it possible to conceive of a kind of authentically democratic politics aspiring beyond the narrow self-interest that Mill believed animated contemporary British parliamentarism.

Mill's tone discussing socialism in the first two editions of the *Principles* in 1848 and 1849 was quite critical, but it softened palpably in the third edition of 1852 and thereafter. In Book 2 of the *Principles*, Mill responded to a series of common objections to socialism. In response to the charge that socialism will produce a universal motive to avoid working, Mill conceded that there is some truth to this, especially with respect to determining in a socialist system how to apportion labour. But he also observed that Saint-Simon allowed for diversity of labour and alternating tasks.[41] Moreover, Mill minimised the importance of ownership providing the incentive to work inasmuch as 'nine-tenths' of workers at present do not work for their own benefit, but as hired labour (CW 2:204). Mill speculated that a socialist system might, in fact, predispose against 'selfish intemperance' because such behaviour negatively impacts the entire community of which one is a member (CW 2:206). To the objection that socialism stifles individual freedom, Mill countered that in some respects the restraints that socialism, and even communism, place on choice of occupations 'would be freedom in comparison with the present condition' of most human beings, who are already heavily dependent upon the will of others (CW 2:209). Mill also pointed to the example of the Owenite and Saint-Simonian support for equal rights for women as a moral victory on behalf of socialism (CW 2:209; CW 1:175).

The other major issue upon which Mill was willing to give socialists credit was inheritance. Here Mill clearly viewed the social interest trumping the individual right to property. While affirming the importance of 'proprietary rights', Mill also added the normative stipulation that 'property is only a means to an end, not itself an end' (CW 2:223). The moral problem of inheritance is the 'incurred advantage' that contradicts the principle of equality of opportunity (CW 2:216). Anything more than making 'moderate' provision for heirs is contrary to 'the permanent interests of the human race' (CW 2:223). This is especially true regarding the transmission of landed estates through generations as Mill declares with a Paine-like rhetorical flourish: 'No man made the land. It is the original inheritance of the whole species' (CW 2:230). At the very least, Mill was sympathetic to the socialist goal of regulating inheritances to diminish large individual-owned estates.

Despite his willingness to defend socialism, at least in part, from some of the most common objections to it, Mill's primary reservation about socialist collectivism in the *Principles* was the tendency towards ethical and intellectual conformity as he warned: 'The question is whether there would be any asylum left for individuality of character' (CW 2:209). In the posthumously published 'Chapters on Socialism', written later in life and edited by his step-daughter Helen Taylor, Mill appeared even more convinced that the main problem with socialism is not economic per se, but rather his doubts about its capacity to produce the 'intellectual and moral condition' necessary for social and individual happiness (CW 5:735). Any advantages produced by a more collectivist approach to economics need to be measured against the real harm caused by 'a delusive unanimity produced by the prostration of all individual opinions and wishes before the decree of the majority' (CW 5:745). As an admirer of Alexis de Tocqueville, Mill was hardly naive about the dangers of rampant majoritarianism in liberal democracy. But his fears were even more acute that in socialism all of the associations of private life 'would be brought in a most unexampled degree within the domain of public authority', and as such the development of 'individual character' and 'individual preferences' would be curtailed enormously (CW 5:746). Thus, while Mill insists that the 'various schemes for managing the productive resources of the country by public instead of private agency' have a case for a trial, it is not surprising that he clearly preferred the moderate form of collectivist social experiments over 'revolutionary' socialists who seek to overthrow the capitalist state.[42] The moderate forms of socialism he associates with Louis Blanc, Robert Owen and Charles Fourier are more realistic because they accept that self-interest will remain the primary human motivation, at least until 'improvements in general education' allow for the gradual establishment of 'higher character' on a societal scale (CW 5:740). The gradualist approach to implementing socialist policies at least has the virtue of trying to calibrate economic change with the hopefully enhanced moral and intellectual capacities of the majority of the people.

The remaining problems Mill identified with socialism are perhaps of a somewhat more instrumental character. Mill insists that in contrast to the expectations of most socialists, the conditions of the working classes – though not improving commensurate with economic and technological progress – were nonetheless not getting much worse (CW 5:728–9). Overpopulation is a looming threat, but in Mill's estimation it had not proven to be as dire a condition as Malthus had prophesied (with the terrible exception of Ireland that we will examine in the following chapter). However, Mill also argued that the poor conditions of the industrial working classes disproves Smith's law of remuneration, by which the most repulsive and painful jobs are rewarded most amply.[43] But for Mill, arguably the greatest measurable flaw in socialist theory is the failure to recognise the serious benefits of competition as even the 'most enlightened' socialists have only a 'very imperfect and one-sided notion of the operation of competition' (CW 5:729). Competition keeps the price of necessities down within reach of the working classes, even if Mill admits that competition is no guarantee for quality (CW 5:731). Thus, for Mill, the importance of freedom of thought and character, no less than the value of free commercial enterprise, established clear set limits on the value of socialism in current times.

The Problem of Laissez faire

Given that Mill's most fundamental objection to socialism was its potential diminution of individual freedom and distinct character formation, it is not surprising that the principle of laissez faire, first popularised by the Physiocrat thinker Vincent de Gournay, would be intrinsically appealing to Mill. Indeed, while the idea of minimalist government interference in the economy was central to early figures in classical political economy such as Smith and Ricardo, arguably it would be Mill's *Principles of Political Economy* that would establish the term laissez faire as a crucial entry in the lexicon of economic usages in the English-speaking world. The economic doctrine of laissez faire seems to flow naturally from the logic of autonomy central to Mill's political theory, and famously expressed in *On Liberty*: 'Over himself, over his own body and mind, the individual is sovereign.'[44] Mill's political economy was no less infused with this spirited defence of liberty insofar as he identified in the *Principles* a zone of privacy as the root of every theory of 'social union', according to which there is a circle around every individual human being 'which no government, be it that of one, of a few, or of the many, ought to be permitted to overstep" (CW 3: 938). This commitment to ethical individualism influenced practically all aspects of Mill's thinking on economic policy whether it be his opposition to the extension of poor relief measures in Ireland for fear of creating a culture of dependency or his contention that public welfare programmes dangerously encourage overpopulation. As he lectured the purportedly profligate and oversexed masses: 'Everyone has a right to live. We will suppose this granted. But no one has a right to bring creatures into life to be supported by other people' (CW 2:358). Mill goes so far as to insist that 'Laisser faire, in short, should be the general practice: every departure from it, unless required by some great good, is a certain evil' (CW 3:938, 945).

Mill's endorsement of the principle of laissez faire did not, however, obviate the need for certain concessions to practical reality. While the individual may be sovereign with respect to actions and ideas that extend only to oneself, government and society do have a legitimate role in preventing harm to others. As such, 'there are some things with which governments ought not to meddle, and other things with which it ought' (CW 3:913). Even in the context of his iconic encomium to freedom in *On Liberty*, Mill conceded that basic economic phenomena such as trade is a 'social act', and thus subject to reasonable regulation to avoid or reduce harm.[45] Mill's reflections upon the social dimension of economic transactions suggest more than simply a prudential application of the harm principle. Rather, in an early essay 'Civilization' (1836), he described the 'gradual rise of the trading and manufacturing classes' as a function of the 'progress of the power of co-operation'.[46] But in contrast to Smith, Mill's account of the historical progress of commerce highlighted both the increased human capacity for cooperation, as well as the logical corollary, some necessary diminution of personal freedom: 'All combination is compromise: it is the sacrifice of some portion of individual will, for a common purpose' (CW 8:122). Moreover, the younger Mill expressed palpable distaste for the more individualistic aspects of commercial life, especially the 'money getting pursuits' that perpetually threaten to reduce modern society to universal materialism characterised by 'the trampling, crushing, elbowing, and treading on each other's heels' (CW 18:129–30; CW 3:754).

Mill's case for laissez faire is not, then, an unambiguous call for complete economic liberation. It involved rather a more speculative conjecture that 'all economical experiments, voluntarily undertaken, should have the fullest licence' with government interfering normally only to prevent harm caused by force or fraud, especially as it impacts 'the less fortunate classes of the community' (CW 3:934). However, even with respect to government involvement in the economy, Mill maintained an overriding presumption in favour of the value of economic freedom. This can be seen in his distinction between authoritative and non-authoritative forms of government intervention; the former involving penal laws and coercive power, and the latter 'that of giving advice, and promulgating information' to enhance the calibre of individual actions and choices (CW 3:937). Mill's preference is that authoritative government strictures should have a 'much more limited sphere of legitimate action' than non-authoritative (CW 3:937). It is, in Mill's view, a matter of 'human freedom and dignity' to maintain 'some space in human existence . . . sacred from authoritative intrusion' (CW 3:938).

Mill framed his argument about laissez faire in contrast to several 'false doctrines' then current among British political economists. The two major doctrines to which Mill objects most vociferously are protectionism and mercantilism. Following Hume and Smith, Mill excoriated the policy of protecting 'native industry' for rendering both labour and capital less efficient (CW 3:913–14). And mercantilism in its basic form, originally spurred by the acquisition of captive colonial markets, was, Mill insists, thoroughly discredited by the mid-nineteenth century.[47] A third erroneous doctrine Mill repudiated on behalf of laissez faire was the establishment of usury laws, whereby governments fixed 'a legal limit to the rate of interest' (CW 3:922). To Mill, this was a matter of freedom of contract, and in this respect he agreed with Bentham rather than Smith, the Scotsman famously having supported a penal offence for 'prodigals and projectors', who lend money above the legal rate.[48] Mill's position resembled John Locke's preference to leave interest rates to determination by the spontaneous play of supply and demand. Another form of deleterious government intervention is price controls. Mill insisted that it is impossible to control the price of a commodity independent of the rate of consumption. As such, in the case of actual scarcity such as what he calls the 'Irish Emergency of 1847', the only measures that can be taken are either to distribute rations through public relief 'as a besieged town', or his preferred solution to encourage 'the richer classes to diminish their own consumption' as an example to the society at large (CW 3:927).

Several other false doctrines Mill rejects in the course of making his case for laissez faire each relate to some form of combination. First, there is the notorious bugbear of Smithian political economy, namely, monopoly. Mill opposed this unhealthy form of combination on the grounds that 'a limitation of competition, however partial, may have mischievous effects quite disproportioned to the apparent cause' (CW 3:928). Another pernicious doctrine Mill exposed was laws against the 'combination of workmen'. These union-breaking measures were essentially laws enacted to keep wages low. Mill's attitude towards working-class associations was complicated. On the one hand, he welcomed the general sign of progress made when 'the better paid classes of skilled artisans' seek common cause with their fellow labourers (CW 3:929, 931). Mill even lauded the importance of strikes as 'the best teacher of the labouring classes on the subject of the relation between wages and the demand and supply of labour' (CW 3:932). However, Mill also insisted that union membership must be voluntary, and no worker should ever be compelled to take part in a strike. Mill's laissez faire predilections also led him to caution against any efforts to restrict business, set salary caps or abolish piece-work (CW 3:933). The final false doctrine Mill considered in this treatment of the principle of laissez faire in the *Principles* is the unhealthy combination comprising a governing body or social majority bound together for purposes of constraining 'mental freedom' (CW 3:934). Clearly, replicating his defence of freedom of thought and speech in *On Liberty*, Mill inveighed against both legal limits on speech and the more insidious 'social penalties' (CW 3:935).

Underlying Mill's repudiation of these pernicious policies is a considerable degree of moral revulsion at the idea of government intervention in the private sphere. These objections were deeply influenced by Mill's appreciation of Alexis de Tocqueville's insight that in modern democracy the power of persons acting in masses is the only substantial power in society.[49] Mill's instinctive resistance to government intervention derived in part from his belief that it habituates people to accepting the legitimacy of compulsion, physical or moral. External compulsion is the antithesis of Mill's ideal of the freedom that inhabits the 'domain of inward consciousness' (CW 3:938). Beyond the problem of compulsion, Mill believed the natural tendency of government power and influence was to extend without any natural limitation. He assumed that as government takes on more tasks, it will perform them all less well. He had confidence in the superior efficiency of private agency due to there normally being a stronger interest in the success or failure of the work at hand: 'the great majority of things are worse done by the intervention of government, than the individuals most interested in the matter would do them, or cause them to be done, if left to themselves' (CW 3:941). But perhaps Mill's most important reason for opposing the expansion of government is his endorsement of Tocqueville's appeal to cultivate habits of collective action among the people themselves. The spectre of the omnicompetent state saps the individual citizens' capacity to join in a 'spontaneous action' for a collective interest with their neighbours and fellow citizens (CW 3:943). In graphic terms unmistakably Tocquevillian in provenance, Mill likened the establishment of technocracy and an all-powerful bureaucratic civil administration to a process of animalisation culminating in the 'government of sheep by their shepherd, without anything like so strong an interest as the shepherd has in the thriving condition of the flock' (CW 3:943).

Even despite the high potential moral stakes he sees in the problem of government intervention, Mill nonetheless always recognised that there are some duties 'most indispensable and unanimously' acknowledged as belonging to the sphere of government (CW 3:936). That is to say, Mill staked out important exceptions to the principle of laissez faire required by 'some great good' (CW 3:945). He fully accepted that there were conditions under which the state was justified to impose a harmony of interest in the economic sphere.[50] Perhaps the most significant exemption to laissez faire relates to education, in particular with respect to imposing legal obligations on parents to provide for the education of their children, albeit with pecuniary support from government if necessary (CW 3:947). But even in this regard Mill maintained a major role for competition as 'government must claim no monopoly' on education, for allowing government complete control over education is to grant a 'despotic' power over the 'opinions and sentiments of the people in their youth' (CW 3:950). Thus, an education system with diverse models of organisation and pedagogical philosophy would appear to be a *sine qua non* of Mill's healthy liberal society. Other related exceptions to the principle of laissez faire are measures designed to protect minors and other vulnerable people, such as laws against child labour and contracts for service long term and in perpetuity (CW 3:952–3). In both cases, the government is justified in assuming that certain individuals are not the best judges of their own interests.

Another major exception to the principle of laissez faire had to do with industrial relations and social welfare. Mill determined that in a complex industrial economy, sometimes government intervention is required to 'give effect' to salutary policy. For instance, the programme of reducing hours of work must be legislated because these rules are effective only if workers demonstrate solidarity (CW 3:957). With respect to the 'Poor Laws', Mill admitted that despite his best efforts to avoid 'metaphysical considerations' about natural law moral obligations, it does seem for all intents and purposes 'to be right that human beings should help one another' (CW 3:960). Indeed, the claim for help issuing from the destitute is 'one of the strongest that can exist' (CW 3:960). But any form of public relief must ensure that it does not produce a feeling of dependence among the recipients: 'there are few things for which it is more mischievous that people should rely on the habitual aid of others, than for the means of subsistence' (CW 3:961). Mill prefers public relief over private charity precisely because intelligent public policy can be modulated to calibrate immediate support with the goal of preserving long-term personal responsibility. The most refined aspect of Mill's treatment of the social welfare exception to the principle of laissez faire is his ringing endorsement of public endowments to support the 'learned class' and state-sponsored projects of scientific and geographic exploration (CW 3:968). A final important exception to the principle of laissez faire related to specific industries such as railways, in which the 'only competition possible is between two or three great companies', and which should be either state-owned or heavily regulated (CW 5:730).

In some respects, Mill's declaration about the great 'general practice' of laissez faire raises more questions than it answers. The list of important exceptions to this principle reminds us that the primary justification for this economic doctrine, in Mill's view, is utility, not a natural right to property or sacrosanct freedom of contract. That is to say, the pure doctrine of laissez faire is no less problematic than socialism, albeit for different reasons. Whereas socialism threatens to stifle mental freedom and individuality for the sake of greater social and economic solidarity, the laissez faire doctrine of economic individualism needs to be corrected by certain forms of government intervention designed to preserve the cooperative dynamic of the social union. Arguably, it is only in the fabled stationary state that Mill provides a fleeting glimpse of a unique polity that combines the virtues of both socialism and capitalism without what he took to be their more harmful tendencies.

The Stationary State

In the old school of classical political economy prior to Mill, the concept of the stationary state was notorious for being at best 'dull' and most commonly a 'hard' or 'dismal' condition for the bulk of the population.[51] In this view, a situation of zero-economic growth and perfect equilibrium of wages and prices is the unfortunate logical end of the progressive state likely thereafter bound to transition from stagnation to eventual decline. One of Mill's most distinctive contributions to liberal political economy was his reimagining of the stationary state as a positive, even desirable, condition that harmonises cultural progress with a comfortable stable standard of living. For Mill, it is the stationary state rather than the doctrine of laissez faire or socialism that comes closest to constituting the natural harmony of interests. Jonathan Riley even goes so far as to call Mill's stationary state a 'liberal social utopia'.[52] To be fair, Mill himself refrained from using such über-idealistic language, but he did signify its importance by describing the stationary state as 'a very considerable improvement on our present condition', that is, the progressive capitalist economy (CW 3:754). Moreover, while Mill made heavy revisions to much of the *Principles* throughout the many editions before his death, it is striking that the brief nine-paragraph treatment of the stationary state in Book 4 of the *Principles* remained largely unaltered over the decades.

In order to appreciate Mill's argument about the connection between stationary economics, and cultural and intellectual progress, we need to distinguish between two kinds of stationary state then common among political economists. First, there was the theoretical zero-economic growth condition characterised by flat wages and overpopulation pressures on labour demand which we saw was associated with Malthus and Ricardo. There was also, however, an historical stationary state that took concrete form in China, according to Adam Smith, or was exemplified by India in John's father James Mill's influential *History of British India* (1817). This historical stationary state is characterised by cultural stagnation and intellectual atrophy. In this sense, 'stationary' signifies an index of factors that extends beyond economics to include the 'want of mental liberty and individuality' taken by many British political economists of the period to be characteristic of 'Asiatic' nations.[53] The historical stationary state is, as one commentator observes, an 'illiberal dystopia' antithetical to Mill's entire philosophical project.[54] Why, then, did Mill seek to rehabilitate a concept with traditional associations to both economic and cultural stagnation?

Mill acknowledged that classical political economists, including Smith and Malthus, viewed the stationary state as an 'apparently stagnant sea' bearing a most 'unpleasing and discouraging prospect' (CW 3:753). He, on the other hand, discovered in the principle of economic equilibrium an important model for encouraging human improvement and social development. In particular, Mill's stationary state served as a theoretical frame within which he grappled with the question of what we have identified as the relative importance of rights and interests. One dimension of this project involved adjudicating the merits of the respective claims of socialism and laissez faire capitalism. Socialism had the virtue of clearly exposing the 'contrariety of interests' among individuals and classes (CW 5:725). But it also bore the grave defect of stifling individual creativity and the advantages of competition, conditions normally associated with the concept of individual rights. Laissez faire capitalism promoted competition and a kind of individual economic freedom, but it required serious forms of government intervention to preserve the relative harmony of interests made possible by the historical achievement of enhanced levels of social cooperation. For Mill, cultural and economic aspects of progress are inseparable because the unmistakable increasing 'spirit of combination among the working classes' will produce effects on the whole range of social activities (CW 18:125). There is, then, a complex dynamic at work in liberal modernity as the increased capacity for cooperation threatens to undermine individual freedom, even as unlimited individual economic freedom in the historical context of this phase of industrial development risked delegitimising the distributive projects necessary to serve the long-term interests of the human being as a progressive species. That is to say, the possibility of the stationary state compelled Mill to reflect upon the tension between a societal model of economic progress and cultural stagnation, on the one hand, and one of cultural vitality, but economic constraints, on the other.

Mill argues that the stationary state is at once the 'ultimate point' of industrial progress, and yet at the same time it is an elusive goal that constantly 'flies before us' (CW 3:752). Industrial development can be measured by a range of factors, including advanced material prosperity, increased productivity, increased population, the reduction in crime and class privilege, and the expansion of human control over nature (CW 3:705–9). In one sense, then, the stationary state represents a kind of end or *telos* of modern political economy insofar as it is a condition enjoyed only by the 'richest and most prosperous countries' (CW 3:752). But in another sense, it can only ever be an end that 'flies before us', because the stationary state is practically never seen as the objective of deliberate policy. As Nadia Urbinati expresses it, for Mill 'economic progress is a permanent work of postponement of its own negation'.[55] As such, the stationary state is not the necessary outcome of an overarching historical progress in the Hegelian sense.[56] Rather, Mill presents it as a theoretical possibility produced by a combination of the mechanical laws of production and the principles of distribution within human control.

Wealthy countries can achieve the stationary state under a few specific conditions. First, when there is no further major technological improvement in the productive arts, and, second, when there is a suspension of the outflow of capital from rich countries to undeveloped ones. The third main factor contributing to the attainment of the stationary state is reaching the optimal level of population density, a condition Mill believes several advanced countries have already achieved (CW 3:756). While Mill recognised that wealthy countries typically still have resources for a great increase in population, he expresses 'very little reason for desiring it' (CW 3:756). Insofar as the perpetual challenge of overpopulation threatens to destroy the economic equilibrium grounding the harmony of interests, regular emigration and the encouragement of birth control among the working classes would be an important feature of the stationary state.

The benefits of the stationary state are both material and moral. Mill rejected Smith's argument that the 'condition of the mass of people' can be satisfactory only in the progressive state (CW 3:753). He, thus, challenged the traditional notion that only the progressive economic state values and rewards creativity.[57] Rather, Mill insisted that rapid industrial progress has not produced any corresponding comparable social progress for the lower classes. Herein Mill employed a very specific idea of progress, one that prioritises distribution over production. In fact, he declares: 'It is only in the backward countries of the world that increased production is still an important object' (CW 3:755). In Mill's refined version of progress, questions about quality of life take on the character of claims of right, whereby the most valuable effect of industrial improvements would be 'that of abridging labour' (CW 3:756). But the egalitarian normative core of the stationary state is unmistakable for it approaches the 'best state for human nature', namely, one in which 'no one is poor, no one desires to be richer, nor has any reason to fear being thrust back, by the efforts of others to push themselves forward' (CW 3:754). Does the stationary state require restrictions on individual economic freedom? Undoubtedly so, especially with regard to limits on inheritance, but, by and large, Mill framed the distributionist imperative of the stationary state in terms compatible with support for the principle of private property.[58] Indeed, Mill's assumption seems to be that the middle classes would predominate politically in the stationary state.[59] The salutary socio-economic effects of stationariness would not arise spontaneously, but would, in Mill's view, require a form of liberal statecraft through which 'just institutions' exercising 'judicious foresight' in planning for population growth and capital accumulation discover a dependable basis to improve 'the universal lot' (CW 3:757).

Clearly, the main advantage of the stationary state is mental and moral, not economic per se. Mill emphasised that a stationary condition of capital and population implies 'no stationary state of human improvement' (CW 3:756). Freed on the individual level from the 'treading on each other's heels' characteristic of the commercial rat-race, as well as the fixation on the political level with constant, hopefully exponential, economic growth, the stationary state adjusts the political vision of the community towards encouraging intellectual diversity, mental cultivation and social progress. Mill's extended discussion of the intellectual and moral advances facilitated by the stationary state model occurred not in his brief chapter on 'The Stationary State', but in the much longer following chapter suggestively titled 'On the Probable Futurity of the Labouring Classes'. The treatment of the stationary state served several purposes in the *Principles*, including presenting a more complex relation between wealth and happiness than in Bentham's utilitarianism, and highlighting the tendency of classical political economy to obsess about production at the expense of thinking about just distribution.[60] But it is in this following chapter that Mill foregrounded what had been largely implicit, namely, his contention that the great question for the future of humanity relates to educating 'the opinions and habits of the most numerous class' (CW 3:758). Mill acknowledged two alternative strategies for achieving the goal of public enlightenment. The first is a paternalistic approach for which Mill admitted some attraction to the seduction of *noblesse oblige*, but he concluded that the increasingly assertive working classes will no longer accept this kind of tutelage (CW 3:758). Thus, the only real path forward is a programme of public education whereby the working classes are taught the 'virtues of independence', especially with respect to justice and moderation (CW 3:763).

Mill is rather optimistic about the prospects for educating the labouring classes in a society that does not prioritise increased production and wealth at the expense of all other considerations. Even in the less than satisfactory condition of industrial Britain, Mill saw evidence of a 'spontaneous education going on in the minds of the multitude', which could be greatly accelerated with state support

(CW 3:754). In the great sacrifices made by the common people in the cause of liberty in the American Civil War, Mill found proof for the continued existence of 'the higher aspirations and the heroic virtues', even in industrial modernity (CW 3:754). Among the enlightened working classes, moderation would become perhaps the cardinal virtue as sexual and material desires would need to be brought under rational self-control. As a consequence, the mass of people would hopefully develop a taste for solitude 'essential to any depth of meditation or of character', and an appreciation for the ecological wonders of nature untrammelled by bricks and mortar (CW 3:756). Mill saw evidence of this mental progress in the pro-liferation of 'Working Men's Associations'' lectures and discussion groups that he concludes have already started to 'awaken public spirit' among the working classes (CW 3:763).[61] Ideas of equality are 'daily spreading more widely among the poorer classes', even as social mobility has largely failed to materialise under conditions in which it remains difficult for the 'labouring classes' to secure 'good work for good wages' (CW 3:767). Thus, in Mill's view, the indus-trial progressive economy state has neither adequately delivered on the promise of greater individual freedom for most people, nor secured the equitable balance of societal interests.

With its own distinctive normative foundation and distribution-ist features, the stationary state, or some approximation of it, per-mits political economists to think beyond the received theoretical framework bounded by capitalism and socialism. Mill's two most important proposals to reform both capitalism and socialism flow out of the logic of the stationary state. The first is the principle of profit-sharing according to which workers share in some propor-tion of a venture's profits. Mill provides the example of Cornish miners and the crew of American merchant vessels, who each share a portion of the company's profits. Profit-sharing presupposes a degree of corporate and individual enlightenment, that is, workers capable of recognising their responsibilities and proprietors enlight-ened enough to see the long-term advantages in giving their workers some measure of ownership in the common project (CW 3:769–70). It was this combination of self-interest and an expanded sense of collective responsibility that made profit-sharing appealing to Mill. Not to mention the fact that it seemed a realistic policy given that it did not challenge the existing legal basis of private property. The more radical proposal Mill endorsed was the idea of workers coop-eratives. This idea did depart from traditional notions of private property inasmuch as it involved workers 'collectively owning the capital with which they carry on their operations' (CW 3:775). Mill provided a host of practical examples of cooperatives in France and England that were successful because they are small-scale, locally owned enterprises that have displayed an admirable capacity to maintain equitable principles of distribution in the course of expansion (CW 3:780). It is characteristic of these cooperatives that wages are set for comfortable subsistence and labour schedules adjusted to prioritise as much as possible leisure for mental cultivation. But the major impact of cooperatives is that they can serve as a school for the working classes to develop habits of 'exertion and self-denial', as well as an appreciation for economic norms beyond 'mere private benefits' (CW 3:783, 775). Both profit-sharing and workers cooperatives can coexist in practically any diversified economic model that is not solely directed towards increased production. Moreover, Mill insists that even these collectivist reforms of capitalism would still retain the advantages of competition, both by competing with private enterprises and among themselves, that the purer forms of socialism would negate.

Mill's speculation about the future improvement of the 'labouring classes' is premised upon the desirability and sustainability of his conception of the stationary state. The normative basis of this new liberal political economy represents an advance from the mechanical metrics of production to a holistic model of distribution animated by an assessment of the material conditions necessary to encourage intellectual and moral development among the majority of people. Mill describes the 'moral revolution' that would accompany this shifting economic paradigm in almost metamorphic terms:

> The healing of the standing feud between capital and labour; the transformation of human life, from a conflict of classes struggling for opposite interests, to a friendly rivalry in the pursuit of a good common to all; the elevation of the dignity of labour; a new sense of security and independence in the labouring class; and the conversion of each human being's daily occupation into a school of the social sympathies and the practical intelligence. (CW 3:792)

Mill's political economy promised, then, nothing less than the possible resolution of class conflict by way of a refined harmony of interests theory that prioritised moral and political ends over economic production and growth. Mill's exercise in redefining the normative presuppositions of political economy bears a certain family resemblance to the Aristotelian model of classical political philosophy which also maintained that economics is subordinate to a substantive political and moral *telos*.[62] But the differences between Aristotle's conception of the 'good life' and Mill's 'art of living' are fundamental. Mill integrated his economic theory into a principle of historical progress unimagined by the classics, according to which industrial society is but one phase of human development. Moreover, the analytic framework for Mill's teleology is the social dynamic governing the interplay of competing organised interests, on the one hand, and a distinctly modern commitment to individual liberty, once again alien to the ancients, on the other.

For Mill, the *telos* embodied in the stationary state supports the proposition that a progressive being only truly flourishes in conditions of intellectual diversity and acute mental energy. Much as the old Benthamite philosophical radicalism failed to incorporate basic insights about human dignity and autonomy, similarly did the venerable classical political economy of Smith, Malthus and Ricardo tend to reduce economics to a science of material causation. Mill's ideal of pluralism stands as a counterpoint to both the socialist and laissez faire models of economics. Neither socialism with its collectivist distrust of spontaneous individuality, nor the capitalist fixation on material pursuits and disregard for the moral and intellectual development of the great mass of people, provide the social conditions for the kind of rich diversity of opinions, beliefs and interests that render the 'art of living' a worthy formula for human happiness and societal progress.

The stationary state, the *bête noire* of classical political economy, was transformed in Mill's *Principles of Political Economy* into the centrepiece of a normative economics intended to promote liberal pluralism. The dyadic teleology embedded in Mill's concept of the *art of living* projected the importance of both individual liberty and societal pluralism as these twin goals are served by the wide range of ideas and lifestyles he believed was endangered by the culturally and socially homogenising effects of both laissez faire capitalism and centralised socialism. Thus, the ideal of the stationary state characterised by economic equilibrium stood as the foundational feature of Mill's account of the aspiration of liberalism to provide not only for individual intellectual, moral and aesthetic freedom, but also for the material prosperity of society.

Mill presented the stationary state as a means to reconcile, and ultimately transcend, prevailing economic ideologies by bringing considerations about production and distribution within the conceptual nexus provided by the *art of living*. One effect of this project was to revise the ideal of the natural harmony of interests inherited from earlier classical political economy insofar as for Mill the state properly conceived in its true material and noetic purpose was justified in imposing a harmony of sorts upon the superstructure of individual interests. This positive conception of the stationary state also compelled Mill's Victorian readers to reconsider their own assumptions about the supposedly superannuated status of natural rights philosophy. Even as the stationary state required restricting a certain form of economic individualism, it also promoted a conception of rights that was at once historically contingent, and yet reflective of a certain commitment to fundamental human freedom and dignity. The rights of the majority of people were in some sense aspirational as their true exercise and enjoyment seemed to depend upon a certain level of material well-being, as well as moral and intellectual development. The radical promise of the stationary state – that instantiation of economic equilibrium – was nothing less than tapping the vast human potential unleashed by the expanding capacity for public spirit among the newly educated and mentally stimulated working classes. Perhaps only once the economic system has been refashioned to support the societal goal of general public enlightenment would the liberal individual truly be born.

Notes

1. E.g., Blyth 2012: 116–17.
2. Capaldi 2004: 201; Mill CW 1:23, 272. Hereafter in notes and text CW 1 and page.
3. For the centrality of the principle of individual liberty in Mill's political economy, see Hollander 1985: 685; Gaus 2016: 489; Riley 1994: xliii. For an alternative reading of Mill that views him as a champion of social control, see Hamburger 1999: 7–9.
4. Mill CW 18:224 and CW 3:938. Hereafter in notes and text CW 18 or CW 3 and page.
5. Mill CW 8:890. Hereafter in notes and text CW 8 and page.
6. Riley 1998: 318. The idea of the stationary or 'steady state' economy has also achieved renewed prominence among environmental theorists since the 1970s, see, e.g., Daly 1973; Daly 2014.
7. Urbinati 2010: 252–53.
8. Levy 1981: 287.
9. Baum 2000: 219–24; Ten 1998: 393–5.
10. Gaus 2016: 489.

11. Riley 1998: 297.
12. Schwartz 1972: 109.
13. Riley 1994: viii.
14. Haakonssen 1981: 41.
15. Bentham 1978: 51–5.
16. Hume 2000: Bk I, Pt 1. However, Hume's insights became a fully developed doctrine of associationism only as a result of David Hartley's *Observations of Man* (1749).
17. Capaldi 2004: 59.
18. CW 1:165.
19. Smith 1981: 96.
20. Robbins (1930: 194) argues that the idea of the stationary state was implicit in physiocrat thought as well.
21. Smith 1981: 90.
22. Smith 1981: 99. See also Hume 1987: 399, for the extreme measures of population control in China.
23. Malthus 2015: 129.
24. Malthus 2015: 132, 142.
25. Malthus 2015: 145.
26. Ricardo 2004: 61.
27. Ricardo 2004: 57.
28. Ricardo 2004: 56, 71.
29. CW 1:31. Cf. Hayek 1978: 270.
30. For an excellent study of Mill's long and complicated relation to the 'Irish Question', see Kinzer 2001. This will also be the subject of further discussion in Chapter 7, below.
31. Mill CW 2:201. Hereafter in notes and text CW 2 and page number.
32. Vallier 2010: 104–6.
33. See Farrant 2011: 82. For Gertrude Himmelfarb's attribution of Mill's supposed radical turn to the seductive impact of Harriet Taylor, see Rees 1977: 372.
34. Cf. Mill CW 5:738. Hereafter in notes and text CW 5 and page.
35. Farrant 2011: 84.
36. Mill followed the Saint-Simonians who advocated that the state should inherit all productive resources. For a good discussion of Mill's treatment of inheritance, see Persky 2016: 91–107.
37. For Mill as an aristocratic liberal, see Boyd 2016: 122; Kahan 1992.
38. Smith 1981: 96.
39. CW 5:726; Baum 2000: 222–3.
40. CW 2:205; CW 5:739–40; CW 1:241. See also Ten 1998: 379.
41. CW 2:207. See also Farrant 2011: 98.
42. CW 5:748, 737, 746, 749.
43. Compare CW 5:729 and Smith 1981: 117.
44. CW 18:224.
45. CW 18:293.

46. CW 18:122.
47. Mill's adoption of the views of the 'Colonial Reformers' in the 1830s and 1840s will be considered in Chapter 7, below.
48. Smith 1981: 357–8.
49. CW 3:939–40. See Tocqueville 2000: 490.
50. Schwartz 1972: 109.
51. Smith 1981: 89–90.
52. Riley 1998: 320; Riley 1994: xxvii.
53. Mill CW 19:396–7. Hereafter in notes and text CW 19 and page.
54. Eisenberg 2018: 157.
55. Urbinati 2010: 242.
56. Eisenberg 2018: 186.
57. Boulding 1973: 97.
58. Daly 1973: 168.
59. Persky 2016: 131.
60. Eisenberg 2018: 182.
61. Mill published cheaper 'People's Editions' of the *Principles* to make it more accessible to the growing working-class readership (CW 1:272).
62. Aristotle 2013: 1252a1–10, 1252b25–30.

Chapter 7

Liberalism on Empire and Emancipation

The circumstances of British liberalism's origins are inextricably linked to both the expansion of modern European imperialism and to the critique of patriarchal divine right monarchy in the cauldron of England's constitutional struggles prior to the Glorious Revolution of 1688–1690. In terms of both empire and the persistence of patriarchy, the egalitarian principles of liberalism were set in stark relief against a background of political, economic and social conditions of radical inequality. The debate in contemporary times is naturally whether British classical liberalism, liberal political economy in particular, was in essence antagonistic towards or complicit with imperialism and patriarchy.

The subject of liberal imperialism is not just of antiquarian interest. In the fairly recent context of reflections upon the challenges and opportunities of the post-Cold War *pax Americana* and post-911 War on Terror even figures as deeply ensconced among the elites of academia as Michael Ignatieff and Niall Ferguson lauded the virtues of liberal imperialism extending democracy and free markets to benighted, illiberal regions of the globe.[1] In terms of early modern historiography, the debate has typically involved those who condemn liberalism as essentially ideological justification of European imperialism, global capitalism and racialist discourse, and others who endorse a more mixed view of liberalism's heritage, including both a noble tradition of anti-imperialism in the eighteenth century associated with Adam Smith, David Hume and Jeremy Bentham, and the later triumphalist colonialism of James Mill, John Stuart Mill and George Wakefield in the nineteenth century marked by the apologia of enlightened despotism and muscular assertions of western cultural superiority.[2] On the question of classical liberalism's relation to patriarchy, the contemporary debate is no less robust as some feminist scholars view early modern liberal thought as integral to justifying de facto social and economic inequality for women, while others turn to classical liberals such as John Locke and John Stuart Mill to identify the early liberal roots of feminism.[3]

This chapter will examine the themes of empire and women's emancipation through the interpretive lens of classical liberal political economy characterised by the two distinct discursive traditions we have identified with natural rights and the harmony of interests. We shall see that classical liberal political economy presented a complex legacy both in support of, and in opposition to, European imperialism, as well as illuminating the emancipatory potential for women's political and civil rights, while also accepting highly gendered structures of economic inequality. For its part, early modern natural rights theory expressed real ambivalence towards colonialism, while the interest-based tradition of liberal political economy shifted dramatically over time from the anti-imperialism of the eighteenth century until in the nineteenth century the expansion of the calculus from the national interest to the interest of humankind per se actually was deployed as a sweeping justification for imperialism.

Classical liberalism is, then, a complicated index of moral resources reflecting ambiguities, contradictions and challenges that arguably still impact international relations and gender relations even to the present. This chapter will proceed first by examining how classical liberalism related to empire and colonisation, especially as evinced in the shift from the natural rights arguments of Hobbes and Locke to the interest-based formula that arguably culminated in John Stuart Mill, the utilitarian philosopher deeply embedded in the apparatus of the Victorian British Empire. The chapter will conclude by considering how classical liberal thinkers such as John Locke, Mary Wollstonecraft and John Stuart Mill provided theoretical inspiration for women's rights and gender equality, but also reveal the limitations of the classical liberal ideal of individualism by placing these canonical thinkers in dialogue with contemporary feminist scholars.

Classical Liberal Anti-Imperialism

On its face, the philosophy of natural equality and self-government animating seventeenth-century classical liberal thought would not appear to be fertile theoretical ground for empire. However, several modern commentators have drawn attention to the important imperial context required to understand English natural rights thinkers such as Hobbes, and especially Locke. The 'colonial reading' of these influential thinkers tends to emphasise what it takes to be early liberalism's role in justifying the dispossession of indigenous peoples' lands,[4] promoting the universalistic rights doctrine that served European imperial ambitions,[5] and the early liberals' aim to incorporate overseas possessions into a system of global capitalism.[6] But when we examine the works of figures such as Hobbes and Locke, the picture is more complicated than a bare apologia for colonialism.

For instance, while Hobbes famously employed the anarchy of international relations as deductive proof of his radically individualistic state of nature theory, imperialism was, despite his personal involvement with the Virginia Company in the 1620s, only peripheral to his political theory.[7] In *Leviathan*, Hobbes described colonies as a form of 'body politic', which is a subordinate system governed by an assembly or appointed officers established by letters patent.[8] Colonies theoretically serve the commonwealth through the advantages of foreign trade that 'supply wants at home, by importation of that which may be had abroad'.[9] There is considerable disagreement about Hobbes' position on colonies. Moloney claims that Hobbes' conceptual dichotomy between the anarchy of the state of nature and the law-based commonwealth was devised to legitimise European colonisation.[10] However, Christov argues that Hobbes expressed deep ambivalence towards the idea of colonies in all cases save as a temporary response to domestic economic and demographic crises, but this did not entail 'any of the Europeans' moral judgements of superiority'.[11] It is perhaps fair to conclude that Hobbes' attitude towards colonies was cautious for, on the one hand, his theory of commodity exchange seemed to allow for a non-exploitive relation between colonists 'transplanted into countries not sufficiently inhabited' and native peoples mutually benefitting from enhanced agricultural development.[12] Yet he also identified over-extension through colonial expansion, 'the insatiable appetite, or Bulimia, of enlarging dominion' as one of the principal causes of the dissolution of the commonwealth.[13] Arguably Hobbes' circumspection about the potential dangers of colonial overreach reflects his prudential approach to political economy as such.

With regard to Locke, his professional and philosophical activities intersected with colonialism more directly. At various points in his career in public life, Locke was Lord Shaftesbury's Secretary for the Proprietors of the Carolina Colony, his Secretary for the

English Council of Trade and Foreign Plantations in the 1670s, and then later served under King William III on the Board of Trade from 1694 to 1700.[14] These positions all involved Locke's participation in a policy-making role on matters of foreign trade and commerce. As we may conclude from his position on English monetary questions, in general Locke's position on trade was mercantilist as exemplified by his recommendation that the English wool industry be protected from Irish competition (and the Irish be encouraged to develop linen manufacture instead).[15] However, the most vexing issues raised by Locke's involvement with colonial trade relate to his attitude towards the rights of indigenous peoples and the practice of slavery in the English colonies in the 'New World'. First, with respect to indigenous peoples it is notable that Locke referred frequently to native Americans in his writings, especially in the hugely influential chapter on property rights in the *Second Treatise*.[16] Some commentators argue that Locke's labour theory of property deliberately undermined and even denied indigenous property rights by dismissing indigenous peoples' claims to nationhood and by excluding them from the normative framework produced by the nearly universal consent to the use of money.[17] There is, however, reason to question these claims about Locke's complicity in the dispossession of native peoples. To start, given the significance Locke placed upon the agreement to use money in the formation of political communities, his acknowledgement that 'the Indians' in his time recognised silver as 'the measure' of exchange would seem to indicate his recognition of some form of indigenous property rights.[18] Moreover, as several commentators have noted there is no evidence that Locke ever believed that indigenous people were intellectually or morally inferior to Europeans, with whom they could negotiate treaties and to whom Locke insisted English authorities should extend the principle of religious toleration.[19]

For Locke, the problem of slavery was both a theoretical and a practical concern. On a theoretical level, Locke's moral premise of natural human equality eliminated any natural or biological arguments for slavery, famously reducing it in the *Second Treatise* to a legitimate form of punishment for violators of the natural law.[20] However, in the *First Treatise* Locke appeared to presuppose the legitimacy of slavery in English colonies in the West Indies and the Carolinas.[21] This is not to mention Locke's personal involvement with slavery as the most likely principal author of the constitution of the Carolina colony that legally enshrined African slavery and hereditary serfdom for a class of English settlers.[22] How can

Locke justify slavery in the colonies given his egalitarian moral philosophy? While Locke seemed to accept the practical existence of slavery in the colonies, Waldron is probably correct to observe that there is no way to reconcile Locke's teaching of natural equality with actual slavery as practiced at the time.[23] That is to say, it is not credible to claim that Locke designed his theory with the intention of defending slavery. To some extent, he even tried to limit slavery in the Carolina Colony by outlawing the enslavement of the indigenous inhabitants.[24] Insofar as Locke ever could hope to reconcile the reality of racial slavery and dispossession of indigenous peoples with his liberal principles of freedom and equality, it would likely have to be on the grounds of the distinction he drew between empire based upon conquest such as Spain's and the commercial imperialism of England.[25] Locke's confidence in the possibility of meaningful commercial relations between Europeans and indigenous people speaks to what Armitage identifies as the 'non-hierarchical and inclusive' moral core of Locke's rationalist philosophy as it applied to the colonial context.[26] It is even possible to detect in Locke's account of the natural basis of commodity exchange an adumbration of Adam Smith's harmony of interests guided by the principle of division of labour inasmuch as 'promises and bargains for truck' between 'a Swiss and an Indian' in the woods of America are binding on them 'for truth and keeping of faith' in economic exchange 'belongs to men as men, and not as members of society'.[27] Thus, Locke's preferred kind of colonial contact would ideally involve mutually beneficial trade.

In the eighteenth century, the question of liberalism's relation to empire assumed increased urgency as the scale and scope of European, especially British, imperialism reached new levels. As we have seen, the Financial Revolution in the first decades of the eighteenth century was deeply implicated in colonial trade. The South Sea Company which provided post-Glorious Revolution England with its first major financial scandal was, we recall, at least ostensibly involved in the Atlantic slave trade to the West Indies, although it did very little actual business of any kind apart from stirring a speculative frenzy among gullible investors.[28] Trenchard and Gordon used the first dozen or so of Cato's Letters to drive home their fear of the corrupting effects that international trading companies could have on the domestic economy and British representative institutions. They did not develop a distinct theory of empire based upon Lockean natural rights principles, but their basic intuition about the corrosive effects of imperial business entanglements and an underlying suspicion that

colonial trade often did not redound to the benefit of the imperial power would become a hallmark of the anti-imperial strain of
eighteenth-century British liberalism.[29]

While eighteenth-century liberal anti-imperialism found clear
expression in the natural rights tradition as seen in Paine's case in
Common Sense for an American war of national liberation against
the British Empire, the most prevalent and important strain of British
liberal anti-imperialism in this period derived from the interest-based
school of liberal political economy. The Scottish political economists'
stadial conjectural history of economic and social development was
especially amenable to 'the language of interests and policy' that
characterised discourse about the British Empire at the time.[30] Thinkers such as Hume and Smith established a model of historical progress that posited modern commercial society as the zenith of social,
political and cultural development.[31] But they associated empire with
mercantilism and all the narrow-minded and short-sighted policies
that implied.[32] Hume dismissed the notion of any great advantages
arising from an expansive territorial empire and insisted that beneficial global trade and commerce are badly injured by imperial wars.[33]
Smith echoed Trenchard and Gordon's deep hostility to commercial
monopolies like the South Sea Company, and the Scotsman did so
in terms of commercial privileges and protectionist policies that he
declared violate 'the most sacred rights of mankind' to produce and
trade freely.[34] As Muthu observes, Smith's rare use of the language
of quasi-natural rights almost exclusively pertained to the right each
individual has to trade and exchange goods.[35] In practice, Smith's
philosophical opposition to the economic case for empire resulted
in both his sympathy for the American cause in the imperial dispute
with Britain in the 1760s and 1770s, for which he proposed a loose
imperial federation as a potential solution, and his harsh condemnation of the slave trade, which he believed victimised a great 'nation of
heroes' in Africa.[36]

Arguably the most complex form of classical liberal anti-
imperialism developed within the context of the utilitarian philosophy pioneered by Jeremy Bentham and James Mill. It was the
utilitarians who made the rejection of empire on the grounds of
economic interests central to their political economy. Bentham was
famously ambivalent about empire, and in this way he influenced
an entire generation of utilitarian thinkers and political reformers.
In his impassioned plea to the French National Assembly in 1793,
Bentham called upon the revolutionary government to 'Emancipate Your Colonies!' because the glories of colonialism are illusory,

and indeed colonies bring no economic benefits at all.[37] Bentham's judgement for Britain was no less categorical: 'It is not the interest of Great Britain to have any foreign dependencies whatsoever.'[38] He also rejected any claims about moral or cultural superiority supposedly derived from natural or biological differences among peoples. The Benthamite commitment to modernisation applied in principle as much to British society (for instance, radical electoral and legal reform) as to peoples overseas. But Bentham's concept of modernisation and progress would in the hands of some of his followers be deployed to provide the cultural, as opposed to purely economic, argument in support of imperialism that would come to characterise British liberal thought well into the nineteenth century.

One of the most important of Bentham's followers was, of course, James Mill. The elder Mill illuminates Bentham's complex imperial legacy because the Scotsman was both hostile to colonialism on economic grounds, but also defended British rule in India as part of the civilisational duty of culturally advanced nations to assist backwards people to attain the capacity for self-government. The Janus-faced character of British liberal attitudes towards empire is exemplified by two very different offerings James Mill published just months apart. In an 1818 article for the *Encyclopaedia Britannica* titled 'Colony', he laid out the classic liberal anti-imperial argument insisting that far from providing economic benefits to Britain, India actually costs 'enormous sums', and joining with 'Dr. Smith' in excoriating commercial monopolies and the military establishment produced by wars of colonial expansion.[39] However, the previous year Mill had published his much heralded *The History of British India* in which he justified British rule of the subcontinent on the grounds of assisting them towards cultural progress. Despite never having visited India, the elder Mill spoke with authority about the backwardness of Hindu customs and laws. For our purposes, it is perhaps most significant that Mill employed a form of conjectural history in the mould of the Scottish political economists of the previous era.[40] But, as Pitts explains, James Mill's version of philosophical history was less sophisticated and graduated than the original in Hume and Smith, with Mill tending towards the reductionist methodology of a simple binary distinction between 'civilised' and 'barbarian' peoples.[41] This simplification of the stadial history of Hume and Smith (not to mention Mandeville) opened astonishing, and shameless, possibilities to justify imperialism largely on non-economic, civilisational grounds. Indeed, Ricardo disagreed with his great friend Mill's position on British rule of India as he believed that 'the English have an interest opposed to that of the people of India'.[42] The utilitarians in the generation prior to John Stuart Mill's philosophical maturation were, then, conflicted over empire and colonialism insofar as they rejected economic justifications for empire even as their penchant for modernisation and reform made them vulnerable to the seductive appeal of serving as crusaders in the cause of civilisational progress. In the thought of John Stuart Mill, we see this deep tension within the utilitarian form of interest-based liberalism raised to its most complex, intriguing and, arguably, contradictory expression.

John Stuart Mill and Liberal Imperialism

Out of all the canonical British liberals, John Stuart Mill is arguably the most deeply implicated in the triumphant imperialism of the Victorian period. In the immediate aftermath of publishing *The History of British India*, his father James Mill achieved great fame as an authority on the politics and culture of the subcontinent and assumed a high-ranking post in the East India Company as a result of this celebrity. The British Empire was, thus, woven into the younger Mill's intellectual DNA as he introduced himself in the opening lines of his *Autobiography* as 'the eldest son of the author of the *History of British India*' (CW 1:5). Through his father's connections he was offered a job in the company office in London as a teenager in 1823 and began decades of service in India House that would only end with the dissolution of the company by Parliament after the Indian Mutinies in 1856–1857. While his connection to the colonies, at least with respect to India, was direct and official, Mill's legacy with regard to the broader constellation of social and moral questions surrounding European imperialism was interconnected with multiple dimensions of his political economy and his political philosophy more generally.

John Stuart Mill is rightly recognised as a central figure in what Jennifer Pitts calls the liberal 'turn to empire'.[43] Undoubtedly, he shed much of the anti-imperial passion of Bentham, and even to some extent of his father. One explanation for this shift was the influence of the group of 'Colonial Reformers' on John Mill's thinking about the empire. These reformers, led by the political economist George Wakefield, rejected the position of Smith, Bentham and James Mill that colonies were synonymous with the negative effects of mercantilism and protectionism. In a series of books published in the 1830s and 1840s, Wakefield linked the solution of social problems in England with economic development in the colonies.[44] Wakefield contended that emigration to settler colonies was a way to manage the problem of excess labour supply in England. As Ince observes, Wakefield's argument for systematic colonisation signified a departure from the orthodox Ricardian doctrine that only productivity gains from the division of labour and free trade can prevent systemic economic decline.[45] In this older view, reinvested profits were thought to activate Says Law by creating demand for labour and raising, or at least sustaining, wage levels. However, Wakefield countered that surplus capital in England did not have profitable avenues in which to invest except in unproductive speculation. The colonies would thus provide both an outlet for surplus labour in Britain, as well as a venue for profitable investment of British capital.

John Mill offered high praise for enlightened 'colonial reformers' such as Wakefield (CW 19:563). Indeed, in Book 5 of the *Principles of Political Economy* Mill lauded Wakefield's plan for systematic colonisation as serving 'the future and permanent interests of civilisation itself' (CW 3:963). Mill considered the Wakefield Plan one of the obvious, necessary limits to the principle of laissez faire inasmuch as because most investors viewed colonising projects as financially risky, it must be a matter of public concern: 'Colonisation should be a National undertaking' (CW 3:964). Mill endorsed Wakefield's specific proposals for constructing a complex 'self-supporting system' of colonisation in which settlers are prevented from buying land for a certain period of time to avoid premature dispersal of the population and to maintain a steady labour supply (CW 3:966). The costs of settlement would be borne principally by the colonial governments who would be required to put a price on unoccupied land to fund emigration. Mill's assumption was that British capital will follow the pool of labour relocating to the colonies.

Mill's association with colonial reformers like Wakefield signified a major shift in classical liberal political economy as it introduced a positive argument for colonisation as an economic boon to the imperial metropole. Moreover, this positive economic argument for colonisation meshed comfortably with a group of liberal reformers already sensitised to James Mill's index of cultural progress according to which the benefits of empire could serve the 'interests of the human race' as a whole, and not merely the narrow economic interests of the imperial power (CW 3:963). John Mill was, however, generally unconcerned about the rights of the indigenous inhabitants of what he called 'the unoccupied continents' under British command: presumably such as Canada and Australia (CW 3:967). This combination of the economic case for colonization in addition to the civilisational justification for promoting cultural progress would produce in Mill's mind the sweeping theoretical rationale for a variegated imperial system of remarkable complexity and under-lying fragility.

The cultural aspect of John Mill's approach to empire was in some respects the continuation of his father's simplification of the stadial conjectural history of Hume and Smith. However, Mill the younger struggled to fashion a measure of sorts to determine where nations stand in the civilisational index of barbarism and progress. In the early essay 'Civilization' (1836) he celebrated the achievements of civilisation and declared that 'the present era is pre-eminently the era of civilisation' (CW 18:119). Mill also high-lighted the important economic dimension of civilisation that dis-tinguished it from barbarism: 'In savage life there is no commerce, no manufacture, no agriculture, or next to none; a country rich in the fruits of agriculture, commerce, and manufactures, we called civilised' (CW 18:120). The moral problem underlying the back-wardness of 'savage life' is a crude kind of ethical individualism that makes it impossible for undeveloped communities to tap 'the power of cooperation' (CW 18:122). Decades later in the essay 'A Few Words on Non-Intervention' (1859), Mill suggested, with-out detailing, a scale of social development between 'civilised nations and barbarians' that hinged upon the capacity to generate and internalise moral obligations such as contracts and treaties. Simply put, 'barbarians will not reciprocate' (CW 21:118).

Mill endorsed the proposition that cultural superiority could be valid moral grounds for one nation to rule another. As is well known, in his masterpiece *On Liberty* (1859), Mill concluded that 'despotism is a legitimate mode of government in dealing with barbarians' (CW 18:224). He hastened to qualify this somewhat with the requirement that this despotic rule must be enlightened such that 'the end be their [the barbarians'] improvement, and the means justified by actually effecting that end' (CW 18:224). Nota-bly, Mill quite explicitly eliminated any consideration of 'abstract right' from the justification of despotic rule over barbarian peoples. He relied solely on the greater interest served with utility being Mill's 'ultimate appeal on all ethical questions' (CW 18:224). A few years later, in Chapter 19 of his *Considerations on Represen-tative Government* (1861) reflecting upon decades of service in the East India Company, Mill would again defend despotism as a form of cultural training; 'A vigorous despotism is in itself the best mode of government for training the people in what is specifically wanting to render them capable of a higher civilisation' (CW 19:567). To some extent, Mill was engaging here in a bout of special pleading as he sought to defend his former employer, the now defunct East India Company, which he insisted set a good example for the 'government of a semi-barbarous dependency by a civilised country' (CW 19:577). However, Mill remained frustratingly vague about the exact criteria for determining whether a people were ripe for self-government, as was true of Canada and Australia, or were like India 'still at a great distance from that state' (CW 19:562).

One way to understand Mill's conception of the connection between economic and social development is to reconsider the 'ethology' introduced in the *System of Logic* (1843). As we saw in the previous chapter, ethology is the science of the development of individual and national character. Mill's political economy had a normative foundation with respect to the role that economic factors play in the moral and intellectual development of individuals, classes and, ultimately, entire nations. Along these lines, it is perhaps helpful to interpret Mill's account of colonies as what Ball terms 'applied ethology'.[46] In the *Principles*, Mill insisted that civilisation is characterised by intellectual diversity and mental energy inasmuch as it brings 'human beings in contact with persons dissimilar to themselves, and with modes of thought and action unlike those with which they are familiar' (CW 3:594). But the methodological challenges of assessing the cultural progress of the working class in industrial Britain would become much more complicated in the context of a multi-cultural empire. To start, in the empire there were manifold historical and economic factors at play that Mill believed caused differing stages of the development of national character. As such, even the potential advantages of enlightened despotism needed to be balanced against the unique social, economic or political conditions that militate against such rule. For example, at an early stage in his career, Mill admitted in a private letter that he has 'always been for a good stout despotism – for governing Ireland like India. But it cannot be done. The Spirit of Democracy has got too much head there, too prematurely.'[47] The Irish situation *c.* 1837 signified just how difficult Mill believed it was to determine when a society is ready to emerge from despotism and assume a greater degree of self-government.[48] Perhaps the only unequivocal feature of Mill's defence of colonialism is his insistence that imperial rule – despotic or otherwise – must be of a temporary nature. But Mill's

'self-abolishing empire' was an instrument responsive to multivari-
ate calculations relating to different factors depending on particular
historical and cultural contexts.[49] Arguably, the three most important colonies in Mill's thought, each reflecting a different stage and
element of his civilisational index were Canada, India and Ireland.

The tripartite colonial model comprised of Canada, India and
Ireland was in reality a complex hybrid of settler colonies and
conquered peoples. Canada was in Mill's estimation the most culturally advanced of the three at the time. The Canadian colony
contained both the descendants of a conquered French people and
British settlers that Mill believed, following Wakefield, produced
economic benefits both in the colony and the mother country. The
origin of British Canada was the 1774 Quebec Act, which was a
remarkably enlightened imperial policy for the day as it guaran-
teed legal protection of both the French language and the Roman
Catholic religion.[50] The later Constitution Act of 1791 established
two provinces with their own legislatures: Lower Canada having a
French Catholic majority and Upper Canada an English Protestant
majority. The government of both provinces was dominated by the
British-appointed governor-general and appointed councils, rather
than elected legislators. The rebellions of 1837 were the culmination of a long simmering constitutional crisis in which reformers
in the Canadian colonies sought to make the government 'responsible' to the elected representatives by refusing to approve 'supply' or taxation required to support the colonial administration. In
response, the Whig ministry of Russell and Melbourne in London
implemented duties without colonial legislative approval, which
led to a serious outbreak of rebellion among the French-Canadian
patriotes in Lower Canada and smaller sporadic risings in English
Upper Canada. By early 1838, British regular troops had crushed
the revolt in both provinces.

The Canadian rebellions of 1837 became a *cause célèbre* among
British radicals critical of the Whig ministry.[51] Mill wrote a series of
articles in 1837 and 1838 published in the *London and Westminster
Review* expressing support and sympathy for the Canadian rebels. In
1837, he defended the Canadian reformers on constitutional grounds
asserting that 'they have a right' of supply that 'we gave them', and
thus 'the people of Canada have against the people of England legitimate cause of war'.[52] Mill's response to the rebels' demands was to
propose that the Canadians be granted greater self-government by
establishing separate responsible legislatures for the two provinces
in a loose federation governed by a 'Federal legislature' restricted to

select matters of common concern (CW 6:432). Later Mill expressed support for Lord Durham's Report published in the wake of the failed rebellions. This report is infamous in Canadian history due to Durham's recommendation that the, in his view, backwards French Canadians be assimilated into the more advanced English Canadian society. But Mill endorsed Durham's plan precisely on the grounds that it would destroy 'the nationality of the French Canadians . . . it would merge their nationality of race in a nationality of country'.[53] It is perhaps remarkable that Durham was considered one of the most progressive British politicians of the age and Mill viewed him as a potential leader of the new Liberal party he hoped to create from the faction of radical Whigs in Parliament.

Mill's response to the Canadian rebellion represents an example of the ethological opportunities available in settler colonies. In Mill's view, Canadian society in 1837 was clearly progressing towards the level of national character required to sustain responsible government. While he was not prepared to accept an imperial parliament per se, and the idea of complete equality within the empire this implied, Mill did, however, encourage accomplished colonial officers to serve in the imperial service as a kind of technocratic, merit-based elite governing the imperial domains, such as the Canadian politician Sir Francis Hincks, who was appointed to serve in a 'West Indian government' (CW 19:566). But greater self-rule for Canada did not translate into self-government for India. On the vast sliding scale of degrees of civilisation, Mill was prepared to accept claims of cultural superiority of the English over the French even in the relatively narrow Eurocentric context of Canada and Durham's assimilationist proposal.[54] With respect to British rule over India, Mill believed that the cultural disparity was much starker.

Given his father's legacy as the expert on Indian culture and history, and his own decades of service in India House, British rule over India was very personal to John Mill. As several commentators have noted, however, it is thus surprising how little he had to say about India in his voluminous writings.[55] By the mid-nineteenth century, the East India Company had effectively ceased to be a purely commercial enterprise – it was now the de facto civil administration of British rule over vast swathes of the Indian subcontinent. There is considerable debate about Mill's attitude towards Indian colonisation. Some scholars argue that Mill adopted a simplistic dualist rubric of barbarism and civilisation to justify British rule over what he took to be the backwards Indians.[56] Others counter that Mill advanced a more nuanced and sophisticated index of cultural progress that emphasised tolerance and recognised the importance of unique historical conditions for cultural formation.[57] Similarly, while some commentators observe a degree of racism in Mill's attitude towards Indian people,[58] others reject the notion that Mill countenanced any idea of inherent biological differences among races and peoples.[59] One thing that does seem clear is that while he was deeply impacted by his father's opinions early in his career, John Mill did come to reject the elder Mill's extremely paternalistic position towards India.[60] The chief piece of evidence for this is probably John Mill's support in the time after his father's death for an approach to education policy that recognised the value of native languages and culture, as opposed to the radical anglicisation programme championed by the Governor-General of India Lord William Bentinck.[61]

The dissolution of the East India Company in the aftermath of the Mutiny of 1856–1857 ended Mill's formal and professional connection to India. In a series of working papers written for parliamentary committees debating the future of the company, Mill defended their administration as enlightened and effective. He also deployed Chapter 19 of the *Considerations on Representative Government* as an extended defence of the company and an opportunity to display the superiority of colonial administration by experts over and against partisan politicians in Parliament. In India, he concludes, the choice is between two despotisms; that of Parliament or India House, and 'it is not certain that the despotism of twenty millions is necessarily between than that of a few, or of one' (CW 19:568). Mill's tone in this episode is more of sadness than anger. In his view, India was too backwards culturally and economically to be capable of the kind of self-government that he advocated for Canada: 'India is still at a great distance from that state' (CW 19:562). Mill doubted whether direct parliamentary rule over India would contribute as much to Indian improvement as the company supposedly had done and could in principle have continued to do. In the case of Ireland, however, any alternative to parliamentary rule was, at least in Mill's time, simply not an option.

With respect to Ireland, the disparity of cultural development with England was a problem, but less important in Mill's view than economic considerations. British colonisation of Ireland was a long and complicated history of centuries of conquest, plantations and periodic rebellions. The traditional hostility between Irish Catholics and British Protestants in some respects only intensified after the 1800 Act of Union dissolved the Irish Parliament in the wake of the 1798 Uprisings and absorbed the country into the Parliament at Westminster. With the achievement of Catholic emancipation in 1829, which allowed Catholics to participate in British public life, Mill believed the main source of conflict between England and Ireland was now the awful economic system whereby most of the majority Catholic Irish population were locked into an arrangement of rent payments to an English landholding class – as Mill described it 'eight thousand persons' – who effectively owned rural Ireland (CW 6:501). Mill believed this 'vicious system, upheld by England' was a Malthusian time bomb primed to explode as the Irish population, which grew from 5 million in 1800 to over 8 million by 1840, put intense pressure on ever smaller parcels of rented land to feed the impoverished Irish cottier class (CW 6:502). As Winch explains, in the Irish countryside 'the subdivision of land-holdings and the use of the potato for subsistence had encouraged early marriages and enabled large families to be supported on a precarious basis'.[62] Whereas in England in 1845 any farm under 100 acres was considered small, in Ireland 70 per cent of tenant farms were less than 15 acres and an astonishing 15 per cent were 1 acre or less.[63]

The event that sparked the Irish crisis was the recurring failure of the potato crop – the staple of the Irish peasantry – beginning in 1846. Mill had begun writing the *Principles* in the months prior to the blight and suspended this work temporarily in the autumn of 1846 to write a series of forty articles for the *Morning Chronicle* to explain to English readers the economic nature of the crisis and how it could be remedied. While it is not clear that Mill fully grasped at this stage the enormous scale of the disaster in rural Ireland that would see a million people die and many more than that emigrate in a three-year period, he was definitive in his attribution of blame: 'The difficulty in governing Ireland lies entirely in our own hands' (CW 6:529). Even in the early phase of the famine, Mill described England and Ireland's tortured relations in radical terms of reparations: 'If ever compensation was due from one people to another, this is the case for it' (CW 24:903).

In the *Principles*, Mill concluded that 'the very foundation of the economic evils of Ireland is the cottier system' (CW 3:989). Mill defined the cottier system as one in which 'the labourer makes his contract for land without the intervention of a capitalist famer, and in which the conditions of the contract, especially the amount of rent, are determined not by custom, but by competition' (CW 2:313). The Irish Catholic peasants were not hired labour. They rented land from a landlord or sublet from a large farmer and paid their rents in money, in kind or by labour service to the landowner. This system of tenant farming had the perverse effect of offering no incentive for the small cottier to improve the land or produce more than was required to provide for one's family. Any improvements due to labour or any surplus production only benefitted the landowner. Rents were set by competition at frequent intervals and on short-term leases. Mill subscribed to Ricardo's rent theory, which held that rent is nothing but the producer's surplus, and thus forecast in the Irish case a perpetual clash between the landlords and the small farmers.[64] Irish cottiers were habitually in arrears and in the event of crop failures were not only unable to pay their rent, but even to feed their families. The combination of this tenant system with the pressures of overpopulation was devastating in Ireland. Whereas in England increased population produced lower wages, in Ireland increased population meant increased rents for ever shrinking holdings. For Mill, the harsh truth is that 'the soil of Ireland can no longer feed anything like its present population' (CW 3:989).

The evils of the cottier system were not solely economic, they were also moral. While Mill rejected any notion of 'national differences' among groups, he nonetheless thought it fair to conclude that the agricultural system in rural Ireland had rendered the Catholic peasantry 'among the most backward of European population in the industrial virtues' (CW 2:319–20). This connection between economic conditions and national moral characteristics set the Irish question firmly within the purview of Mill's ethology. That is, Mill viewed agrarian reform in Ireland as a means to produce, what Zastoupil calls a more 'active personality' among the downtrodden Catholic population, in order to facilitate nothing less than the 'social and moral reconstruction of Ireland'.[65] Mill's proposed solution to the problem in Ireland involved radical reform of the land tenure system. In a best-case scenario, Mill would have preferred to see Irish overpopulation lessen through emigration, Irish farms considerably expand in acreage, and the Irish peasant to become hired labourers as in England. But the 'best in itself is purely theoretical interest', and the solution to Ireland's problems in 1846–1848 had to have as its premise acceptance of the practical reality of the great harm caused by centuries of tenant farming (CW 3:991). Strikingly, Mill dramatised the deficiencies of the Irish cottier system by declaring it worse than the *ryotwari* practice of landownership in India in which peasant farmers pay rent directly to the state, which is the only landowner. Whereas in

Ireland the competitive basis for rent rates tended to drive up rents, in India the British administrators or their local proxies set the rates because 'the government itself is the landlord' (CW 3:993). The upshot, for Mill, was that in the Irish context simply extending longer leases would be insufficient to reverse the debilitating effects of the cottier system: the peasant farmers themselves must become proprietors (CW 3:327). Mill insists that in Irish culture the status of a day labourer has no charm as Irish 'moral feelings' believe the right to hold land is tied to the right to till it.[66] But how did Mill propose to execute this massive transfer of land ownership?

Mill's preferred method for instituting perpetuity of land tenure for Irish cottiers was through a programme of 'waste reclamation'. This would involve the British government allocating uncultivated land in rural Ireland to peasant proprietors. The waste lands are 'happily so extensive, and a large proportion of them so improvable as to afford a means by which, nearly the whole surplus population might be converted into peasant proprietors elsewhere' (CW 3:997). This measure would reduce the immediate pressure on rents and the demand for ever smaller plots. While Mill was open to the possibility of reclaiming land left uncultivated by English landlords, he supported the wasteland reclamation scheme in large part because it was a way to reform land tenure that did not require the politically volatile idea of expropriating the current British landholders.[67] Unsurprisingly, the utilitarian Mill did not oppose expropriation of the landlords on grounds of the sacred right of property, but rather on the basis of sound practicable policy. Indeed, Mill was prepared to countenance the 'complete expropriation of the higher classes in Ireland', but only 'if it were the sole means of effecting a great public good' (CW 2:329).

Mill also anticipated that a programme of waste land reclamation in Ireland would require government involvement to drain the bogs, build roads and in essence modernise the country's medieval transportation infrastructure (CW 3:1000). Arguably, the greatest transformation would, in Mill's view, be to the mentality of the Irish peasant, who would now be on the path to greater self-reliance and productivity. Mill opposed the extension of the Poor Law to Ireland, even during the famine, precisely because he feared it would produce long-term dependence on government assistance. Regardless, Mill's proposal for wasteland reclamation was denounced by British leaders such as Lord Palmerston for being 'communistic'.[68] Mill did not deny that the permanent transfer of land to peasant ownership was a 'radical change', but he insisted that 'revolutionary measures are the things now required';[69] and he pointed to the radical agrarian reforms of revolutionary France to highlight a successful land transfer on a massive scale.

Mill's thinking on Irish agrarian reform evolved somewhat in the years following the Famine of 1846–1849. His initial waste-land reclamation proposal presupposed that severe overpopulation would continue to strain Irish agriculture for the foreseeable future. But in the 1862 edition of the *Principles*, Mill speculated that an English-style system of hired labour was now more feasible in Ireland due to the sudden and dramatic decline in population due to death and emigration caused by the famine.[70] In the later editions of *Principles*, Mill looked beyond peasant proprietorship to a fuller integration of Irish agriculture into a complex modern economy in which the economic advantages of large-scale enterprises would be able to conjoin with the moral and social benefits of a variegated system of ownership, including partnerships and cooperatives.[71] But perhaps the most profound impact that the Irish crisis had on Mill related to his ethological science of character formation. In the years following the famine, Mill reflected deeply on the economic foundations not only of personal character development, but also of national identity: 'The land of Ireland, the land of every country, belongs to the people of that country' (CW 2:326). Policies setting a nation's distribution of land must not be determined by claims of proprietary rights alone, but rather by the mode of appropriation 'most useful to the collective body of its inhabitants' (CW 2:326). In the 1858 edition of the *Principles*, Mill predicted that with the introduction of peasant proprietorship on a wide scale, from 'the present lazy, apathetic, reckless, improvident and lawless Ireland, a new Ireland [will] arise' (CW 3:1003).

Sadly, practically none of Mill's proposals for agrarian reform were palatable to the corrupt and short-sighted, but politically influential, English landowning class in Ireland. The radical de-population caused by the famine only delayed the struggle over land ownership into the future. In the final analysis, Mill was disappointed by Britain's failure to resolve, or even truly understand, the profound economic, political and social problems in Catholic Ireland. He declared that 'the loss and disgrace, are England's . . . to retain the mere soil of Ireland, but to lose its inhabitants' (CW 2:326). However, confident that Irish emigrants would go forth to help build 'a higher state of civilisation' in America, Mill continued throughout his life to show concern for Ireland languishing under a particularly destructive form of colonisation. Indeed, he was not completely unsympathetic even to the Fenian rebels and cited the 1867 Risings as evidence for the urgency with which 'liberal Englishmen' need to support radical change to the land system in Ireland. He continued to defend the Union, but he did so purely on the grounds of short-term interests. Irish political leaders were not, in Mill's view, ready for self-rule, and thus separation at this time was undesirable (CW 6:526). On the scale of cultural progress, the Irish were stuck somewhere between India and Canada, and Mill left for a future generation of British liberals the perhaps impossible task of resolving the empire's Irish Problem.

The Liberal Critique of Patriarchy

Classical liberalism was practically born in the critique of patriarchalist arguments for absolute monarchy in seventeenth-century England. But over the course of time, English, and later British, liberal thinkers established different grounds for their arguments both against patriarchy and for greater equality for women. In the early modern period in England the patriarchal motif fused with other authoritarian doctrines to form a formidable absolutist political ideology that rejected the principle of natural equality. In this period, traditional male rule in families (i.e., the ubiquity of patriarchy) was viewed as support for foundational ideas of classical and Christian thought, such as Aristotle's account of the organic webs of hierarchical relations that comprise the human *telos* and scriptural-based theological arguments for patriarchy deduced from Adam's rule over Eve and her children.[72] Both Hobbes and Locke launched their natural rights teaching in the context of the critique of patriarchy, albeit for varying reasons. Hobbes sought to defend the foundational principle that all forms of rule must be based on consent, and thus inasmuch as patriarchy exists it is nonetheless artificial in this sense. For Locke, the need to respond to patriarchy was more direct and more urgent given that by the late 1670s the volatile blend of traditional patriarchalist and scriptural divine-right monarchy popularised by Robert Filmer's writings had become a potent weapon in the rhetorical arsenal of the Whig Locke's Tory opponents in England's constitutional struggles of the time. With both Hobbes, but especially Locke, we see thinkers reflecting on the emancipatory potential of natural rights theory, but also recognising the radical implications for the family, not just political society.

Political economy was not a direct concern in Hobbes' scattered discussions of gender. Indeed, feminist scholars are often struck by the noticeable absence of references to women in Hobbes' political theory purportedly based upon human psychology. Some commentators argue that Hobbes' individualism constitutes a new modern form of patriarchy that always results in male rule despite the theoretical premise of equal natural rights,[73] while others insist that Hobbes' account of radical individualism in the state of nature suppressed motherhood and distinctive feminine aspects of human experience.[74] There are also, however, commentators who view Hobbes' general acceptance of the conventional basis of male rule in families as actually subverting traditional patriarchy.[75] Nonetheless, feminist scholars have ably demonstrated Hobbes' difficulty in reconciling the ubiquitous historical practice of patriarchy with the theoretical principle of natural equality.

The key to understanding Hobbes' position on sexual equality is, of course, the state of nature. Hobbes famously described the state of nature as the condition in which human beings appeared 'as if they had just emerged from the earth like mushrooms and grown up without any obligation to each other'.[76] The effect of these fully-formed beings co-habiting without prior engagement is to produce a deep sense of insecurity generated, perhaps counterintuitively, precisely by the similarity of beings relatively equal both in terms of mental capacity and physical strength.[77] For our purposes, the most striking feature of the state of nature is Hobbes' revelation that there are no matrimonial laws in it, and his insistence that fathers of children cannot be known 'but by the testimony of the mother'.[78] Hobbes takes his egalitarian principles seriously as applied to women, at least in the natural condition, as he explicitly rejects the assumption of Aristotle, Thomas Aquinas and Hugo Grotius that men naturally rule women because they are 'the most excellence sex'.[79] As such, Hobbes insisted (rather implausibly) that dominion over the child derives originally from the little one's consent. In principle, a child can be 'equally subject to both parents' because there is 'not always that difference of strength between a man and a woman' that can be settled as a matter of right; if, however, there is no matrimonial contract, then Hobbes concludes that 'the dominion is in the mother'.[80] Hobbes' natural primal matriarchy means that every woman becomes a ruler if she decides to raise a child, much like the mythical female warriors the Amazons, who contracted with neighbouring men and sent back the male children, even as they ensured that 'the dominion of the females was in the mother'.[81] For Hobbes, then, if there is any basis at all for natural or quasi-natural rule, it would seem to be natural maternal right.

How does Hobbes account for the common practice of patriarchal families? He explains that while it is true that dominion in the family is set by contract, not nature, he admits civil laws 'for the most part (but not always)' favour male heads of households because 'for the most part commonwealths have been erected by the fathers, not by the mothers of families'.[82] Hobbes' assumption is that male rule in the family, if not natural in the strict sense, is in important respects pre-civil: 'For the father and master being before the institution of the commonwealth absolute sovereigns in their own families, they lose afterward no more of their authority than the law of the commonwealth taketh from them.'[83] As several feminist critics observe, it makes little sense in Hobbist terms that women would consent to a contractual arrangement that practically always (Amazons notwithstanding) concludes in their subservient role in the family and civil society.[84] Perhaps Hobbes assumed a natural competitive disadvantage that women experience due to pregnancy and the demands of childbearing, but he never says so. What seems undeniable is that Hobbes' primary theoretical concern was to undermine traditional claims to political rule, whether religious or naturalistic, and was relatively unconcerned about disturbing the practice of male rule in the family. For Hobbes, patriarchy did not contradict absolute sovereignty in the commonwealth insofar as the family is absorbed politically into 'the unity of the representer', who is the sovereign.[85] Thus, the family, however constituted, will exist as 'a regular and lawful private body' subject to the sovereign and enmeshed in the political economy of the *Leviathan*.[86]

The issue of gender is more directly implicated in Locke's political economy because of the pervasiveness of his teaching on property rights. The main elements of Locke's critique of divine-right monarchy are familiar: the powers of government derive from the natural powers of individuals in a state of nature – not from divine donation – and are limited by the purpose for which government is created; namely, to secure the rights to life, liberty and property. Whereas Hobbes and Filmer reached arguably the same constitutional conclusion – absolute sovereignty – by way of radically different premises, Hobbes and Locke reached a very different constitutional conclusion on the same basic premise of natural rights (with the major difference being Locke's natural right of property derived originally from labour). Locke famously declared that the 'state all men are naturally in' is a 'state of perfect freedom' and a 'state also of equality'.[87] Feminist scholars have taken Locke's theoretical egalitarianism to task in recent times. Some claim that

Locke's abstract case for equality conceals deeper underlying patri-archalist assumptions about male rule in the family as 'the abler and stronger' sex and the presumed disadvantage women experi-ence due to reproduction.[88] Another line of criticism charges that Locke's theory of property rights in the family is a rejection of women's capacity to acquire property on equal terms with men, which then deprives them of access to the public sphere and thus perpetuates their subjection in the private family.[89] However, other commentators determine that while Locke retained some patriar-chal assumptions, his individualist principles were potentially trans-formative for women in that they compelled later liberal thinkers to bring their views on women in line with their ideas of equality.[90]

Upon examination, it is clear that greater equality for women is central to Locke's project to undermine 'natural' claims to rule and to transform the historical patriarchal family, long a buttress for authoritarian politics into a *natural rights family* based on Locke's individualist principles. Locke's theory of property is integral to this reformulation of gender relations and the family. The first step in this process was Locke's redefinition of marriage or 'con-jugal society' as a voluntary compact between man and a woman directed to the goal of raising children. In this de-sacralised account of marriage, the scope and duration of the institution is set by the demands of human biology, which require a longer conjunction than for faster maturing creatures.[91] For Locke, conjugal society does not presuppose male rule inasmuch as 'the master or mistress' may have 'some sort of rule proper to a family'.[92] But how in this naturalised account of the family is it possible to explain the his-torical subjection of women? One obvious source for Filmer was the biblical injunction to Eve at Genesis 3:16 that 'thy desire shall be to thy husband, and he shall rule over thee'.[93] Locke's response to this venerable claim for male superiority is instructive. First, he denied that Genesis 3:16 involves a command at all. It was more a matter of a prediction of 'what should be the woman's lot'.[94] But this only begs the question why would it be the lot of all, or at least most, women to be ruled by men? Locke concedes that this biblical prediction is not wholly mysterious inasmuch as 'there is I grant, a foundation in nature for it'.[95]

What is the normative bearing of this putative natural 'founda-tion' for sexual inequality? Frustratingly, Locke never answered this question definitively, but he did allude to some possible expla-nations. First, there is the supposed disadvantage for women due to pregnancy: 'She should bring forth children in sorrow and pain.'[96]

But Locke questions the moral status of this condition insofar as there is no requirement that childbirth must be debilitating, 'if there could be found a remedy for it'.[97] Another more significant possible explanation for the inequality of men and women is Locke's suggestion in the *Second Treatise* that in the event that spouses disagree on a course of action, the final determination falls to the man as the 'abler and stronger'.[98] Locke never clarified the sense in which men are supposedly 'abler and stronger' than women. Physical strength alone does not seem to carry much normative weight as Locke dismissed this as the 'rule of beasts'.[99] And even this supposed male superiority is limited by virtue of the fact that the wife retains full possession of what is her 'peculiar right', and even has 'in many cases a liberty to separate from him'.[100]

Given that the most characteristic feature of Locke's political theory is his treatment of property rights, it is perhaps not surprising that the possibility for sexual equality in Locke's thought hinges on his perception of women's capacity to acquire and own property. The moral meaning of property is a theme throughout Locke's political writings. In terms of the historical origins of patriarchy, Locke somewhat anticipated the stadial history of the Scottish Enlightenment by framing it in terms of a distinct stage of economic and social development. In the first ages of the world, the father was ruler of his family. Locke admits that this simple form of government may have been suitable in that 'poor but virtuous age', but as property holdings expanded it led to the establishment of limits on the arbitrary power of these father rulers.[101] From this anthropological perspective, the historical form of the patriarchal family was already obsolete economically and morally problematic even in Locke's time. Locke indicates that women in the contemporary period can and do in fact retain title to property both in their own right and as members of a family. One example of this is illustrated by the case of conquest. Locke argued that a just conqueror may rightfully kill and even enslave an aggressor, but the conqueror has no claim to the goods of his 'wife and children' even as reparation because 'as to the wife's share, whether her own labour, or compact, gave her a title to it, it is plain, her husband could not forfeit what was hers'.[102]

The notion that women can possess property in their own right is confirmed by Locke's account of inheritance. The natural right of dependant children to inherit their parent's property exists as an extension of the fundamental right of self-preservation.[103] But Locke not only rejected the practice of primogeniture so beloved by patriarchalists like Filmer, he also defended a parent's right to choose to bequeath his or her estate on the adult children or whomever happens to 'please them best'.[104] In Locke's individualistic moral calculus, the prospect of inheritance provides the most reliable incentive for adult children to honour their parents, and Locke insists that this honour must extend to women as 'the Father's authority cannot dispossess the Mother' of that right she has to the honour of her children.[105] For this right of maternal honour to have any practical effect, women must have property of their own or a share in the common family property.

Locke's declarations about the property rights of women were clearly more prescriptive than an accurate account of seventeenth-century English life. In this sense, reformulating inherited conceptions of the family in terms of natural rights philosophy was a central part of Locke's critique of patriarchal divine-right monarchy. But the success of any major reform of the family structure would ultimately depend on whether women are capable of exercising the degree of reason necessary to generate a right to property (i.e., animals do not have a right to property) and to participate fully in both the private and public realms of life. There is no evidence that Locke ever entertained the idea that women were less rational than men. To the contrary, he soundly rejected one of the long-cherished tenets of Aristotelian biology speculating: 'The Rational Soul . . . of the yet unformed embrio . . . if it must be supposed to derive anything from the parents, it must certainly owe most to the mother.'[106] Furthermore, in *Some Thoughts Concerning Education* (1693) in which Locke outlined the education for a young gentleman to prepare him for a life in business, the professions and politics, it is remarkable how little he thought it should differ from the education of girls. Locke confided where the 'difference of sex' requires different treatment for boys and girls ''twill be no hard matter to distinguish'.[107] A few sections later, Locke reveals the essential similarity of the proper education of boys and girls when he proposes that with regard to the education of daughters, 'the nearer they come to the Hardships of their brothers in their Education, the greater advantage will they receive from it all the remaining Part of their Lives'.[108] For an education ostensibly intended for the training of young gentlemen, Locke retained only minor, non-intellectual differences for girls. As he confided to one young mother: 'I acknowledge no difference of sex in your (daughter's) mind relating . . . to truth, virtue, obedience, I think I will have no thing altered in it from what is (writ for the son).'[109]

204 | RECOVERING CLASSICAL LIBERAL POLITICAL ECONOMY

There is, thus, perhaps a tension in Locke's argument by which he extends individualist principles to women, but also appears to accept some vague basis, at least historically, for male rule in the family. But this presumed male dominance is circumscribed considerably by Locke's defence of women's property rights and his progressive attitude towards female education as a means to produce rational, autonomous female agents in the family and political society. Locke concluded that real societal progress requires reforming the traditional family in a manner consistent with natural rights. Liberal government and a liberalised family would be mutually interdependent.

Later Liberalism and the Subjection of Women

The question of women's rights was not a direct focus of the Scottish Enlightenment thinkers we have considered such as David Hume and Adam Smith. However, part of their argument in rejecting Mandeville's hedonistic moral philosophy involved reworking his conjectural stadial history in a manner that did speak indirectly to issues of gender. In particular, in their account of the progress of civilisation the Scottish philosophers articulated a narrative of gradual, albeit never complete, female emancipation in the transition from hunter-gatherer to the later commercial stage of economic development.[110] In the essay 'Of the Rise and Progress of the Arts and Sciences', Hume cited the status of women as an index of the measure of cultural progress:

> Nature has given men the superiority above women, by endowing him with greater strength both of mind and body ... Barbarous nations display this superiority, by reducing their females to the most abject slavery ... But the male sex, among a polite people, discover their authority in a more generous, though a not less evident manner; by civility, by respect, by complaisance, and in a word gallantry.[111]

Hume's sexist assumptions, akin to Locke's 'abler and stronger' argument, are moderated somewhat by the historical evolution of commerce and *politesse* rather than by women's assertion of equal rights. Smith discovered a similar process in the most advanced stage of economic development in which 'commerce and manufactures gradually introduced order and good government, and with them, the liberty and security of individuals'.[112] Smith identified the gradual softening of mores and, with it, improved conditions for women as a function of the increased hospitality offered by the 'rich and the great' in the commercial era.[113] The emancipation of women in the legal, political and economic sense was not, however, a serious concern for Hume and Smith.

By contrast, Mary Wollstonecraft was undoubtedly a seminal figure in the liberal struggle for women's rights. Writing in the context of the Age of Revolutions in France and America, Wollstonecraft is widely acknowledged as one of the grandmothers of modern feminism. But there is nonetheless considerable debate among scholars about the content of her thought and her intellectual influences. Some commentators view her argument for women's rights as the product of the Christian theology of radical dissenting English Protestantism,[114] while others identify her approach with the Enlightenment rationalism of Lockean natural rights,[115] or as a 'novelised polemic' influenced by the literary conventions of the period.[116] She has been called a champion of republican radical democracy,[117] a proponent of Scottish Enlightenment moral philosophy,[118] and even a classical Aristotelian.[119] For our purposes, it is perhaps wise to recognise the eclectic range of intellectual influences in Wollstonecraft's sweeping argument for equality in her masterpiece *A Vindication of the Rights of Woman* (1792). In particular, I want to highlight the complex manner in which she deployed discursive techniques and strategies familiar to us from both the natural rights and interest-based traditions of liberalism.

The title of her major works reminds us that the *Vindication* emerged in the context of the French Revolution. Wollstonecraft's 'Rights of Woman' are the unspoken and forgotten complement to the *Declaration of the Rights of Man and Citizen* announced by the French National Constituent Assembly in August 1789. Wollstonecraft's anonymously published *A Vindication of the Rights of Man* (1790) was actually the first rejoinder to Edmund Burke's *Reflections on the Revolution in France*, appearing several months before Tom Paine's celebrated *Rights of Man Part I*. However, *A Vindication of the Rights of Woman* was inspired not by animosity to Burke, but rather by French minister Talleyrand's report on educational policy submitted to the National Assembly in 1791, which called for the introduction of a system of free public education for boys to promote republican values, but did not extend the recommendation to the education of girls. The rights of women that Wollstonecraft believed were denied or injured by depriving them the same educational opportunities as men are certainly recognisable as part of the discourse of rights, but she described them in a complicated way. In Wollstonecraft's rendering, rights are inseparable from duties, but the latter are typically associated with the classical republican or Christian tradition, rather than the individualistic secular natural rights doctrine of Hobbes and Locke.[120] But while Wollstonecraft's conception of rights would depart in significant ways from the earlier liberal arguments of her English predecessors over the importance of moral duties, she never rejected the fundamental liberal premise about the logical priority of rights over duties: 'take away natural rights, and duties become null'.[121] But what constitutes the moral core of both human and women's rights?

Talleyrand's Report on Education struck such a profound chord with Wollstonecraft precisely because she believed that improving the faculty of reason is essential to human character development in general and for virtue in particular. She declared: 'In what does man's pre-eminence over brute creation consist? The answer is as clear as that half is less than the whole; in Reason. What acquirement exalts one being over another? Virtue, we spontaneously reply.'[122] The dichotomy between reason and sensuality is central to Wollstonecraft's account of virtue. By depriving females of the opportunity for serious education, in effect 'cramping their understandings and sharpening their senses', even societies putatively committed to natural rights such as France (not to mention England) are treating women and girls as little better than animals.[123] This injustice assumed theological significance for Wollstonecraft as she insists that the 'stamen of immortality . . . is the perfectability of human reason'.[124] Reason, as opposed to our sensual nature, is, according to Wollstonecraft, the source of our common humanity independent of any patriarchalist assumptions about male superiority: 'If women are by nature inferior to men, their virtues must be the same in quality, if not in degree . . . consequently, their conduct should be founded on the same principles, and have the same aim.'[125] Clearly, the rights of women that Wollstonecraft contextualised in terms of duty, virtue, and the priority of reason and passions differ significantly from the natural rights evoked by Hobbes and Locke.

Wollstonecraft did, however, continue the earlier liberal appeal to nature because of its powerful rhetorical appeal as a counterpart to what she took to be the social construction of gender. Her penetrating reflections on the way sexual identity is in large measure a product of social customs and practices is perhaps what Wollstonecraft is best known for today. She cast her conception of universalist reason as the antithesis of the misogynist arguments that attempt to 'give sex to mind'.[126] The deontological tenor animating her rationalist appeal to inspire the total reform of sexual identities is unmistakable. Wollstonecraft declared that only the societal commitment to the cultivation of reason can result in making men more chaste, women more modest and persuade women to renounce the arbitrary, demeaning and ultimately self-destructive 'sovereignty of beauty'.[127] The cause of women's rights is woven into the promise of global revolution against aristocracy and inequality of all kinds, for 'to effect a revolution in female manners' is the vital first step in drawing women into the progressive struggle 'to reform the world'.[128]

There are, however, important elements of Wollstonecraft's argument that do not appear to rest upon a rationalist metaphysical foundation of natural rights. There is, for example, a decidedly empirical dimension to her views about progress akin to the conceptual stadial history of Hume and Smith: 'Brutal force has hitherto governed the world, and the science of politics is in its infancy.'[129] For Wollstonecraft, rights are both good in themselves, but also instrumental to certain measurable individual and social goods.[130] In this sense, Wollstonecraft anticipated John Mill's version of enlightened utility. In the opening letter of the *Vindication of the Rights of Woman* addressed personally to Talleyrand, Wollstonecraft made the case that it is in the national interest of the revolutionary government in France to advance female education, for if woman 'be not prepared by education to become companions of man, she will stop the progress of knowledge and virtue . . . If children are to be educated to understand the true principles of patriotism, their mother must be a patriot.'[131] In order to prevent women from becoming a permanent reactionary force in a democratic republic, they must be educated to become full participants in public life as 'an active citizen' and even 'ought to have representatives' in government.[132]

There is also an important economic dimension to Wollstonecraft's argument for equal educational opportunities for females. Women who have been properly educated will be better wives and mothers. In one sense, Wollstonecraft's argument is quite conservative as she seems to presume that woman's nature is to be in the family: 'whatever tends to incapacitate the maternal character, takes woman out of her sphere'.[133] However, she also advocates reimagining marriage in terms of a partnership between autonomous agents 'equally necessary and independent of each other'.[134] Thus, even in the context of family life, Wollstonecraft's central claim is to render women more independent and capable of civil existence 'married or single'.[135] As such, the professions should be open, at least to 'women of a superior cast'.[136] Only with a measure of economic independence will women no longer accept 'legal prostitution' as a means to acquire support from men they do not love.[137] The examples of lines of employment that should be opened to women include nursing, medicine, studying politics and 'business of various kinds'.[138] Ultimately, then, Wollstonecraft's goal extends beyond liberating a few select women of 'superior cast' towards a universal call for women's emancipation: 'I speak of the improvement and emancipation of the whole sex.'[139] Economic independence for women is a *sine qua non* for social progress towards a democratic future.

John Stuart Mill is justly celebrated as an early male supporter of women's emancipation. He introduced an unsuccessful bill for female suffrage in 1867 in his single term as a Member of Parliament, and his last major work *The Subjection of Women* (1869) made an eloquent and powerful case for the equal legal, political and economic rights of women. His relationship both as Platonic friend and married partner with pioneer of the women's rights movement Harriet Taylor was well known.[140] Indeed, early in his philosophical career John Mill broke from his father James Mill on the issue of women's rights, as the elder Mill dismissed the idea of female suffrage in his influential utilitarian tract *Essay on Government* (1820). Feminist scholars have interpreted Mill's protofeminism in several ways. His secular liberal utilitarian approach has been contrasted to Wollstonecraft's more theological argument.[141] Some scholars view Mill's as a notable, but incomplete, argument for women's rights that failed to address the gendered division of labour in the family,[142] denied the value of women's distinctive experiences such as childbearing and rearing,[143] and retained basic sexist assumptions about respective intellectual and emotional 'natures' of men and women.[144] Still other commentators argue that Mill's primary goal in the *Subjection of Women* was not in fact political equality for women, but rather the redefinition of marriage as rational friendship.[145] For our purposes, it is useful to examine Mill in relation to Wollstonecraft, specifically as an example of the complex use of the discourse of rights and interests. Arguably, out of all of the subjects of inquiry in his long and varied career, the issue of women's emancipation is the one that brought Mill closest to the very brink of a deontological rights argument. I will also investigate how Mill's political economy sheds light on his advocacy for women's rights, especially in relation to the moral and intellectual advancement of the working class.

The interplay of the logic of rights and interests is a feature of the *Subjection* from its opening lines in which Mill declared that 'the legal subordination of one sex to the other – is wrong in itself, and now one of the chief hindrances to human improvement'.[146] Published six years after his classic *Utilitarianism* (1863), the *Subjection* presented women's emancipation as a major test case for the validity of utilitarian principles inasmuch as the argument for women's equality confronts the dual challenges of the emotional opposition of the 'mass of feeling' among men and the lack of any measurable experience with alternative arrangements for sexual relations.[147] On its face, the subjection of women in law is a clear violation of the 'greatest happiness principle' central to utilitarian philosophy.[148] In Mill's reform of the Benthamite original, happiness is redefined in terms of the intellectualised forms of pleasure and pain produced by the 'higher faculties'.[149] The causes of unhappiness are intrinsically social; namely, the 'present wretched education and institutions'.[150] While he indicates that reflecting upon such a deeply entrenched social pathology as patriarchy can be depressing, Mill also encouraged a degree of optimism insofar as social ills are 'conquerable by human care and effort'.[151]

Women are perhaps the major constituent block among the 'large portions of mankind whose happiness it is still practicable to disregard'.[152] While Mill quite easily framed the issue of women's rights in the rubric of utilitarian happiness, it is nonetheless striking the degree to which he also described this issue as a matter of rights. As Botting observes, the *Subjection* is, uncharacteristically for Mill, saturated with the terms 'rights' and 'moral right'.[153] Does the normative conclusion that the inequality of women is 'wrong in itself' signify an abandonment of the utility principle in favour of a rights-based argument? In part it does, but with the caveat that Mill always seems to interpret rights claims in instrumental terms. A right is 'something which society ought to defend me in possession of'. In answer to the question why society bears this obligation, Mill's response is: 'I can give no other reason than general utility.'[154] He reiterated frequently his contention that there is no value in resorting to the 'fiction of a contract' in the manner of Hobbes and Locke.[155] For Mill, rights are modified by the utilitarian logic of interest in two distinct ways. First, with respect to individuals, rights discourse can be deployed pragmatically as a tool for realising personal development. But rights are also useful as a way to describe the measurable promotion of the permanent interests of humankind as a progressive being.[156] *Utilitarianism* points towards the *Subjection*, as the former practically concluded with an appeal to historical progress and the overthrowing of the 'aristocracies of colour, race and sex'.[157] Mill, then, displayed some kinship to the conjectural stadial history of Hume and Smith, even as the discourse of rights provided a rhetorically potent idiom for advancing an empirically grounded call for reform.

Another example of Mill's relation to Hume is his insistence that even though moral feelings 'are not innate, but acquired, they are not for that reason the less natural'.[158] Mill's emphasis on the social basis of the acquired virtues served the larger aims of his 'ethology' or science of character development generally, but it also provided a more specific model for his sceptical examination of the prevalent claims about the putative 'nature' of women. As Ball suggests, the *Subjection* can be understood as an exercise in applied 'ethology' given that Mill sought to expose the limits of contemporary knowledge about the science of character formation.[159] Mill agreed with Wollstonecraft that the psychic damage caused to the development of women's character and personality is a deeper problem even than the visible civil and economic disabilities.[160] Men want women to be willing subordinates, and therefore 'they have put everything in practice to enslave their minds'.[161] It is for this reason, echoing Wollstonecraft, that Mill concludes that what is now called the nature of women is an 'eminently artificial thing'.[162]

Mill's programme for women's emancipation is well-known and includes such measures as overturning the laws of coverture to allow married women to retain their legal personality and individual rights; introduce laws against domestic abuse; make divorce accessible to middle- and working-class women; extend the franchise to women; and, perhaps most controversially, open all professions and educational opportunities to qualified women. Mill asserts that legal exclusion of women from jobs and professions can be justified only if no woman is capable of successfully performing the job, in which case legal prohibitions are redundant.[163] The benefits of equal opportunity for women extend both to general society, which effectively doubles the talent pool, and will improve the moral development of males who Mill insists are also victims of patriarchy due to the malformation of their character development caused by the pernicious effects of an unwarranted feeling of superiority over half the human race.[164] Once again, similarly to

Wollstonecraft, Mill placed great emphasis on the gradual reform of marriage, and by extension the family as a whole, as friendship among equals becomes the model for marriage as opposed to subservience and dependence.[165] Yet notwithstanding his call for equal opportunity for women and for rational friendship as the model for married life, Mill still, as feminist commentators have noted, retained some sexist assumptions about women's supposedly more 'practical' way of thinking and his judgement that most women will choose domestic roles as 'the one vocation in which there is nobody to compete with them'.[166] However, probably Mill's most powerful and moving argument for women's rights is profoundly progressive and emancipatory as he extolled 'the unspeakable gain in private happiness to the liberated half of the species that would enjoy the effects of greater social and economic independence'.[167]

Mill's argument for women's rights is tightly interwoven in his broader political economy. He was convinced that the 'power of earning is essential to the dignity of a woman, if she has not independent property'.[168] Mill was impressed early in his career by the Saint Simonian socialists who were committed to 'the perfect equality of men and women'.[169] Later in the important chapter in the *Principles of Political Economy* titled 'Of the Probable Futurity of the Labouring Classes', Mill maintained that the increased social and economic independence of women is a necessary condition for improving the moral habits of the working class as such, especially as liberal society grapples with the unrelenting problem of overpopulation.[170] Channelling the spirit of Malthus and Ricardo, Mill expressed confidence in the *Principles* that improved education of the working classes will 'manifest itself in provident habits of conduct with the result that population, therefore will bear a gradually diminishing ratio to capital employment'.[171] That there is no other career option for the great majority of women than that of wife and mother is 'a flagrant social injustice', but in addition to the individual satisfaction of women themselves, 'the individual and social independence of women' will produce 'a great diminution of the evil of over-population'.[172] The 'improved intelligence' of the working class serves as a metaphor for the entire human race, which Mill concludes suffers enormously when one half of the species is exclusively devoted to the 'animal instinct' of reproduction, while this same base physicality insinuates itself into practically every potentially elevating activity of both sexes.[173] What is at stake, then, in the economic and social independence of women in the largest segment of the population is nothing less than the liberation of the distinctively human moral and intellectual life from mere biology.

In the twenty-first century, in which the harmful effects of imperialism and patriarchy have still not been completely effaced from the political and social experience of advanced liberal democracies, it is perhaps useful to look back to the origins of liberalism. We have seen that classical liberal political economy presents a complex legacy on the historical problem of imperialism and the struggle for the emancipation of women. The natural rights and interest-based strands of liberal political economy provide a rich index of concepts and rhetorical strategies both in support of, and opposition to, colonisation and empire. Similarly, liberalism, which was practically born in the critique of patriarchal divine-right monarchy, can be condemned for allowing sexist institutions and practices to continue for centuries, even while prominent liberals such as Wollstonecraft and John Mill provided inspiration for modern feminism by compelling later liberals to apply basic principles of freedom and equality to women in the family and political society. Reflecting upon the tensions, ambiguities, and even contradictions embedded in the history of liberal thought may put the challenges of today in stimulating perspective.

Notes

1. Bell 2016: 25.
2. For the root-and-branch condemnation of classical liberalism's connection to imperialism, see Tully 2008: 127–8; Ince 2018; Parekh 1995; Dossa 2002. For a more mixed liberal legacy on empire, see Pitts 2005; U. Mehta 1999; Muthu 2003; Armitage 2000; Winch 1965.
3. For important works on the connection between liberalism and patriarchy, see Pateman 1988; Brennan and Pateman 2007; Okin 1979; Coole 1988. For the early liberal roots of feminism, see Butler 1991; Ward 2010: ch. 4.
4. See Tully 1995; Arneil 1996; Parekh 1995.
5. Pagden 2003.
6. Ince 2018.
7. For Hobbes' connection to the Virginia Company as an associate of the powerful Cavendish family, see Malcolm 2002: 53–79.
8. Hobbes 1994: 22.3–7.146–7, 24.14.164.
9. Hobbes 1994: 24.4.159–600.
10. Moloney 2011.

11. Christov 2015: 130–5, 134.
12. Springborg 2015: 160; Hobbes 1994: 30.19.228.
13. Hobbes 1994: 29.22.218.
14. Armitage 2013: 91.
15. Armitage 2000: 165.
16. Locke 2016 II:26, 30, 37, 41.
17. Parekh 1995: 86; Ince 2018: 47–69.
18. Locke 1991: 423. My reading generally follows Corcoran's assessment of Locke's support for the 'indefeasible native right to property and possession' (Corcoran 2018: 225–50, 226). For the view that Locke's theory of property was devised, at least in part, to justify dispossession of indigenous peoples, see Arneil 1994; Hsueh 2008.
19. Armitage 2013: 83; Armitage 2012: 88; Farr 2008: 509–10.
20. Locke 2016 II:22–4.
21. Locke I:144, 130–1.
22. See Farr 2008: 497–98; Armitage 2013: 96–9.
23. Waldron 2002: 202, 206.
24. Farr 2008: 504–6
25. Parekh 1995: 88.
26. Armitage 2012: 109.
27. Locke 2016 II:14; and see Ince 2018: 66.
28. Balen 2003: 34–5.
29. Trenchard and Gordon 1995: 748–50
30. Armitage 2000: 148.
31. Hume 1987: 253–67; Smith 1981: 412.
32. Pitts 2005: 1–2; Sullivan 1983: 600.
33. Winch 1965: 19; Rothschild 2012: 488.
34. Smith 1981: 582. Pitts is correct to highlight the role of conjectural history in Smith's argument against colonialism, but she perhaps exaggerates somewhat by calling it 'highly original' (2005: 28) given the clear evidence of a stadial history in Hume and Mandeville.
35. Muthu 2003: 191. See also Smith 1978: 8.
36. See Smith 1981: 152 and Smith 1984: 206. In this regard, Smith shared the view of Turgot and other French Physiocrats who also criticised imperial expansion and condemned slavery (see Rothschild 2012: 189).
37. Bentham 1793: 300–6. Bentham uncharacteristically employed the discourse of rights in this address, but this rhetorical device was likely more a function of appealing to his French revolutionary audience than a genuine endorsement of natural rights philosophy.
38. Pitts 2005: 111. Winch argues that Bentham was unable to hold a consistent position regarding colonies (1965: 25).
39. Mill 1818: 17, 19, 31. See also Majeed 1999: 56.
40. Forbes 1951: 24, 31; Eisenberg 2018: 158–62.
41. Pitts 2005: 128–9.

42. Winch 1965: 161.
43. Pitts 2005, see also Sullivan 1983.
44. For an excellent discussion of Wakefield, see Ince 2018: ch. 4.
45. Ince 2018: 118.
46. Ball 2000: 31.
47. Mill CW 12:365.
48. P. Mehta 2012: 252.
49. Ryan 1999: 15.
50. Tully 1995: 142–52.
51. For an excellent treatment of the impact of the Canadian rebellions of 1837 in British radical politics, see Turner 2006.
52. Mill CW 6:418; hereafter in notes and text CW 6 and page.
53. CW 6:458–9. See also Bell 2010: 48; Winch 1965: 117–21.
54. Tully 1995: 159–62; Parekh 1995: 95.
55. E.g., Schwartz 1972: 5; Ambirajan 1999: 223.
56. See Pitts 2005; U. Mehta 1999; Parekh 1995.
57. See Tunick 2006: 597; Marwah 2011: 352–4.
58. Dossa 2002: 739; Pitts 2005: 20.
59. Meha 1999: 234; Muthu 2003: 279; Tunick 2006: 106–7.
60. Zastoupil 1999: 113.
61. Harris 1965: 197–8, Ambirajan 1999: 229; Tunick 2006: 605.
62. Winch 1965: 69.
63. Kinzer 2001: 91.
64. Ricardo 2004: 33. See also Kinzer 2001: 57, 61.
65. Zastoupil 1983: 708; Kinzer 2001: 64.
66. CW 3:326; CW 6:513.
67. See Hollander 1985: 848; Kinzer 2001: 97.
68. Schwartz 1972: 206. Kinzer argues that in his opposition to an extension of the Poor Law in Ireland, Mill displayed a 'dogmatic streak' that put him at odds even with most British liberals at the time (2001: 69–70).
69. CW 3:1003; CW 6:518, 503.
70. CW 2:33. See Hollander 1985: 852.
71. Schwartz 1972: 207–8.
72. For the classic study of patriarchalism in seventeenth-century England, see Schochet 1975.
73. Pateman 1991: 56
74. Di Stefano 1991: 83–5; Coole 1988: 81–2.
75. Makus 1996: 53; Zvesper 1985.
76. Hobbes 1998: 102.
77. Hobbes 1994: 13.1.74.
78. Hobbes 1994: 20.4.129; Hobbes 1998: 108.
79. Hobbes 1994: 20.4.125.
80. Hobbes 1994: 20.4–5.128–9.
81. Hobbes 1994: 20.4.129.

82. Hobbes 1994: 20.4.128–9.
83. Hobbes 1994: 22.26.153.
84. Coole (1988: 84) and Pateman (1991: 61–2) suggest the disadvantages supposedly arising from pregnancy.
85. Hobbes 1994: 16.13.104.
86. Hobbes 1994: 22.26.152.
87. Locke 2016 II:4.
88. Locke II:82. See Clark 1977: 701; Brennan and Pateman 2007: 63; Coole 1988: 88.
89. Gatens 1991: 34–5; Clark 1977: 715–16; Brennan and Pateman 2007: 61–6.
90. Butler 1991: 74–94; Grant 2003: 286–306; Walsh 1995: 252; Ward 2010: 134–70.
91. Locke 2016 II:79.
92. Locke 2016 II:77.
93. Locke 2016 I:47.
94. Locke 2016 I:47.
95. Locke 2016 I:47.
96. Locke 2016 I:47.
97. Locke 2016 I:47.
98. Locke 2016 II:82.
99. Locke 2016 II:1.
100. Locke 2016 II:82.
101. Locke 2016 II:110, 105, 111.
102. Locke 2016 II:183.
103. Locke 2016: I:88.
104. Locke 2016 I:91; II:72.
105. Locke 2016 II:69.
106. Locke 2016 I:55.
107. Locke 1996: 12.
108. Locke 1996: 14.
109. See Ward 2010: 167.
110. O'Brien 2009: 78–82.
111. Hume 1987: 133.
112. Smith 1981: 412.
113. Smith 1981: 413.
114. Botting 2016: 1, 14, 18; O'Brien 2009: 174.
115. Gatens 1991: 112–13; Muller 1996: 48–53.
116. Kelly 1992: 114.
117. Zerilli 2018: 433–4; Sapiro 1996: 38–41.
118. De Lucia 2014: 114–25; O'Neill 2007: 8–9, 103–7.
119. Taylor 2014: 108.
120. Botting (2016: 78, 80) discovered that 'duties' appears three times more than 'rights' in the *Vindication of the Rights of Woman*.
121. Wollstonecraft 2009: 155.

122. Wollstonecraft 2009: 14.
123. Wollstonecraft 2009: 25.
124. Wollstonecraft 2009: 57.
125. Wollstonecraft 2009: 29.
126. Wollstonecraft 2009: 46.
127. Wollstonecraft 2009: 14, 24, 59, 131.
128. Wollstonecraft 2009: 49.
129. Wollstonecraft 2009: 41.
130. Abbey 2018: 427.
131. Wollstonecraft 2009: 6.
132. Wollstonecraft 2009: 154, 156.
133. Wollstonecraft 2009: 186.
134. Wollstonecraft 2009: 151.
135. Wollstonecraft 2009: 151.
136. Wollstonecraft 2009: 155.
137. Wollstonecraft 2009: 157.
138. Wollstonecraft 2009: 157.
139. Wollstonecraft 20009: 185.
140. But Abbey (2018: 429) and Okin (1979: 204) both observe that Mill had practically nothing to say about his own mother in his *Autobiography*.
141. Botting 2016: 1, 95, 102.
142. Okin 1979: 215–17.
143. Di Stefano 1991: ch. 4; Coole 1988: 117.
144. Annas 1977: 184–6; Gatens 1991: 33; Makus 1996: 95.
145. Urbinati 1991: 626–48; Shanley 1991: 164–80.
146. Mill 2002: 123.
147. Mill 2002: 133, 143.
148. Mill 2002: 239.
149. Mill 2002: 241.
150. Mill 2002: 246.
151. Mill 2002: 248.
152. Mill 2002: 266.
153. Botting 2016: 89.
154. Mill 2002: 290.
155. E.g., Mill 2002: 292.
156. Botting 2016: 90–5.
157. Mill 2002: 300.
158. Mill 2002: 264.
159. Ball 2000: 37–40.
160. Baum 2000: 173.
161. Mill 2002: 137.
162. Mill 2002: 144.
163. Mill 2002: 175.
164. Mill 2002: 207.

165. Mill 2002: 169.
166. Mill 2002: 175, 184. See Annas 1977: 184–6; Makus 1996: 95; Okin 1979: 215–17.
167. Mill 2002: 223.
168. Mill 2002: 173.
169. Mill CW 1:175
170. Baum 2000: 183.
171. Mill CW 3:765.
172. Mill CW 3:766.
173. Mill CW 3:766.

Conclusion: Towards a Political Economy of Rights and Interests

John Maynard Keynes famously observed, with no small hint of irony, that one of the characteristics of the relation between modern politics and modern economics is that: 'Practical men, who believe themselves to be quite exempt from any intellectual influences, are usually the slaves of some defunct economist.'[1] I do not mean to suggest that any of the major figures of classical liberal political economy that we have examined in this book are 'defunct' or somehow only of antiquarian interest. Rather, the object of my recovery project has been to challenge a narrow and reductive interpretation of the legacy of classical liberal political economy that remains influential among a key segment of the political and economic elites in contemporary liberal democracies (Keynes' 'practical men'). This distorted view of classical liberal political economy continues to hover over our economic debates as the purported intellectual forbear of the laissez faire doctrine that provides academic pedigree and philosophical heft for the policies of austerity and unrestrained capitalism in our times. In contrast, what we have seen in our careful reading of figures ranging from Hobbes to John Stuart Mill is a complex narrative that interweaves distinct forms of economic reasoning based upon the morally and politically infused discourses of both natural rights and the harmony of interests.

This study arraigned an influential philosophical anthropology claiming to expose the origins of liberalism, which tends to reduce the state and political life primarily into an instrument designed to secure the conditions required for free market economics. I have tried to demonstrate that this account of classical liberalism depends upon an historical appropriation of this complex intellectual tradition that proves inadequate upon serious re-engagement with the economic, political and philosophical writings of the most important liberal thinkers of the seventeenth century to the mid-nineteenth century. But this misreading of what classical liberal political economy means, even by sophisticated commentators, is in itself both instructive and consequential as it speaks to the general problem of delimiting intellectual traditions that necessarily draw upon multiple, diverse influences. On the one hand, despite the enormous social and technological changes in the past four centuries, there remain clear aspects of continuity in the way we talk about the relation between the individual and government in liberal societies. Yet, on the other hand, the very recognition of intellectual traditions often occludes theoretical possibilities embedded in the complex relation of philosophical speculation, prudential judgement and empirical observation, as well as historical and social context.

How is classical liberal political economy still relevant today? One aim of this study has been to point broadly towards the possibility that recovering classical liberal political economy may help us to understand and critique contemporary liberal democratic theory and practice as we confront new economic and political challenges, as well as continue to grapple with the painful legacies of imperialism and patriarchy. In recent times perhaps the most theoretically significant critique of the liberal democratic state from the perspective of democratic theory has come from proponents of *agonistic* democracy, who contrast the characteristically 'liberal' ideals of the rule of law, individual autonomy and the sanctity of private property rights to the quintessentially 'democratic' tradition of equality and popular sovereignty.[2] These radical democrats draw a direct connection between the formal, legal and hierarchical restrictive practices of liberal constitutionalism and the perpetuation of deep structural socio-economic inequalities.

While this democratic critique has contributed much to our understanding of the profound challenges facing liberal democracy in the age of austerity, there is also something lacking in this formulation of liberalism as being limited to a largely formal idea of equality. Practically all of the classical liberal political economists we have presented in this book (with the possible exception of Thomas Paine) were not democrats in the broadly inclusive, twenty-first-century sense of the term, but we have seen that many of them were keenly aware of the dangers of inequality and defended substantive normative principles underlying their political economy, even as they advanced notions of equity and the goal of individual moral and intellectual development to guide liberal statecraft. Admittedly, a classical liberal such as Hobbes' emphasis on equity or J. S. Mill's promise of an 'ethological' science of character formation differs from contemporary concerns about 'recognition'.[3] However, classical liberal political economy deployed strategies of rights claiming with sufficient moral force to require some form of legal recognition by the civil state, as well as presenting issues such as trade, taxation and public debt as matters of prudential judgement drawing from a complex index of social and individual interests, rather than the stark economic determinism of many current neoliberal policies. That is, classical liberal political economy contains theoretical resources that draw upon both the normative ground of rights and a mode of thinking about the harmonisation of interests in a pluralistic liberal society. Thus, contrary to received opinion, classical liberal political economy could actually be a valuable potential theoretical source for constructing a liberal critique on egalitarian grounds of the austerity policies of contemporary liberal democratic states.

This study sought to uncover important features of the classical liberal tradition often neglected. However, it is important to conclude by once again reminding ourselves that intellectual traditions are historically contestable models with their own internal diversity and rhetorical possibilities. Arguably, the current populist challenge to the neoliberal order represents a rejection of the influential libertarian strain of political economy that has resurfaced as neoliberalism today, which emphasises privatisation, deregulation and policies of austerity, and tends to suppress or marginalise the egalitarian aspects of classical liberalism. Our fresh re-examination of classical liberal political economy, hopefully freed somewhat from the prejudices produced by nearly two centuries of a narrow and distorting interpretation, illuminates a kind of authentically, even 'classical', liberalism, which could in principle support redistributionist and social investment policies. In contrast to what Hungarian Prime Minister Viktor Orbán notoriously termed 'illiberal democracy', marked by populist intolerance towards civil liberties, the classical liberal political economy we have recovered highlights the important contribution that both the rights-based and interest-based forms of liberalism historically made towards our understanding not only of equal rights, non-discrimination and fair treatment, but also our substantive moral commitments to political and economic justice. The recovery of classical liberal political economy promises, then, potentially to supply a corrective principle of moderation and an instrument of critique for both the radical libertarian neoliberal and the populist majoritarian extremes in the debate over the future of the modern democratic state. That is to say, recovering our sense of wonder about the complex legacy of classical liberal political economy may help us better understand the periodic crises of liberal democracy through insights drawn from forgotten chambers within the liberal tradition itself.

Notes

1. Keynes 1964: 383.
2. E.g., Tully 2008: 91–100; Mouffe 2018: 14.
3. Mouffe 2018: 15; Tully 2008: 226–31.

Bibliography

Abbey, Ruth. 2018. 'Symposium on Eileen Hunt Botting's *Wollstonecraft, Mill and Women's Human Rights*', *Political Theory* 46(3): 426–9.

Abizadeh, Arash. 2004. 'Historical Truth, Nationals Myths, and Liberal Democracy: On the Coherence of Liberal Nationalism', *Journal of Political Philosophy* 12(3): 291–313.

Abizadeh, Arash. 2011. 'Hobbes on the Causes of War: A Disagreement Theory', *American Political Science Review* 105(2): 298–315.

Abizadeh, Arash. 2012. 'On the Demos and its Kin: Nationalism, Democracy, and the Boundary Problem', *American Political Science Review* 106(4): 867–82.

Abizadeh, Arash. 2018. *Hobbes and the Two Faces of Ethics*. New York: Cambridge University Press.

Ambirajan, S. 1999. 'John Stuart Mill and India', in Martin I. Moir, Douglas Peers and Lynn Zastoupil (eds), *J. S. Mill's Encounter with India*. Toronto: University of Toronto Press, 221–64.

Anderson, Benedict. 1991. *Imagined Communities*. London: Verso.

Annas, Julia. 1977. 'Mill and the Subjection of Women', *Philosophy* 52, 200 (April): 179–94.

Appleby, Joyce O. 1976. 'Locke, Liberalism and the Natural Law of Money', *Past & Present* 71 (May): 43–69.

Appleby, Joyce. 1978. *Economic Thought and Ideology in Seventeenth-Century England*. Princeton, NJ: Princeton University Press.

Arendt, Hannah. 1966. *The Origins of Totalitarianism*, new edn. New York: Harcourt, Brace & World.

Arendt, Hannah. [1958] 1998. *The Human Condition*. Chicago, IL: University of Chicago Press.

Aristotle. 1934. *The Nicomachean Ethics*, trans. Henry Rackham. Cambridge, MA: Harvard University Press.

Aristotle. 2013. *Politics*, 2nd edn, ed. Carnes Lord. Chicago, IL: University of Chicago Press.

Armitage, David. 2000. *The Ideological Origins of the British Empire*. Cambridge: Cambridge University Press.

Armitage, David. 2012. 'John Locke: Theorist of Empire', in Sankar Muthu (ed.), *Empire and Modern Political Thought*. Cambridge: Cambridge University Press, 84–111.

Armitage, David. 2013. *Foundations of Modern Political Thought*. Cambridge: Cambridge University Press.

Arneil, Barbara. 1994. 'Trade, Plantations and Property: John Locke and the Economic Defence of Colonialism', *Journal of the History of Ideas* 55(4): 591–609.

Arneil, Barbara. 1996. *John Locke and America: The Defence of English Colonialism*. Oxford: Clarendon Press.

Baier, Annette C. 2010. *The Cautious Jealous Virtue: Hume on Justice*. Cambridge, MA: Harvard University Press.

Bailyn, Bernard. 1967. *The Ideological Origins of the American Revolution*. Cambridge, MA: Harvard University Press.

Balen, Malcolm. 2003. *The Secret History of the South Sea Bubble*. London: Fourth Estate.

Ball, Terence. 2000. 'The Formation of Character: Mill's "Ethology" Reconsidered', *Polity* 33(1): 25–48.

Baum, Bruce. 2000. *Rereading Power and Freedom in J. S. Mill*. Toronto: University of Toronto Press.

Bell, Duncan. 2010. 'John Stuart Mill on Colonies', *Political Theory* 38(1): 34–64.

Bell, Duncan. 2014. 'What is Liberalism?' *Political Theory* 42(6): 682–715.

Bell, Duncan. 2016. *Reordering the World: Essays on Liberalism and Empire*. Princeton, NJ: Princeton University Press.

Bellarmine, Roberto. 1928. *De Laicis*, trans. Kathleen Murphy. New York: Fordham University Press.

Bentham, Jeremy. 1978. 'Security and Equality of Property', *Property: Mainstream and Critical Positions*, ed. C.B. Macpherson. Toronto: University of Toronto Press, 41–58.

Bentham, Jeremy. [1793] 2002. 'Emancipate your Colonies!' *The Collected Works of Jeremy Bentham*, ed. Philip Schofield, Catherine Pease-Wilkin and Cyprain Blamires. Oxford: Oxford University Press, 289–316.

Berlin, Isaiah. 1964. 'Hobbes, Locke and Professor Macpherson', *Political Quarterly* 35 (October): 444–68.

Berry, Christopher J. 1992. 'Adam Smith and the Virtues of Commerce', in John W. Chapman and William A. Galston (eds), *Virtue NOMOS XXXIV*. New York: New York University Press, 69–88.

Biebricher, Thomas. 2018. *The Political Theory of Neoliberalism*. Stanford, CA: Stanford University Press.

Blyth, Mark. 2012. *Austerity: The History of a Dangerous Idea*. Oxford: Oxford University Press.

Botting, Eileen Hunt. 2016. *Wollstonecraft, Mill, and Women's Human Rights*. New Haven, CT: Yale University Press.

Boulding, Kenneth E. 1973. 'The Shadow of the Stationary State', *Daedalus* 102(4): 89–101.

Boyd, Richard. 2016. 'John Stuart Mill on Economic Liberty and Human Flourishing', in Michael R. Strain and Stan A. Veuger (eds), *Economic Freedom and Human Flourishing: Perspectives from Political Philosophy*. Washington, DC: American Enterprise Institute, 108–28.

Bray, Michael. 2007. 'Macpherson Restored? Hobbes and the Question of Social Origin', *History of Political Thought* 28(1): 56–90.

Brennan, Theresa and Carole Pateman. 2007. '"Mere Auxiliaries to the Commonwealth": Women and the Origins of Liberalism', in Nancy J. Hirschmann and Kirstie M. McClure (eds), *Feminist Interpretations of Locke*. University Park, PA: Penn State University Press, 51–73.

Brewer, John. 1988. *The Sinews of Power: War, Money and the English State, 1688–1783*. Cambridge, MA: Harvard University Press.

Burke, Edmund. [1790] 1987. *Reflections on the Revolution in France*. Buffalo, NY: Prometheus Books.

Burtt, Shelley. 1992. *Virtue Transformed: Political Argument in England 1688–1740*. Cambridge: Cambridge University Press.

Butler, Melissa. 1991. 'Early Liberal Roots of Feminism: John Locke and the Attack on Patriarchy', in Mary Lyndon Shanley and Carole Pateman (eds), *Feminist Interpretations and Political Theory*. University Park, PA: Penn State University Press, 74–94.

Caffentzis, George. 1989. *Clipped Coins, Abused Words, and Civil Government: John Locke's Philosophy of Money*. New York: Autonomedia.

Canavan, Francis. 1987. 'Thomas Paine', in Leo Strauss and Joseph Cropsey (eds), *The History of Political Philosophy*, 3rd edn. Chicago, IL: University of Chicago Press, 680–6.

Canavan, Francis. 1995. *The Political Economy of Edmund Burke: The Role of Property in His Thought*. New York: Fordham University Press.

Capaldi, Nicholas. 2004. *John Stuart Mill: A Biography*. Cambridge: Cambridge University Press.

Carey, Daniel. 2011. 'John Locke, Money, and Credit', in Daniel Carey and Christopher J. Finlay (eds), *Empire of Credit: The Financial Revolution in the British Atlantic World, 1688–1815*. Dublin: Irish Academic Press, 25–51.

Carey, Daniel. 2014. 'John Locke's Philosophy of Money', in Daniel Carey (ed.), *Money and Political Economy in the Enlightenment*. Oxford: Voltaire Foundation, 57–81.

Carswell, John. 1960. *The South Sea Bubble*. Stanford, CA: Stanford University Press.

Casson, Douglas John. 2011. *Liberating Judgment: Fanatics, Skeptics and John Locke's Politics of Probability*. Princeton, NJ: Princeton University Press.

Castiglione, Dario. 1983. 'Mandeville Moralized', *Annali della Fondazione Luigi Einaudi* 12: 239–90.

Castiglione, Dario. 1992. 'Excess, Frugality and Spirit of Capitalism: Readings of Mandeville on Commercial Society', in Joseph Melling and Jonathan Barry (eds), *Culture in History: Production, Consumption and Values in Historical Perspective*. Exeter: University of Exeter Press, 155–79.

Champion, Justin. 2014. '"Mysterious politicks": Land, Credit and Commonwealth Political Economy, 1655–1722', in Daniel Carey (ed.), *Money and Political Economy in the Enlightenment*. Oxford: Voltaire Foundation, 117–62.

Chown, John. 1994. *A History of Money from AD 800*. London: Routledge.

Christian, William. 1973. 'The Moral Economics of Tom Paine', *Journal of the History of Ideas* 34(3): 367–80.

Christov, Theodore. 2015. *Before Anarchy: Hobbes and His Critics in Modern International Thought*. Cambridge: Cambridge University Press.

Church, Jeffrey. 2007. 'Selfish and Moral Politics: David Hume on Stability and Cohesion in the Modern State', *Journal of Politics* 69(1): 169–81.

Claeys, Gregory. 2003. *Thomas Paine: Social and Political Thought*. London: Routledge.

Clark, Lorene. 1977. 'Women and John Locke: Or, Who Owns the Apples in the Garden of Eden?' *Canadian Journal of Philosophy* 7(4): 699–724.

Collins, Gregory M. 2017. 'Edmund Burke on the Question of Commercial Intercourse in the Eighteenth Century', *Review of Politics* 79(4): 565–95.

Colman, John. 1972. 'Bernard Mandeville and the Reality of Virtue', *Philosophy* 47(180): 125–39.

Coole, Diana. 1988. *Women in Political Theory: From Ancient Misogyny to Contemporary Feminism*. Boulder, CO: Lynne Rienner.

Corcoran, Paul. 2018. 'John Locke on Native Right, Colonial Possession, and the Concept of *Vacuum domicilium*', *The European Legacy* 23(3): 225–50.

Cowles, Virginia. 1960. *The Great Swindle: The Story of the South Sea Bubble*. London: Collins.

Cropsey, Joseph. 2001. *Polity and Economy: With Further thoughts on the Principles of Adam Smith*. South Bend, IN: St. Augustine's Press.

Daly, Herman. E. (ed.). 1973. *Toward a Steady State Economy*. San Francisco, CA: W. H. Freeman.

Daly, Herman E. 2007. *From Uneconomic Growth to a Steady State Economy*. Northampton, MA: Edward Elgar.

Danford, John. 1990. *David Hume and the Problem of Reason: Recovering the Human Sciences*. New Haven, CT: Yale University Press.

Dawson, Hannah. 2007. *Locke, Language and Early Modern Philosophy*. Cambridge: Cambridge University Press.

De Lucia, JoEllen. 2014. 'A Delicate Debate: Mary Wollstonecraft, the Bluestockings and the Progress of Women', in Enit Karafili Steiner (ed.), *Called to Civic Excellence: Mary Wollstonecraft's A Vindication of the Rights of Woman*. Amsterdam: Brill, 113–30.

Deneen, Patrick. 2018. *Why Liberalism Failed*. New Haven, CT: Yale University Press.

Desan, Christine. 2014. *Making Money: Coin, Currency, and the Coming of Capitalism*. Oxford: Oxford University Press.

Dickinson, H. T. 1975. 'The Politics of Bernard Mandeville', in Irwin Primer (ed.), *Mandeville Studies*. The Hague: Martinus Nijhoff, 80–97.

Dickson, P. G. M. 1967. *The Financial Revolution in England: A Study of the Development of Public Credit 1688–1756*. New York: St. Martin's Press.

Di Stefano, Christine. 1991. *Configurations of Masculinity*. Ithaca, NY: Cornell University Press.

Dorfman, Joseph. 1938. 'The Economic Philosophy of Thomas Paine', *Political Science Quarterly* 53(3): 372–86.

Dossa, Shiraz. 2002. 'Liberal Imperialism? Natives, Muslims, and Others', *Political Theory* 30(5): 738–45.

Douglass, Robin. 2015. *Rousseau and Hobbes: Nature, Free Will, and the Passions*. Oxford: Oxford University Press.

Douglass, Robin. 2017. 'Morality and Sociability in Commercial Society: Smith, Rousseau – and Mandeville', *Review of Politics* 79(4): 597–620.

Douglass, Robin. 2020. 'Mandeville on the Origins of Virtue', *British Journal for the History of Philosophy* 28(2): 276–95.

Dumont, Louis. 1977. *From Mandeville to Marx: The Genesis and Triumph of Economic Ideology*. Chicago, IL: University of Chicago Press.

Dunn, John. 1969. *The Political Thought of John Locke*. Cambridge: Cambridge University Press.

Dunn, John. 1983. 'From Applied Theology to Social Analysis: The Break between John Locke and the Scottish Enlightenment', in Istvan Hont and Michael Ignatieff (eds), *Wealth and Virtue: The Shaping of Political Economy in the Scottish Enlightenment*. Cambridge: Cambridge University Press, 119–35.

Dunn, John. 1995. *The History of Political theory and Other Essays*. Cambridge: Cambridge University Press.

Dworetz, Steven. 1990. *The Unvarnished Doctrine: Locke, Liberalism, and the American Revolution*. Durham, NC: Duke University Press.

Eich, Stefan. 2020. 'John Locke and the Politics of Monetary Depoliticisation', *Modern Intellectual History* 17(1): 1–28.

Eisenberg, Jay M. 2018. *John Stuart Mill: Human Nature, Progress, and the Stationary State*. Lanham, MD: Lexington Books.

Englert, Gianna. 2016. 'Liberty and Industry: John Locke, John Stuart Mill, and the Economic Foundations of Political Membership', *Polity* 48(4): 551–79.

Epstein, Richard. 2014. *The Classical Liberal Constitution*. Cambridge, MA: Harvard University Press.

Farr, James. 2008. 'Locke, Natural Law, and New World Slavery', *Political Theory* 36(4): 495–522.

Farrant, Andrew. 2011. 'A Renovated Social Fabric: Mill, Hayek, and the Problem of Institutional Change?' in Andrew Farrant (ed.), *Hayek, Mill and the Liberal Tradition*. London: Routledge, 81–129.

Fatovic, Clement. 2015. *America's Founding and the Struggle over Economic Inequality*. Lawrence: University Press of Kansas.

Feavearyear, Albert. 1931. *The Pound Sterling: A History of English Money*. Oxford: Oxford University Press.

Finnis, John. 1980. *Natural Law and Natural Rights*. Oxford: Oxford University Press.

Fleischaker, Samuel. 2004. *On Adam Smith's 'Wealth of Nations': A Philosophical Companion*. Princeton, NJ: Princeton University Press.

Foner, Eric. 1977. *Tom Paine and Revolutionary America*. Oxford: Oxford University Press.

Foot, Michael and Isaac Kramnick. 1987. 'Editor's Introduction', *The Thomas Paine Reader*, Michael Foot and Isaac Kramnick (eds). London: Penguin Classics, 7–36.

Forbes, Duncan. 1951. 'James Mill and India', *The Cambridge Journal* 5: 19–33.

Forbes, Duncan. 1975. *Hume's Philosophical Politics*. Cambridge: Cambridge University Press.

Forsyth, Murray. 1981. 'Thomas Hobbes and the Constituent Power of the People', *Political Studies* 29(2): 191–203.

Frost, Samantha. 2008. *Lessons from a Materialist Thinker: Hobbesian Reflections on Ethics and Politics*. Stanford, CA: Stanford University Press.

Franklin, Benjamin. 1996. *The Autobiography of Benjamin Franklin*. Mineola, NY: Dover.

Fruchtman, Jack. 1993. *Thomas Paine and the Religion of Nature*. Baltimore, MD: Johns Hopkins University Press.

Fruchtman, Jack. 2009. *The Political Philosophy of Thomas Paine*. Baltimore, MD: Johns Hopkins University Press.

Gatens, Moira. 1991. *Feminism and Philosophy: Perspectives on Difference and Equality*. University Park, PA: Penn State University Press.

Gatens, Moira. 1991. '"The Oppressed State of My Sex": Wollstonecraft on Reason, Feeling and Equality', in Mary Lyndon Shanley and Carole Pateman (eds), *Feminist Interpretations and Political Theory*. University Park, PA: Penn State University Press, 112–28.

Gaus, Gerald. 2016. 'Mill's Normative Economics', in Christopher Mcleod and Dale E. Miller (eds), *A Companion to Mill*. London: John Wiley, 488–503.

Gauthier, David P. 1969. *The Logic of Leviathan: The Moral and Political Theory of Thomas Hobbes*. Oxford: Clarendon Press.

Gellner, Ernest. 1997. *Nationalism*. New York: New York University Press.

Goldsmith, M. M. 1985. *Private Vices, Public Benefits: Bernard Mandeville's Social and Political Thought*. Cambridge: Cambridge University Press.

Gray, John. 1996. *Post-liberalism: Studies in Political Thought*. New York: Routledge.

Grant, Ruth. 2003. 'John Locke on Women and the Family', in Ian Shapiro (ed.), *Two Treatises of Government and a Letter on Toleration*. New Haven, CT: Yale University Press, 286–308.

Griswold, Charles L. 1999. *Adam Smith and the Virtues of Enlightenment*. Cambridge: Cambridge University Press.

Grotius, Hugo. [1625] 2005. *The Rights of War and Peace, Book I*, ed. Richard Tuck Indianapolis, IN: Liberty Fund Books.

Gunn, J. A. W. 1983. *Beyond Liberty and Property*. Kingston and Montreal: McGill-Queens University Press.

Haakonssen, Knud. 1981. *The Science of a Legislator: The Natural Jurisprudence of David Hume and Adam Smith*. Cambridge: Cambridge University Press.

Haakonssen, Knud. 1993. 'The Structure of Hume's Political Theory', in David Fate Norton and Jacqueline Taylor (eds), *The Cambridge Companion to Hume*. Cambridge: Cambridge University Press, 182–221.

Haakonssen, Knud. 2006. 'Introduction: The Coherence of Smith's Thought', in Knud Haakonssen (ed.), *The Cambridge Companion to Adam Smith*. Cambridge: Cambridge University Press, 1–21.

Habermas, Jürgen. 1996. *Between Facts and Norms: Contributions to a Discourse Theory of Law and Democracy*, trans. William Rehg. Cambridge, MA: MIT Press.

Hamburger, Joseph. 1999. *John Stuart Mill on Liberty and Control*. Princeton, NJ: Princeton University Press.

Hamowy, Ronald. 1990. 'Cato's Letters, John Locke, and the Republican Paradigm', *History of Political Thought* 11(2): 274–94.

Hanley, Ryan Patrick. 2009. *Adam Smith and the Character of Virtue*. Cambridge: Cambridge University Press.

Hanley, Ryan Patrick. 2011. 'David Hume and the "Politics of Humanity"', *Political Theory* 39(2): 205–33.

Hanley, Ryan Patrick. 2017. *Love's Enlightenment: Rethinking Charity in Modernity*. New York: Cambridge University Press.

Hanvelt, Marc. 2012. *The Politics of Eloquence: David Hume's Political Rhetoric*. Toronto: University of Toronto Press.

Hardin, Russell. 2007. *David Hume: Moral and Political Theorist*. Oxford: Oxford University Press.

Harris, Abram L. 1965. 'John Stuart Mill: Servant of the Easy India Company', *Canadian Journal of Economics and Political Science* 30(2): 185–202.

Harrison, Jonathan. 1981. *Hume's Theory of Justice*. Oxford: Clarendon Press.

Hayek, Friedrich A. 1960. *The Constitution of Liberty*. Chicago, IL: University of Chicago Press.

Hayek, Friedrich A. 1978. *New Studies in Philosophy, Politics, Economics and the History of Ideas*. Chicago, IL: University of Chicago Press.

Hillyer, Richard. 2002. 'Keith Thomas' "Definitive Refutation" of C. B. Macpherson: Revisiting "The Social Origins of Hobbes' Political Thought"', *Hobbes Studies* 15: 32–44.

Hirschman, Albert O. 1977. *The Passions and the Interests: Political Arguments for Capitalism before its Triumph*. Princeton, NJ: Princeton University Press.

Hobbes, Thomas. [1668] 1840. *Behemoth: The History of the Causes of the Civil War*, in *The English Works of Thomas Hobbes, Volume 6*, ed. William Molesworth. London: John Bohn, 161–417.

Hobbes, Thomas. [1640] 1969. *Elements of Law: Natural and Politic*, ed. Ferdinand Tonnies. New York: Barnes & Noble.

Hobbes, Thomas. [1658] 1991. *Man and Citizen (De Homine and De Cive)*, ed. Bernard Gert. Indianapolis, IN: Hackett.

Hobbes, Thomas. [1651] 1994. *Leviathan*, ed. Edwin Curley. Indianapolis. IN: Hackett.

Hobbes, Thomas. [1642] 1998. *On the Citizen*, ed. Richard Tuck and Michael Silverthorne. Cambridge: Cambridge University Press.

Hobsbawm, E. J. 1990. *Nations and Nationalism since 1780*. Cambridge: Cambridge University Press.

Hollander, Samuel. 1985. *The Economics of John Stuart Mill*. Toronto: University of Toronto Press.

Hont, Istvan. 1983. 'The "Rich Country–Poor Country" Debate on Scottish Classical Political Economy', in Istvan Hont and Michael Ignatieff (eds), *Wealth and Virtue: The Shaping of Political Economy in the Scottish Enlightenment*. Cambridge: Cambridge University Press, 271–315.

Horne, Thomas A. 1978. *The Social Thought of Bernard Mandeville*, New York: Columbia University Press.

Horsefield, J. Keith. 1960. *British Monetary Experiments, 1650–1710*. Cambridge, MA: Harvard University Press.

Hsueh, Vicki. 2008. 'Unsettling Colonies: Locke, "Atlantis" and the New World Knowledges', *History of Political Thought* 29(2): 295–319.

Hume, David. [1751] 1961. *Enquiries Concerning the Human Understanding and Concerning the Principles of Morals*, ed. L. A. Selby-Bigge. Oxford: Clarendon Press.

Hume, David. 1983. *The History of England*, 6 vols. Indianapolis, IN: Liberty Fund Books.

Hume, David. 1987. *Essays Moral, Political and Literary*, ed. Eugene F. Miller. Indianapolis, IN: Liberty Fund Books.

Hume, David. 2000. *A Treatise of Human Nature*, ed. David Fate Norton and Mary J. Norton. Oxford: Oxford University Press.

Hundert, E. G. 1994. *The Enlightenment's Fable: Bernard Mandeville and the Discovery of Society*. Cambridge: Cambridge University Press.

Hundert, Edward J. 1977. 'Market Society and Meaning in Locke's Political Philosophy', *Journal of the History of Philosophy* 15(1): 33–44.

Ince, Onur Olas. 2011. 'Enclosing in God's Name, Accumulating for Mankind: Money, Morality, and Accumulation in John Locke's Theory of Money', *Review of Politics* 73(1): 29–54.

Ince, Ulas Onur. 2018. *Colonial Capitalism and the Dilemmas of Liberalism*. Oxford: Oxford University Press.

Israel, Jonathan. 2001. *Radical Enlightenment: Philosophy and the Making of Modernity, 1650–1750*. Oxford: Oxford University Press.

Jefferson, Thomas. [1789] 1950. 'Letter to James Madison, September 6, 1789', *The Papers of Thomas Jefferson, Vol. 15*, ed. Julian Boyd et al. Princeton, NJ: Princeton University Press, 392–7.

Jones, Gareth Steadman. 2004. *An End to Poverty? A Historical Debate*. New York: Columbia University Press.

Josephson, Peter B. 2002. *The Great Art of Government: Locke's Use of Consent*. Lawrence: University Press of Kansas.

Josephson, Peter B. 2016. 'Hobbes, Locke and the Problems of Political Economy', in Michael R. Strain and Stan A. Veuger (eds), *Economic Freedom and Human Flourishing: Perspectives from Political Philosophy*. Washington, DC: American Enterprise Institute, 9–29.

Kahan, Alan S. 1992. *Aristocratic Liberalism: The Social and Political Thought of Jacob Burckhardt, John Stuart Mill, and Alexis de Tocqueville*. Oxford: Oxford University Press.

Kalyvas, Andreas and Ira Katznelson. 2008. *Liberal Beginnings: Making a Republic for the Moderns*. Cambridge: Cambridge University Press.

Kant, Immanuel. 1991. *Political Writings*. Cambridge: Cambridge University Press.

Kavka, Gregory. 1988. 'Some Neglected Liberal Aspects of Hobbes' Philosophy', *Hobbes Studies* 1: 89–108.

Kaye, Fredrick. [1924] 1988. 'Introduction', in *The Fable of the Bee or Private Vices, Publick Benefits*. Indianapolis. IN: Liberty Fund Books, vii–cxlvi.

Kaye, Harvey J. 2006. *Thomas Paine and the Promise of America*. New York: Hill & Wang.

Kelly, Duncan. 2011. *The Propriety of Liberty: Persons, Passions and Judgment in Modern Political Thought*. Princeton, NJ: Princeton University Press.

Kelly, Gary. 1992. *Revolutionary Feminism: The Mind and Career of Mary Wollstonecraft*. New York: St. Martin's Press.

Kelly, Patrick. 1988. '"All Things Richly to Enjoy": Economics and Politics in Locke's *Two Treatises of Government*', *Political Studies* 36(2): 273–93.

Kelly, Patrick. 1991. 'Introduction', in Patrick Kelly (ed.), *The Clarendon Edition to the Works of John Locke: Locke on Money, Volume 1*. Oxford: Oxford University Press, 1–106.

Keynes, John Maynard. [1935] 1964. *The General Theory of Employment, Interest, and Money*. San Diego. CA: First Harvest/Harcourt.

Kinzer, Bruce. 2001. *England's Disgrace: J. S. Mill and the Irish Question*. Toronto: University of Toronto Press.

Kleer, Richard. A. 2004. '"The Ruin of their Diana": Lowndes, Locke and the Bankers', *History of Political Economy* 36(2): 533–56.

Klimchuk, Dennis. 2012. 'Hobbes on Equity', in David Dyzenhaus and Thomas Poole (eds), *Hobbes and Law*. Cambridge: Cambridge University Press, 165–85.

Kohn, Margaret and Daniel O'Neill. 2006. 'A Tale of Two Indias: Burke and Mill on Empire and Slavery in the West Indies and America', *Political Theory* 34(2): 192–228.

Kramer, Matthew. 1997. *John Locke and the Origins of Private Property*. Cambridge: Cambridge University Press.

Kraynak, Robert P. 1990. *History and Modernity in the Thought of Thomas Hobbes*. Ithaca, NY: Cornell University Press.

Lamb, Robert 2015. *Thomas Paine and the Idea of Human Rights*. Cambridge: Cambridge University Press.

Landreth, Harry. 1975. 'The Economic Thought of Bernard Mandeville', *History of Political Economy* 7(2): 193–208.

Laslett, Peter. 1957. 'John Locke, the Great Recoinage, and the Origins of the Board of Trade: 1695–1698', *William and Mary Quarterly* 14(3): 370–402.

Letwin, William. 1963. *The Origins of Scientific Economics: English Political Thought 1660–1776*. Westport, CT: Greenwood Press.

Letwin, William. 1972. 'The Economic Foundations of Hobbes' Politics', in Maurice Cranston (ed.), *Hobbes and Rousseau: A Collection of Critical Essays*. Garden City, NY: Anchor Books, 143–64.

Levy, Michael B. 1981. 'Mill's Stationary State and the Transcendence of Liberalism', *Polity* 14(2): 273–93.

Li, Ming-Hsun. 1963. *The Great Recoinage of 1696 to 1699*. London: Weidenfeld & Nicolson.

Locke, John. [1690] 1975. *Essay Concerning Human Understanding*, ed. Peter Nidditch. Oxford: Oxford University Press.

Locke, John. [1692] 1991a. 'Some Considerations of the Consequences of the Lowering of Interest and Raising the Value of Money', in *The Clarendon Edition to the Works of John Locke: Locke on*

Money, Volume 1, ed. Patrick Kelly. Oxford: Oxford University Press, 203–342.

Locke, John. [1695] 1991b. 'Further Considerations Concerning Raising the Value of Money', in *The Clarendon Edition to the Works of John Locke: Locke on Money, Volume 1*, ed. Patrick Kelly. Oxford: Oxford University Press: 399–481.

Locke, John. 1996. *Some Thoughts Concerning Education and Of the Conduct of the Understanding*. ed. Ruth W. Grant and Nathan Tarcov. Indianapolis, IN: Hackett.

Locke, John. [1695] 1997. 'Venditio', in *Locke: Political Essays*, ed. Mark Goldie. Cambridge: Cambridge University Press, 339–43.

Locke, John. [1689] 2016. *Two Treatises of Government*, ed. Lee Ward. Indianapolis, IN: Hackett.

Lopata, Benjamin. 1973. 'Property Theory in Hobbes', *Political Theory*1(2): 203–18.

MacArthur. Neil. 2013. '"Thrown Amongst Many": Hobbes on Taxation and Fiscal Policy', in S. A. Lloyd (ed.), *Hobbes Today: Insights for the 21st Century*. Cambridge: Cambridge University Press, 178–89.

Macaulay, Thomas Babington. 1866. *The Complete Works of Lord Macaulay in Eight Vols. Volume 4*, ed. Lady Trevelyan. London: London, Green.

Machiavelli, Niccolò. [1532] 1985. *The Prince*, trans. Harvey Mansfield. Chicago, IL: University of Chicago Press.

Macpherson, C. B. 1962. *The Political Theory of Possessive Individualism: Hobbes to Locke*. Oxford: Clarendon Press.

Macpherson, C. B. 1985. 'Do We Need a Theory of the State?' in *The Rise and Fall of Economic Justice and Other Essays*. Oxford: Oxford University Press, ch. 5.

Majeed, Javed. 1999. 'James Mill's the History of British India: A Reevaluation', in Martin I Moir, Douglas Peers and Lynn Zastoupil (eds), *J. S. Mill's Encounter with India*. Toronto: University of Toronto Press, 53–71.

Makus, Ingrid. 1996. *Women, Politics, and Reproduction: The Liberal Legacy*. Toronto: University of Toronto Press.

Malcolm, Noel. 2002. *Aspects of Hobbes*. Oxford: Oxford University Press.

Malthus, Thomas. [1798] 2015. *An Essay on the Principle of Population and Other Writings*. London: Random House.

Mandeville, Bernard. [1729] 1988. *The Fable of the Bees or Privates Vices, Publick Benefits*, ed. Frederick Kaye. Indianapolis, IN: Liberty Fund Books.

Mansfield, Harvey C. 1971. 'Hobbes and the Science of Indirect Government', *American Political Science Review* 65(1): 97–110.

Martinich, A. P. 1997. *Thomas Hobbes*. New York: Cambridge University Press.

Marwah, Inder. 2011. 'Complicating Barbarism and Civilization: Mill's Complex Sociology of Human Development', *History of Political Thought* 32(2): 345–66.

Marx, Karl. 1978. 'On the Jewish Question', in Robert C. Tucker (ed.), *The Marx–Engels Reader*, 2nd edn. New York: W. W. Norton, 26–51.

Marx, Karl. [1867] 1990. *Capital: A Critique of Political Economy, Volume I*. New York: Penguin.

Mathie, William. 1987. 'Justice and Equity: An Inquiry into the Meaning and Role of Equity in the Hobbesian Account of Justice and Politics', in Craig Walton and Paul Johnston (eds), *Hobbes' Science of Natural Justice*. Dordrecht: Martinus Nijhoff, 257–76.

Mathiowetz, Dean. 2011. *Appeals to Interest: Language, Contestation, and the Shaping of Potential Agency*. University Park, PA: Penn State University Press.

Maxwell, J. C. 1954. 'Ethics and Politics in Mandeville', *Philosophy* 26(98): 242–52.

May, Larry. 2013. *Limiting Leviathan: Hobbes on Law and International Affairs*. Oxford: Oxford University Press.

McArthur, Neil. 2007. *David Hume's Political Theory: Law, Commerce, and the Constitution of Government*. Toronto: University of Toronto Press.

McKean, Benjamin L. 2020. *Disorienting Neoliberalism: Global Justice and the Outer Limit of Freedom*. Oxford: Oxford University Press.

McNamara, Peter. 1998. *Political Economy and Statesmanship: Smith, Hamilton, and the Foundations of the Commercial Republic*. DeKalb, IL: Northern Illinois University Press.

Mehta, Pratap Bhanu. 2012. 'Liberalism, Nation, and Empire', in Sankar Muthu (ed.), *Empire and Modern Political Thought*. Cambridge: Cambridge University Press, 232–60.

Mehta, Uday Singh. 1999. *Liberalism and Empire: A Study in Nineteenth-Century British Liberal Thought*. Chicago, IL: University of Chicago Press.

Mill, James. 1818. 'Colony', in *Essays from the Supplement to the Encyclopaedia Britannica. Collected Works*. London: J. Innes.

Mill, John Stuart. 1965–1991. *Collected Works of John Stuart Mill*, ed. J. M. Robson et al. 33 vols. Toronto: University of Toronto Press. The form of referencing is CW, volume and page numbers (CW 1:123).

CW 1 'The Autobiography' (1873)
CW 2 and 3 'The Principles of Political Economy' (1848)
CW 4 'Essays on Some Unsettled Questions of Political Economy' (1844)
CW 5 'Chapters on Socialism' (1879)
CW 6 'Radical Party and Canada: Lord Durham and the Canadians', 'What Is to be Done with Ireland?' (1848), 'England and Ireland' (1868).
CW 8 'System of Logic, Parts IV–V' (1843)

CW 12 'Letter to John Pringle Nichol' (1837)
CW 18 'Civilisation' (1836), 'De Tocqueville on Democracy in America' (1835, 1840), 'On Liberty' (1859)
CW 19 'Considerations on Representative Government' (1861)
CW 21 'A Few Words on Non-Intervention' (1859)
CW 24 'The Condition of Ireland [7]' (1846)

Mill, John Stuart. 2002. *The Basic Writings of John Stuart Mill: On Liberty, The Subjection of Women, and Utilitarianism.* New York: Modern Library.

Miller, David. 1981. *Philosophy and Ideology in Hume's Political Thought.* Oxford: Clarendon Press.

Miller. David. 1982. 'The Macpherson Version', *Political Studies* 30(1): 120–7.

Miller, David. 1995. *On Nationality.* Oxford: Clarendon Press.

Mitchell, Annie. 2003. 'Character of an Independent Whig – "Cato" and Bernard Mandeville', *History of European Ideas* 29: 291–311.

Mitchell, Neil J. 1984. 'John Locke and the Rise of Capitalism', *History of Political Economy* 18(2): 291–305.

Moloney, Pat. 2011. 'Hobbes, Savagery, and International Anarchy', *American Political Science Review* 105(1): 180–204.

Mouffe, Chantal. 2018. *For a Left Populism.* London: Verso.

Muldrew, Craig. 1998. *The Economy of Obligation: The Culture of Credit and Social Relations in Early Modern England.* New York: St. Martin's Press.

Muller, Virginia L. 1996. 'What can Liberals Learn from Mary Wollstonecraft?' in Maria J. Falco (ed.), *Feminist Interpretations of Mary Wollstonecraft.* University Park, PA: Penn State University Press, 47–60.

Muthu, Sankar. 2003. *Enlightenment against Empire.* Princeton, NJ: Princeton University Press.

Muthu, Sankar. 2008. 'Adam Smith's Critique of International Trading Companies: Theorizing "Globalization"', *Political Theory* 36(2): 185–212.

Myers, Milton L. 1983. *The Soul of Modern Economic Man: Ideas and Self-Interest Thomas Hobbes to Adam Smith.* Chicago, IL: University of Chicago Press.

Nacol, Emily. 2016. *An Age of Risk: Politics and Economy in Early Modern Britain.* Princeton, NJ: Princeton University Press.

Nelson, Craig. 2006. *Thomas Paine: Enlightenment, Revolution and the Birth of Modern Nations.* New York: Viking Penguin.

Nelson, Eric. 2019. *The Theology of Liberalism.* Cambridge, MA: Harvard University Press.

Norton, David Fate. 1993. 'Hume, Human Nature, and the Foundations of Morality', in David Fate Norton and Jacqueline Taylor (eds), *The*

Cambridge Companion to Hume. Cambridge: Cambridge University Press, 148–81.

O'Brien, John. 2007. "John Locke, Desire, and the Epistemology of Money." *British Journal for the History of Philosophy*. Vol. 15, No. 4: 685–708.

O'Brien, Karen. 2009. *Women and Enlightenment in Eighteenth-Century Britain*. Cambridge: Cambridge University Press.

Okin, Susan Moller. 1979. *Women in Western Political Thought*. Princeton, NJ: Princeton University Press.

Olsthoorn, Johan. 2013. 'Hobbes' Account of Distributive Justice as Equity', *British Journal for the History of Philosophy* 21(1): 13–33.

Olsthoorn, Johan. 2015. 'Hobbes on Justice, Property Rights and Self-Ownership', *History of Political Thought* 26(3): 471–98.

O'Neill, Daniel I. 2007. *The Burke–Wollstonecraft Debate: Savagery, Civilization, and Democracy*. University Park, PA: Penn State University Press.

Orwin, Cifford. 1975. 'On the Sovereign Authorization,' *Political Theory* 3(1): 26–44.

Outram, Dorinda. 2013. *The Enlightenment*, 3rd edn. Cambridge: Cambridge University Press.

Pagden, Anthony. 2003. 'Human Rights, Natural Rights, and Europe's Imperial Legacy', *Political Theory* 21(2): 171–99.

Paine, Thomas. 1987a. 'The Rights of Man, Parts I and II', *The Thomas Paine Reader*, ed. Michael Foot and Isaac Kramnick. London: Penguin Classics, 201–364.

Paine, Thomas. 1987b. 'Common Sense', *The Thomas Paine Reader*, ed. Michael Foot and Isaac Kramnick. London: Penguin Classics, 65–115.

Paine, Thomas. 1987c. 'Dissertation on Government, the Affairs of the Bank, and Paper Money', *The Thomas Paine Reader*, ed. Michael Foot and Isaac Kramnick. London: Penguin Classics, 167–200.

Paine, Thomas. 1987d. 'Dissertation on First Principles of Government', *The Thomas Paine Reader*, ed. Michael Foot and Isaac Kramnick. London: Penguin Classics, 452–70.

Paine, Thomas. 1987e. 'Agrarian Justice', *The Thomas Paine Reader*, ed. Michael Foot and Isaac Kramnick. London: Penguin Classics, 471–89.

Parekh, Bhiku. 1995. 'Liberalism and Colonialism: A Critique of Locke and Mill', in Jan Nederveen Pieterse and Bhiku Parekh (eds), *The Decolonization of imagination: Culture, Knowledge, and Power*. New York: Zed Books, 81–99.

Pateman, Carole. 1988. *The Sexual Contract*. Stanford, CA: Stanford University Press.

Pateman, Carole. 1991. '"God hath Ordained to Man a Helper": Hobbes, Patriarchy and Conjugal Right', in Mary Lyndon Shanley and Carole Pateman (eds), *Feminist Interpretations and Political Theory*. University Park, PA: Penn State University Press, 53–73.

Pech, Carol. 2007. '"His Nuts for a Piece of Metal": Fetishism in the Monetary Writings of Locke', in Nancy J. Hirschmann and Kirstie M. McClure (eds), *Feminist Interpretations of John Locke*. University Park, PA: Pennsylvania State University Press, 269–95.

Persky, Joseph. 2016. *The Political Economy of Progress: John Stuart Mill and Modern Radicalism*. Oxford: Oxford University Press.

Philp, Mark. 2013. 'Revolutionaries in Paris: Paine, Jefferson, and Democracy', in Simon P. Newman and Peter S. Onuf (eds), *Paine and Jefferson in the Age of Revolutions*. Charlottesville: University of Virginia Press, 136–60.

Pincus, Steven. 2009. *1688: The First Modern Revolution*. New Haven, CT: Yale University Press.

Pitkin, Hanna. 1964. 'Hobbes' Concept of Representation – I', *American Political Science Review* 58(2): 328–40.

Pitts, Jennifer. 2005. *A Turn to Empire: The Rise of Imperial Liberalism in Britain and France*. Princeton, NJ: Princeton University Press.

Pocock, J. G. A. 1975. *The Machiavellian Moment: Florentine Political thought and the Atlantic Republican Tradition*. Princeton, NJ: Princeton University Press.

Pocock, J. G. A. 1993. 'A Discourse on Sovereignty', in Nicholas Phillipson and Quentin Skinner (eds), *Political Discourse in Early Modern Britain*. Cambridge: Cambridge University Press, 377–428.

Polanyi, Karl. 1944. *The Great Transformation: The Political and Economic Origins of Our Time*. Boston, MA: Beacon Press.

Rahe, Paul. 1992. *Republics Ancient and Modern: Classical Republicanism and the American Revolution*. Chapel Hill: University of North Carolina Press.

Rasmussen, Dennis C. 2013. *The Pragmatic Enlightenment: Recovering the Liberalism of Hume, Smith, Montesquieu and Voltaire*. Cambridge: Cambridge University Press.

Rasmussen, Dennis C. 2017. *The Infidel and the Professor: David Hume, Adam Smith and the Friendship that Shaped Modern Thought*. Princeton, NJ: Princeton University Press.

Rees, John. 1977. 'The Thesis of the Two Mills', *Political Studies* 25(3): 369–82.

Ricardo, David. [1817] 2004. *The Principles of Political Economy and Taxation*. Garden City, NY: Dover Publishing.

Riley, Jonathan. 1994. 'Introduction', in *John Stuart Mill: Principles of Political Economy with Chapters on Socialism*. Oxford: Oxford University Press, vii–xlvii.

Riley, Jonathan. 1998. 'Mill's Political Economy: Ricardian Science and Liberal Utilitarian Art', in John Skorupski (ed.), *The Cambridge Companion to Mill*. Cambridge: Cambridge University Press, 293–337.

Robertson, John. 1983. 'The Scottish Enlightenment at the Limits of the Civic Tradition', in Istvan Hont and Michael Ignatieff (eds), *Wealth and Virtue: The Shaping of Political Economy in the Scottish Enlightenment*. Cambridge: Cambridge University Press, 137–78.

Robbins, Caroline. 1968. *The Eighteenth Century Commonwealthmen*. New York: Atheneum.

Robbins, Lionel. 1930. 'On a Certain Ambiguity in the Conception of Stationary Equilibrium', *The Economic Journal* 40(158): 194–214.

Ron, Amit. 2006. 'The "Market" and the "Forum" in Hobbes' Political Philosophy', *Polity* 38(2): 235–53.

Rosenberg, Nathan. 1963. 'Mandeville and Laissez-Faire', *Journal of the History of Ideas* 24(2): 183–96.

Rosenblatt, Helena. 2018. *The Lost History of Liberalism: From Ancient Rome to the Twentieth Century*. Princeton, NJ: Princeton University Press.

Rothschild, Emma. 2012. 'Adam Smith in the British Empire', in Sankar Muthu (ed.), *Empire and Modern Political thought*. Cambridge: Cambridge University Press, 184–98.

Rothschild, Emma and Amartya Sen. 2006. 'Adam Smith's Economics', in Knud Haakonssen (ed.), *The Cambridge Companion to Adam Smith*. Cambridge: Cambridge University Press, 319–65.

Rotwein, Eugene. 1955. 'Introduction', in *David Hume: Writings on Economics*. Madison: University of Wisconsin Press, ix–cxi.

Rousseau, Jean-Jacques, [1750, 1754] 1964. *The First and Second Discourses*, trans. Roger D. Masters and Judith R. Masters. New York: St. Martin's Press.

Runciman, David. 1997. *Pluralism and the Personality of the State*. Cambridge: Cambridge University Press.

Runciman, David. 2000. 'Debate: What kind of Person is Hobbes' State? A Reply to Skinner', *Journal of Political Philosophy* 8(2): 268–78.

Ryan, Alan. 1999. 'Introduction', in Martin I. Moir, Douglas Peers and Lynn Zastoupil (eds), *J. S. Mill's Encounter with India*. Toronto: University of Toronto Press, 3–17.

Sabl, Andrew. 2012. *Hume's Politics: Coordination and Crisis in the 'History of England'*. Princeton, NJ: Princeton University Press.

Sapiro, Virginia, 1996. 'Wollstonecraft, Feminism, and Democracy: "Being Bastilled"', in Maria J. Falco (ed.), *Feminist Interpretations of Mary Wollstonecraft*. University Park, PA: Penn State University Press, 33–45.

Schochet, Gordon. 1975. *Patriarchalism in Political Thought*. Oxford; Oxford University Press.

Schumpeter, Joseph. 1954. *A History of Economic Analysis*. New York: Oxford University Press.

Schwarze, Michelle 2020. *Recognizing Resentment: Sympathy, Injustice, and Liberal Political Thought*. Cambridge: Cambridge University Press.

Schwartz, Pedro. 1972. *The New Political Economy of J. S. Mill*. Durham, NC: Duke University Press.

Seaman, John W. 1988. 'Thomas Paine: Ransom, Civil Peace and the Natural Right to Welfare', *Political Theory* 16(1): 120–42.

Seligman, Edwin. 1921. *The Shifting and Incidence of Taxation*, 4th edn. New York: Columbia University Press.

Shaftesbury, Anthony 3rd Earl of. 2001. *Characteristicks of Men, Manners, Opinions, Times*, 3 vols. Indianapolis, IN: Liberty Fund Books.

Shanks, Torrey. 2019. 'The Rhetoric of Self-Ownership', *Political Theory* 47(3): 311–37.

Shanley, Mary Lyndon. 1991. 'Marital Slavery and Friendship: John Stuart Mill's *The Subjection of Women*', in Mary Lyndon Shanley and Carole Pateman (eds), *Feminist Interpretations and Political Theory*. University Park, PA: Penn State University Press, 164–80.

Simmons, John A. 1983. 'Inalienable Rights and Locke's Treatises', *Philosophy and Public Affairs* 12: 175–204.

Simmons, John A. 1992. *The Lockean Theory of Rights*. Princeton, NJ: Princeton University Press.

Skinner, Andrew S. 1993. 'David Hume: Principles of Political Economy', in David Fate Norton and Jacqueline Taylor (eds), *The Cambridge Companion to Hume*. Cambridge: Cambridge University Press, 222–54.

Skinner, Quentin. 2007. 'Hobbes on Persons, Authors and Representatives', in Patricia Springborg (ed.), *The Cambridge Companion to Hobbes' Leviathan*. Cambridge: Cambridge University Press, 157–80.

Sklansky, Jeffrey. 2012. 'The Elusive Sovereign: New Intellectual and Social Histories of Capitalism', *Modern Intellectual History* 9(1): 233–48.

Smith, Adam. 1978. *Lectures on Jurisprudence*, ed. R. L. Meek, D. D. Raphael and P.G. Stein. Indianapolis. IN: Liberty Fund Books.

Smith, Adam 1981. *An Inquiry into the Nature and Causes of the Wealth of Nations*, 2 vols, ed. R. H. Campbell and A. S. Skinner. Indianapolis, IN: Liberty Fund Books.

Smith, Adam. 1984. *The Theory of Moral Sentiments*, ed. D. D. Raphael and A. L. MacFie. Indianapolis, IN: Liberty Fund Books.

Somos, Mark. 2019. *American States of Nature: The Origins of Independence, 1761–1775*. New York: Oxford University Press.

Sorrell, Tom. 2011. 'Hobbes, Public Safety, and Political Economy', in Gabriella Slomp and Raia Prokhovnik (eds), *International Political Theory after Hobbes: Analysis, Interpretation and Orientation*. New York: Palgrave Macmillan, 42–55.

Sparling, Robert. 2013. 'Political Corruption and the Concept of Dependence in Republican Thought', *Political Theory* 41(4): 618–47.

Sparling, Robert. 2019. *Political Corruption: The Underside of Civic Morality*. Philadelphia: University of Pennsylvania Press.

Springborg, Patricia. 2015. 'Hobbes, Donne and the Virginia Company: Terra Nullius and "The Bulimia of Dominium"', *History of Political Thought* 36(1): 113–63.

Sreedhar, Susanne. 2010. *Hobbes on Resistance: Defying the Leviathan*. Cambridge: Cambridge University Press.

Stanton, Timothy. 2018. 'John Locke and the Fable of Liberalism', *Historical Journal* 61(3): 597–622.

Stasavage, David. 2011. *States of Credit: Size, Power, and the Development of European Polities*. Princeton, NJ: Princeton University Press.

Stauffer, Devin. 2018. *Hobbes' Kingdom of Light: A Study of the Foundations of Modern Political Philosophy*. Chicago, IL: University of Chicago Press.

Steuart, James. [1767] 2020. *An Inquiry into the Principles of Political Economy*. Coppell, TX: Amazon Books.

Stewart, John B. 1963. *The Moral and Political Philosophy of David Hume*. New York: Columbia University Press.

Strauss, Leo. 1936. *The Political Philosophy of Hobbes: Its Basis and Its Genesis*, trans. Elsa Sinclair. Chicago, IL: University of Chicago Press.

Strauss, Leo. 1953. *Natural Right and History*. Chicago, IL: University of Chicago Press.

Suarez, Francisco. 1950. *Extracts on Politics and Government*, trans. George Moore. Chevy Chase, MD: Country Dollar Press.

Sullivan, Eileen. 1983: 'Liberalism and Imperialism: J. S. Mill's Defence of the British Empire', *Journal of the History of Ideas* 44(4): 599–617.

Sullivan, Vickie B. 2004. *Machiavelli, Hobbes, and the Formation of Liberal Republicanism in England*. New York: Cambridge University Press.

Taylor, Natalie Fuehrer. 2014. '"Mistaken Notions of Female Excellence": Mary Wollstonecraft's Vindication of Virtue', in Enit Karafili Steiner (ed.), *Called to Civic Excellence: Mary Wollstonecraft's A Vindication of the Rights of Woman*. Amsterdam: Brill, 93–112.

Ten, C. L. 1998. 'Democracy, Socialism and the Working Classes', in John Skorupski (ed.), *The Cambridge Companion to Mill*. Cambridge: Cambridge University Press, 372–95.

Thomas, Keith. 1965. 'The Social Origins of Hobbes' Political Thought', in Keith Brown (ed.), *Hobbes Studies*. Cambridge, MA: Harvard University Press, 185–236.

Thompson, Michael J. 2007. *The Politics of Inequality: A Political History of the Idea of Economic Inequality in America*. New York: Columbia University Press.

Tocqueville, Alexis de. 2000. *Democracy in America*, trans. Harvey Mansfield and Delba Winthrop. Chicago, IL: University of Chicago Press.

Townshend, Jules. 1999. 'Hobbes as Possessive Individualist: Interrogating the C. B. Macpherson Thesis', *Hobbes Studies* 12: 52–72.

Trenchard, John and Thomas Gordon. [1720–1723] 1995. *Cato's Letters*, 2 vols, ed. Ronald Hamowy. Indianapolis, IN: Liberty Fund Books.

Tribe, Keith. 1981. *Genealogies of Capitalism*. London: Palgrave Macmillan.

Tuck, Richard. 1979. *Natural Rights Theories*. Cambridge: Cambridge University Press.

Tully, James. 1980. *A Discourse on Property: Locke and his Adversaries*. Cambridge: Cambridge University Press.

Tully, James. 1993. *An Approach to Political Philosophy: Locke in Contexts*. Cambridge: Cambridge University Press.

Tully, James. 1995. *Strange Multiplicity*. Cambridge: Cambridge University Press.

Tully, James. 2008. *Political Philosophy in a New Key*, 2 vols. Cambridge: Cambridge University Press.

Tunick, Mark. 2006. 'Tolerant Imperialism: John Stuart Mill's Defence of British Rule of India', *Review of Politics* 68(4): 586–611.

Turner, Michael J. 2006. 'Radical Agitation and the Canada Question on British Politics, 1837–41', *Historical Research* 79(203): 90–114.

Urbinati, Nadia. 1991. 'John Stuart Mill on Androgyny and Ideal Marriage', *Political Theory* 19(4): 626–48.

Urbinati, Nadia. 2010. 'An Alternative Modernity: Mill on Capitalism and the Quality of Life', in Ben Eggleston, Dale Miller and David Weinstein (eds), *John Stuart Mill and the Art of Life*. Oxford: Oxford University Press, 236–63.

Vallier, Kevin. 2010. 'Production, Distribution, and J. S. Mill', *Utilitas* 22(2): 105–25.

Vaughn, Karen Iverson. 1980. *John Locke, Economist and Social Scientist*. Chicago, IL: University of Chicago Press.

Vaughn, Karen Iverson. 1992. 'The Economic Background to Locke's *Two Treatises of Government*', in Edward J. Harpham (ed.), *John Locke's Two Treatises of Government: New Interpretations*. Lawrence: University Press of Kansas. 118–47.

Vickers, Douglas. 1959. *Studies in the Theory of Money, 1690–1776*. Philadelphia, PA: Chilton.

Viner, Jacob. 1958. *The Long View and the Short*. Glencoe, IL: The Free Press.

Waldron, Jeremy. 2001. 'Hobbes and the Principle of Publicity', *Pacific Philosophical Quarterly* 82: 447–74.

Waldron, Jeremy. 2002. *God, Locke and Equality*. Cambridge: Cambridge University Press.

Walsh, Mary. 1995. 'Locke and Feminism on Private and Public Realms of Activities', *Review of Politics* 57(2): 251–77.

Ward, Lee. 2004. *The Politics of Liberty in England and Revolutionary America*. Cambridge: Cambridge University Press.

Ward, Lee. 2010. *John Locke and Modern Life*. Cambridge: Cambridge University Press.

Ward, Lee. 2017. 'Thomas Hobbes and John Locke on a Liberal Right of Secession', *Political Research Quarterly* 70(4): 876–88.

Warrender, Howard. 1957. *The Political Philosophy of Hobbes*. Oxford: Clarendon Press.

Wei, Ja. 2017. *Commerce and Politics in Hume's History of England*. Woodbridge: Boydell & Brewer.

Wilson, Douglas L. 1989. 'Jefferson v. Hume', *William and Mary Quarterly* 46(1): 49–70.

Winch, Donald S. 1965. *Classical Political Economy and Colonies.* Cambridge, MA: Harvard University Press.

Winch, Donald S. 1978. *Adam Smith's Politics: An Essay in Historiographical Revision* Cambridge: Cambridge University Press.

Winch, Donald S. 1992. 'Adam Smith: Scottish Moral Philosopher as Political Economist', *The Historical Journal* 35(1): 91–113.

Wollstonecraft, Mary. [1792] 2009. *A Vindication of the Rights of Woman*, 3rd edn, ed. Deidre Shauna Lynch. New York: W. W. Norton.

Wood, Gordon. 2013. 'The Radicalism of Thomas Jefferson and Thomas Paine Reconsidered', in Simon P. Newman and Peter S. Onuf (eds), *Paine and Jefferson in the Age of Revolutions.* Charlottesville: University of Virginia Press, 13–25.

Woolhouse, Roger. 2007. *Locke: A Biography.* Cambridge: Cambridge University Press.

Zagorin, Perez. 2009. *Hobbes and the Law of Nature.* Princeton, NJ: Princeton University Press.

Zastoupil, Lynn. 1983. 'J. S. Mill on Ireland', *The Historical Journal* 26(3): 7077–717.

Zastoupil, Lynn. 1999. 'India, J. S. Mill and Western Culture', in Martin I Moir, Douglas Peers and Lynn Zastoupil (eds), *J. S. Mill's Encounter with India.* Toronto: University of Toronto Press, 111–48.

Zerilli, Linda M. G. 2018. 'Symposium on Eileen Hunt Botting's *Wollstonecraft, Mill and Women's Human Rights*', *Political Theory* 46(3): 429–36.

Zuckert, Michael. 1994. *Natural Rights and the New Republicanism.* Princeton, NJ: Princeton University Press.

Zuckert, Michael. 2013. 'Two Paths from Revolution: Jefferson, Paine, and the Radicalization of Enlightenment Thought', in Simon P. Newman and Peter S. Onuf (eds), *Paine and Jefferson in the Age of Revolutions* Charlottesville: University of Virginia Press, 252–76.

Zvesper, John. 1985. 'Hobbes' Individualistic Analysis of the Family', *Politics* 5: 28–33.

Index

EU representative:
Easy Access System Europe
Mustamäe tee 50, 10621 Tallinn, Estonia
Gpsr.requests@easproject.com

www.ingramcontent.com/pod-product-compliance
Lightning Source LLC
Chambersburg PA
CBHW051959270326
41929CB00015B/2710